The British new towns

International Library of Sociology

Founded by Karl Mannheim

Editor: John Rex, University of Aston in
        Birmingham

Arbor Scientiae
Arbor Vitae

A catalogue of the books available in the **International Library of Sociology** and
other series of Social Science books published by Routledge & Kegan Paul will be
found at the end of this volume.

The British new towns

A programme without a policy

Meryl Aldridge

Department of Social Administration and Social Work,
University of Nottingham

Routledge & Kegan Paul

London, Boston and Henley

First published in 1979
by Routledge & Kegan Paul Ltd
39 Store Street, London WC1E 7DD,
Broadway House, Newtown Road,
Henley-on-Thames, Oxon RG9 1EN and
9 Park Street, Boston, Mass. 02108, USA
Set in 10/11 Times by
Oxprint, Oxford
and printed in Great Britain by
Lowe and Brydone Ltd
Thetford, Norfolk
© Meryl Aldridge 1979

British Library Cataloguing in Publication Data

Aldridge, Meryl

The British new towns. — (International
library of sociology).
1. New towns — Great Britain
2. Urban policy — Great Britain
I. Title II. Series
309.2'62'0941   HT169.G7   79–40866

ISBN 0 7100 0356 0

For my parents

Kenneth and Betty Horrocks

Contents

Preface and acknowledgments

Background

Between 1969 and 1972 I was involved, with three colleagues at the University of Birmingham Centre for Urban and Regional Studies, in an SSRC financed project originally concerned with the planning process and the development of new communities. During the three years, the objective of the study was narrowed to the more manageable one of studying social development staff in British new towns and in some expansion schemes and elsewhere. The four members of the research team visited all the new towns between them, and therefore became familiar not only with the post-war decentralization policy expressed through the New Towns Act and the Town Development Act 1952, but with the physical and aesthetic qualities of the towns themselves.

After I left the Centre and moved into a teaching post I found, as is often the case, that my interest in the new towns policy was increased rather than diminished, reinforced by requests from colleagues to 'do' the new towns for their courses of lectures and seminars. Students seem fascinated by the whole idea of new towns, so while I enjoyed being a pundit on the topic, I became increasingly frustrated by the literature available. Attempts to deal with the policy from a detached and evaluative perspective have been few. Some are now historical documents (Orlans, 1952; Rodwin, 1956). More recent appraisal is scattered amongst journals (Heraud, 1966 and 1968) or government papers of daunting scale and detail (Cullingworth and Karn, 1968; Expenditure Committee, 1974 and 1974−5a). The annual reports of the development corporations and occasional parliamentary debates are also rich potential sources of data, but finding enough material with which to construct an argument is rather like panning for gold, and not an activity that a teacher can reasonably expect of a student preparing for a seminar or an essay.

There are, of course, a number of recent books dealing with the British new towns, notably: Evans (1972), Osborn and Whittick (1969) and Schaffer (1972). All are lively and informative, but all overlook or evade discussion of the more controversial elements of the policy. They have also tended to emphasize continuities rather than changes and contradictions, and to reject examination of that aspect of new towns policy which to a sociologist is most fascinating: its ideological content. This book is an attempt to rectify this, from a position of detachment, although the new towns defy impartiality. They have a fascination which arouses emotions powerful enough to transcend the turgid format of annual reports and select committee hearings. Simply reading and writing about new towns provides some insight into why people should devote a lifetime to their cause.

The book does not attempt to deal with the history or objectives of particular new towns. For this, the reader should turn to Osborn and Whittick (1969), Schaffer (1972) and Thomas (1969a and b).

Northern Ireland new towns are omitted from the discussion, because their circumstances, and in particular their local government powers, bear no comparison with those in the rest of the United Kingdom.

The plan of the book

Chapters 1 to 4 and 8 form a chronological account of the development of the policy, from the publication in 1898 of Ebenezer Howard's *Garden Cities of Tomorrow* under the title *Tomorrow: a Peaceful Path to Real Reform,* until 1978. Chapters 5 to 7 deal with elements of the new towns policy which merit detailed attention: the ownership of the assets, the concepts of 'balance' and 'self-containment' and the new towns in relation to the regions. Chapter 9 contains a review of the main themes and some remarks about the future.

Chapter 1 is a highly selective outline history of the early years of the garden city movement, concentrating on the philosophy of Howard himself and that of his most influential successor, F. J. Osborn. The growth of the Garden City Association into a highly effective lobby in the years 1918 to 1939 is sketched. The chapter concludes with the mounting public concerns in the 1930s about regional imbalances of wealth and the consequences of large-scale housing development. Readers with a particular interest in the historical background to the new towns may also wish to refer to Howard himself (1965) and to Ashworth (1954), Cherry (1972),

Petersen (1968) and Purdom (1949). (The last describes in detail the building of Letchworth and Welwyn Garden City.)

Chapter 2 examines the recommendations of the three famous wartime committees: 'Barlow' (1940), 'Scott' (1942) and 'Uthwatt' (1942). It then moves on to review both the recommendations and the underlying philosophy of the New Towns Committee (1946a, b and c) under Lord Reith, suggesting that wartime conditions produced a vision of new towns more centralized and collectivist than that of the earlier propagandists — and yet equally apolitical.

The development of the 'Mark One' new towns between 1946 and 1959 is examined in chapter 3. During this early period certain crucial characteristics of the new towns were established, notably a tendency to high rents and a concentration on industrial development, together with the rigid application of employment criteria for housing allocation. Despite this, the relations of the ministry concerned and the Board of Trade remained informal.

After 1960 there was a sudden renewal of interest in new towns, arising from expanding affluence and rapidly increasing population projections. Chapter 4 covers this phase of the 'Mark Two' new towns, during which existing problems and contradictions were compounded by a new emphasis on profitability and the use of private capital to finance new developments.

Chapter 5 deals in more detail with a particular issue during the Mark Two phase: that of the ownership and management of the housing, industrial and commercial assets of the new towns. It describes the setting up of the Commission for the New Towns in 1959 and subsequent party political ambivalence towards it. It then moves on to examine the adoption of a policy of greater owner-occupation.

'Balanced' and 'self-contained' towns were a part of the New Towns Committee's remit. The twin concepts have generated more attention from researchers than any other aspect of new towns policy. Some of this literature and more recent census data is evaluated in chapter 6 in the light of disputes about both the redistributive intent and potential of the policy. The chapter concludes with a brief discussion of the neighbourhood community idea in new towns.

Chapter 7 deals with the role of new towns as part of intra- and inter-regional strategies. It draws attention to the longstanding lack of contact between the Department of Industry and Department of the Environment over Industrial Development Certificates (which are part of the policy to redirect wealth away from the Midlands and South East England). Recent alarm on the part of urban local authorities at the effect of intra-regional decentralization on their tax-base and services, and the subsequent switch of central-government attention and resources to the inner city is described.

Chapter 8 returns to the historical theme. It describes the consultative documents (DOE, 1974; Scottish Office, 1975), the deliberations of the House of Commons Expenditure Committee (1974 and 1974–5a) hearings on the new towns and the government's response to this (Cmnd 6616). The first section concludes with the 1977 review of new towns targets in the light of the inner-city 'crisis' and policy. An account of the 1976 New Towns (Amendment) Act, legislating for disposal of the new towns' rented housing, completes the chapter.

Concluding, chapter 9 draws attention to the early decline in central-government commitment to the new towns idea, producing incremental decision-making inimical to laying down or reaching any consistent social objectives. This is explained partly by the persistent refusal of both central government and the Town and Country Planning Association to recognize the political content of the new towns and their administration, which has resulted in a lack of informed public debate about the overall policy and a legacy of local hostilities over the development corporations' democratic accountability. It argues that some decisions, especially in relation to owner-occupation and the use of private finance, have been regressive, but finally declares that the weaknesses of the new towns programme have been due more to lack of resources and of resolve by central government than to any inherent defect in the concept itself.

Unfortunately, it is indicative of the problems of the thirty years of new towns as a part of public policy that I cannot, without qualification, thank the DOE for help in this project. Between 1976 and 1978 I asked via three different routes to be allowed to read the New Town circulars and the New Towns Handbook. All requests were met with blank refusal. The replies included a number of curious arguments including that the circulars, which are confidential, are similar in content to the department's Local Authority circulars, which are public. I was also assured that they would be of no interest to a researcher, a judgment which I had hoped to make for myself. The final approach, through my head of department, produced a slightly sinister phone call, asking him who I was and why I was writing the book. It was followed by a letter again refusing me official access to the documents, remarking that much of the information in them is out of date and 'could therefore be misleading'. The letter did, however, promise help with any specific questions I might have and this was instantly and generously forthcoming when I telephoned with several such questions. In the event, the New Town circulars at least were most informative. They are not, incidentally, available to the new town local authorities, nor were they to the Select Committee.

On a more positive note I should like to acknowledge a small grant from Allied Breweries, which helped towards travel, photocopying and books. Professor D. C. Marsh has provided a great deal of practical advice and support. Sue Barratt, Maurice Bradley, Michael Buttery, Michael Harloe, Professor J. R. James, David Jones, Helen Kirby, Randall Smith, Professor Murray Stewart and Tony Veal have all helped and advised me in various ways, but should not be blamed for the outcome. Jo Wilson and Kate Castleton typed the manuscript.

The author and publishers would like to thank the following for permission to reproduce illustrations: Faber and Faber Ltd (plates 1 and 2); Letchworth Museum (plates 3 to 8); the estate of Arthur Wragg (plate 8); *London Evening News* (plate 9); Corby Development Corporation (plate 10); Aycliffe Development Corporation (plate 11); Stevenage Development Corporation (plate 12); Henk Snoek and Basildon Development Corporation (plate 13); Irvine Development Corporation (plate 14); Pineham Photographers and Milton Keynes Development Corporation (plate 15); Peterlee Development Corporation (plate 16); Cumbernauld Development Corporation (plate 17).

Without my husband Alan Aldridge I would probably never have started, and certainly never finished, this project.

Nottingham
July 1978

Abbreviations

ANTLA	Association of New Town Local Authorities
CDP	Community Development Project
CHAC	Central Housing Advisory Committee
CLA	Community Land Act
CLNT	Central Lancashire New Town
CNT	Commission for the New Towns
DC	Development Corporation
DEA	Department of Economic Affairs
DOE	Department of the Environment
D(T)I	Department of (Trade and) Industry
GCTPA	Garden City and Town Planning Association
IDC	Industrial Development Certificate
ISS	Industrial Selection Scheme
MHLG	Ministry of Housing and Local Government
MTCP	Ministry of Town and Country Planning
NETS	New and Expanded Towns Scheme
NIB	National Industry Board
ODP	Office Development Permit
RSG	Rate Support Grant
TCPA	Town and Country Planning Association
TPP	Transport Policies and Programmes

1 The new town idea 1898–1939

The dream is broken, the ugly nineteenth century has been wiped off the slate and the country has resumed its natural evolution from the eighteenth century . . . (MacFadyen, 1933, p. 29).

I think it was the persistency with which our group struck to one objective, and even over-simplified it, that lodged the idea in the public mind (Mumford and Osborn, 1971, p. 145).

British new towns are famous throughout the world as an ambitious government initiative. They are among the earliest examples of comprehensive urban planning and have a reputation as social experiments. Yet it was the tenacity and even eccentricity of two men that transformed, over the course of nearly fifty years, an inventor's obsession into a major piece of public policy. Ebenezer Howard had the idea; F. J. Osborn had the dedication, the political acumen and the longevity to keep it on the public agenda until new towns were enshrined in legislation.

The idea

Britain's nineteenth-century urban problems are now well documented. Between 1801 and 1901 the population of England, Wales and Scotland grew from 10,501,000 to 37,000,000 (Ashworth, 1954, p. 7) by a combination of rising fertility and falling mortality. At the same time the population was moving from the countryside to the towns. The percentage of the population living in towns of more than 100,000 residents grew from nil in 1801 to 17·3 in 1891, and that in towns of 20,000 to 100,000 tripled to 21·8 per cent (*ibid.*, p. 8). The quality of city life became a major preoccupation of social philosophers, philanthropists and public administrators alike in the

1

Figure 1 Towns in England and Wales, designated under the New
Towns Acts

second half of the century. Ashworth (1954), Cherry (1972) and Petersen (1968) have described how hatred of the new cities brought together strange political bedfellows. Those who feared insurrection by the uncontrolled hordes, and those who were appalled at the exploitation of the urban working class shared a conviction that radical measures were needed. Early public intervention centred on health. Precipitated by the cholera epidemic of 1848, the Public Health Act of that year gave local authorities powers over sewerage, water supply, cemeteries and a number of other matters. Gradually regulation was applied to building standards and the provision of working-class housing. (See Ashworth, 1954, for a comprehensive history of the development of town planning legislation.)

By the turn of the century a new dimension had been added to the urban question. Whereas the problems had been those of concentration, suddenly the development of public transport systems allowed an explosion in the area of towns and cities (Hall *et al.*, 1973, vol. 1, pp. 76ff). It is hardly surprising, therefore, that when Ebenezer Howard published *Tomorrow: a Peaceful Path to Real Reform* in 1898 his devastatingly simple – even simplistic – scheme attracted so much interest. It seemed at once to solve the problems of overcrowding and ill-health, of congestion and of sprawl.

Ebenezer Howard left school at the age of fifteen, in 1865. For the next six years he drifted 'from one insignificant job to another' before he went to the United States with two friends. Finding himself a failure at farming, he returned to office work in Chicago, where he became a reporter for the courts and press. In 1876 he came home to England, where he joined Gurney's as a parliamentary reporter. He stayed in this type of work for the rest of his career. F. J. Osborn writes of him, in the Preface to the 1965 edition of *Garden Cities of Tomorrow:*

> His life was always one of hard work and little income; his interest was never seriously in his own economic prosperity, but was divided between mechanical invention and the movement that made him famous . . . almost always he had a small workshop somewhere in which a mechanic was working on his ideas. . . . In his spare time the young Howard moved in earnest circles of nonconformist churchmen . . . overlapping with others of mild reformists who in those days were largely concerned with the land question (Howard, 1965, pp. 19–20).

Apparently Howard, although mild-mannered and ordinary in appearance, was a natural orator. 'On the platform he was most impressive and seemed of a dominating type' (*ibid.*, p. 23).

As a young man, Howard had been a Fabian. The philosophy of

his scheme would today be considered liberal in that he advocated a degree of collective action to provide improved urban facilities and opportunities, but favoured a mixed economy to provide the housing, industry and commerce for his garden cities. Howard did not, however, have an explicit political platform which undoubtedly explains the heterogeneity of his support. Nor was he interested in aesthetics. The garden city idea was part of Howard's fascination with technical invention and he presented it essentially as a complex and innovative machine. This is certainly not to suggest that Howard was unaware of, or uninterested in, human problems. One could describe his vision as 'organic' but the imagery would lack the sense of the positive application of the new human skills and knowledge by which Howard was so fascinated.

The physical plan presented in *Tomorrow: a Peaceful Path to Real Reform* is brief. It suggests cities of 6,000 acres. About 1,000 acres would be devoted to the city itself, in a circular form, and the rest to an agricultural estate. The two would be interdependent and together virtually self-sufficient (Howard, 1965, pp. 50ff.). In due course a cluster of such cities would grow up, linked by rapid rail transport, although each would be administratively autonomous, thus forming a 'social city' (*ibid.*, pp. 138ff.). Howard suggested that the population of the garden cities would be about 32,000, and speculated briefly on the advantages of a peripheral railway, circular boulevards and a central park surrounded by a 'Crystal Palace' (*ibid.*, p. 54) or wide glass arcade to tempt people outdoors whatever the weather. He remarks, however, that these ideas are 'merely suggestive and will probably be much departed from' (*ibid.*, p. 51). Clearly he felt his real contribution was in the administrative devices that he recommended. Land would be purchased by a company formed for the purpose and owned by the municipality. Other organizations and individuals would lease sites for building. The 'rate rent' that they paid would then be used to repay the loan, and the surplus (he was confident that there would be one) ploughed into the provision of municipal facilities. Considerable space in the book is devoted to issues of, for example, temperance, the advantages of limited competition for tradesmen and the recycling of the city's sewage for the agricultural estate. Today the scheme seems naïve and utopian, as it did to many contemporary commentators, yet the watchword was always practicality.

Howard came to be a well-known and respected public figure, but it is clear that, while he provided the inspiration, most of the initiatives were taken by others. In 1901 the Garden City Association was founded, under the chairmanship of Ralph (later Mr Justice) Neville, KC. In turn, the Pioneer Company was formed and, in 1903, bought 3,818 acres in Hertfordshire to found Letchworth.

4

(Detailed accounts of this period can be found in the preface to Howard, 1965; MacFadyen, 1933; and Purdom, 1949.)

F. J. Osborn joined the staff at Letchworth in 1912 as a housing manager and quickly established himself in the small group dedicated to promoting the garden-city idea. With Howard, C. B. Purdom and W. G. Taylor, who together formed the National Garden Cities Committee, he wrote *New Towns After the War* (1942) in 1918. He remained at Letchworth and later Welwyn until 1936 when he transferred to a part-time directorship with a local firm. He thus had time to work for the (by then) Garden City and Town Planning Association as Secretary and then Chairman of the Executive, until 1961. F. J. Osborn edited the Association's journal *Town and Country Planning* until 1965 when he was 80. Like Howard, Osborn was a ferocious self-educator, reading, going to night-school and belonging to the Fabians as a young man. From his *Letters* with Lewis Mumford (Mumford and Osborn, 1971), though, he appears more humorous, more politically astute and more this-worldly than does Howard as described by MacFadyen (1933) and others.

The philosophy of the founders

Ebenezer Howard was undoubtedly influenced by nineteenth-century utopian authors, specifically Bellamy (1851) and Buckingham (1849) and presumably also by the writings and public statements of William Morris, John Ruskin, H. G. Wells and G. K. Chesterton (Petersen, 1968). F. J. Osborn has specifically noted the influence of Wells and Chesterton on his own youth and yet has rejected the utopian element in the new towns idea: 'There was no utopianism in my book of 1918 or in the first Garden City prospectus of 1903 or in the New Towns Committee's report of 1946 or in the propaganda of the TCPA since 1899' (Mumford and Osborn, 1971, p. 253).

Yet some vision of a better life, still to be created, must have informed Osborn in his years of effort for the new towns cause, as it did Howard in his book and his work. The tension between this vision of a changed life and the practical use of existing institutions which runs through his book has been perpetuated in the policies of the TCPA, became embodied in the New Towns Act of 1946 and has characterized the new towns programme to the present time. The British new towns are seen as an experiment in social living, when Howard and Osborn were in many ways conservative about social and family structures, and as redistributive when there is little in the 1946 legislation or subsequent action to bear this out.

It has been suggested that there was created in Britain in the

5

nineteenth century an anti-urbanism that has profoundly affected urban policy and town planning practice ever since. This may be accurate of some intellectuals. William Morris, in *News from Nowhere* (1891) described his vision of a post-industrial return to a society where medieval face-to-face society combined with egalitarianism. In it the lower Thames is fished for salmon and the Palace of Westminster has become a fruit and vegetable market.

Reading Howard and Osborn, however, it is clear that what motivated much of their rejection of city life was not so much the fear of social disorganization or hatred of industrialism as a conviction that the city by its very nature destroyed physical health, impaired the quality of the race and reduced fertility. The belief about fertility became an even greater preoccupation during the 1930s when the birthrate reached an unprecedentedly low level, thus appearing to lend support to the case of the decentralists. Lewis Mumford, writing to Osborn, expresses this conviction vividly: '. . . the big city not merely devours population, but because of its essential nature prevents new babies coming into the world' (Mumford and Osborn, 1971, p. 61).

From the time that Letchworth was founded, until after the Second World War physical health had much the same status as the major social problem confronting legislators and philanthropists as crime and violence has today.

The solution to both the social and health problems of the urban population was seen by Howard and Osborn to be largely achievable by the provision of a better physical environment. Indeed it also formed part of public policy via the 1918 Tudor Walters report to which Raymond Unwin, an influential early member of the garden cities movement, was a major contributor. Low-density cottage-style developments became the official orthodoxy (Mumford and Osborn, 1971, p. 16). Better housing, more space for recreation, convenient work and welfare facilities undoubtedly have a major influence on health and well-being, but these ideas acquired more than mere practical status in the writings of Howard and Osborn. Contact with nature and the countryside was seen as having a fundamental, almost mystical, significance for the state of mankind. Despite his protestations of practicality, rather than utopianism, Osborn became almost obsessively attached to the idea of these low-density cottage developments at twelve houses to an acre. It is over this that he and Mumford quarrelled more than once, face-to-face and by letter − the only issue that seemed to divide them in more than thirty years' friendship.

The position you seem to have taken, dear F. J. seems to you an impregnable one because you simply cannot imagine any reasonable man having another point of view than your own, or proceeding from another set of axioms than those which seem to you self-evident (*ibid.*, p. 275).

Propounding his famous 'two magnets' principle, Ebenezer Howard too was quite unequivocal:

> our kindly mother earth, at once the source of life, of happiness, of wealth and of power. . . . The country is the symbol of God's love and care for man. All that we are and all that we have comes from it. Our bodies are formed of it; to it they return. . . . It is the source of all health, all wealth, all knowledge. But its fullness of joy and wisdom has not revealed itself to man. Nor can it as long as this unholy, unnatural separation of society and nature endures. Town and country *must be married* (Howard, 1965, pp. 46, 48, emphasis in original).

This passionate advocacy of the countryside as a source of spiritual, as well as physical, regeneration must be the source of one of the recurrent themes of the new towns movement: collective ownership of land. Howard proposes the interim measure of municipal purchase and ownership of the new town sites, but his ultimate aim is clearly that private ownership of land should end. He criticizes 'our friends, the socialists' (with whom he had, as did Osborn, extensive sympathies) for placing too much emphasis on the means of production and too little on land. They 'have thus missed the true path of reform' (Howard, 1965, pp. 135, 136).

Forty years later, Osborn commended the Uthwatt Committee's proposals for land reform (Mumford and Osborn, 1971, p. 58) and later still referred, quite seriously, to a conspiracy between the LCC architects with their monumental and high-density aesthetic and the countryside preservationists (*ibid.*, p. 204). The conviction of many members of the TCPA that collective ownership of land is an essential precursor to a better life reappears in Schaffer's *The New Town Story* (1972). In the middle of a careful — almost bland — history of the new towns, the author attacks a system which allows vast unearned profits to be made as a consequence of planning decisions. The thinly veiled passion contrasts oddly with the tone of the rest of the book.

For Howard, his supporters and his colleagues, action was, however, more important than the careful refining of a consistent philosophy. The eclecticism of their ideas reflects the eclecticism of the influences upon them. Howard had been impressed by Bellamy's *Looking Backward 2000—1887*; he had read it in its American edition and was instrumental in having it published in England.

7

When the novel was published in 1887 it was, according to the introduction of the 1951 edition 'the most widely read book of [the]
times' (Bellamy, 1951, p. xv). The utopia is described through the
medium of a novel. Boston in 2000 is a city of great beauty where
private property, wages and, indeed, all forms of money are absent.
Although family and household structure is unaltered, there are
municipal eating places and other facilities which contribute to the
emancipation of women, a dominant theme of the novel (as it is in
William Morris's *News from Nowhere*, 1891). All citizens are
allotted an equal amount of credit to obtain goods and services,
unrelated to their work because 'all who do their best, do the same'
(Bellamy, 1951, p. 74).

Despite the strong emphasis on the collectivity, the author's
sympathies are clearly not with centralized socialism. His utopia has
only a vestigial judiciary and legislature because, he claims, once
private property disappears most of the need for the apparatus of
law disappears, as does taxation. Industry is, however, completely
monolithic — a sort of corporate state, regulating its production by
demand. Opportunities and incentives for individual effort are
introduced by an elaborate system of honours which Bellamy sees
as reward enough in a society which has made 'patriotism a national
devotion' (*ibid.*, p. 206).

Somehow Bellamy contrived a system that combined collectivism
and individual incentive, decentralized power and a sophisticated
industrial system, equality and a rigid meritocracy. These themes
reappeared strongly in Howard's book although his campaign was
for a less centralized society in a quiet literal sense. He quite clearly
believed that adoption of his plan would result in the redundancy of
the great cities.

Ebenezer Howard was not unaware that he was trying to integrate two political philosophies that were then, and still are, defined
in terms of their opposition to one another, but he hoped that some
blend of individual and municipal effort could be found by
experiment:

With a growing intelligence and honesty in municipal enterprise, with greater freedom from control of the central
government, it may be found — especially on municipally
owned land — that the field of municipal activity may grow so
as to embrace a very large area and yet the municipality claim
no rigid monopoly and the fullest rights of combination exist
(Howard, 1965, p. 90).

I have made it abundantly clear that on a small scale society
may readily become more individualistic than now — if by
individualism is meant a society in which there is fuller and

free opportunity for its members to do and to produce what
they will . . . while it may also become more socialistic − if
by socialism is meant a condition of life in which the well-
being of the community is safe-guarded, and in which the collective spirit is manifested by a wide extension of the area of
municipal effort . . . Not content with *urging* the necessity of
increased production, I have shown *how it can be achieved*
. . . *(ibid.,* p. 131, emphasis on original).

F. J. Osborn's philosophy can be partly reassembled from the
fascinating collection of letters he exchanged with Lewis Mumford
(Mumford and Osborn, 1971), unfortunately only starting in 1938.
Osborn clearly has socialist sympathies, but specifically rejects the
idea of revolutionary change. Despite his disdain for inherited
wealth − especially in the form of land − and for the monarchy, he
does not wish for an enlargement of central state control, rejecting
the 'current mechanical leftism' in 1946 almost as much as the
'urbanized, café-lounging, quasi-communist, quasi-technocrat
types' *(ibid.,* p. 46) that he feels sure eviscerated the *County of
London Plan* (Forshaw and Abercrombie, 1943). Socialism, while
embodying many of the human values he wishes to endorse, is too
conservative in organization, too doctrinaire, too bureaucratic and
too inclined to endanger the voluntary initiatives that produce the
'biological competition' through which he feels society matures
(Mumford and Osborn, 1971, p. 132).

Osborn's vision of new towns is populist rather than socialist. The
rejection of the notion that new towns are a utopian concept reappears constantly in his correspondence with Lewis Mumford. The
new towns movement and in particular Osborn's advocacy of it had
a strong ideological content nevertheless. It was perhaps the more
powerful for remaining implicit. This combination of a passionately
supported ideology and the conviction that its benefits are self-
evident and without political content is a prominent feature of
British public life. Presumably both the pan-political position of the
TCPA and its success can be attributed to this assumption amongst
its most influential members.

Despite Osborn's obvious pleasure in the weakening of class
barriers, his better world emerges clearly as healthier, more in
touch with nature, but having essentially the same social structure
and institutions as before. He is particularly opposed to those who
see planning as accommodating fundamental changes in family life
− an error committed by one of his particular *bêtes noires,* the
Architectural Review, in 1943: 'the idea that we are passing into an
age when buildings express the communal life which is to replace
rather than supplement, the family life' (Mumford and Osborn,

9

1971, p. 46). The battle continued in 1949:

> There exists in their mind an idea that the family home is a
> dying institution, and that we are on the threshold of a new
> world in which, somehow, man will be born again as a social
> animal in a way different from past and present ways. When I
> was a young member of the Fabian Society I was surrounded
> by people who felt like that; I scoffed at it then as I do
> now . . . (*ibid.*, p. 171).

While Osborn acknowledges that urban café society may offer
more intellectual culture and that high-density modern architecture
may be more aesthetically coherent and striking, his conviction is
that ordinary people want neither. The new towns are to provide a
house and garden – within easy journey of work and social facilities
– for everyone. In 1943 he refers to a survey of preferences that
showed that '90 to 95 per cent want houses and gardens and don't
want flats' (*ibid.*, p. 40). Indeed the whole issue of architectural
aesthetics played little part in the new towns movement. The prime
consideration was the provision of low-density, conventional,
popular housing. Vernacular building and public architecture have
had remarkably little to do with one another, especially in housing,
for many years (Perks, 1974) and the propagandists for new towns
opted for the vernacular. The early housing in Letchworth and
Welwyn was largely privately and not publicly built, by building
firms and by subsidiaries of the Garden City companies. Much of it
was built in local style from local traditional materials (Mumford
and Osborn, 1971, p. 46). 'The speculative builder's name is mud,
but he stands far closer to the ordinary man' (*ibid.*, p. 185).

By the late 1930s the supposed anomie of life on public-housing
estates had joined the ranks of the social problems to be solved by
a new towns policy. The idea of community came to be a central
preoccupation of the post-war New Towns Committee and a recurrent topic of debate up to the present time. Yet again, however,
Osborn is a heretic; in 1956 he was writing:

> The fact is that a home-centred culture, which is healthy, does
> to some extent conflict with . . . theatres, lectures, eating,
> Johnsonian coffee-house celebration – and that most people
> value more highly the former if they can't have both
> (Mumford and Osborn, 1971, pp. 260–1).

Speaking of the idea of the neighbourhood, Osborn is even less in
step with the social planning orthodoxies of the time. Writing in
February 1956 he commends the usefulness of small halls but says:
'None of them function [to] bring together the neighbours as a geographical social group. The only thing that did that in Welwyn was

the air-raid warden service during the war' (*ibid.*, p. 244). He continues that the pioneering element in new settlements brings the newcomers together for a short spell, but is then superseded by interest groups:

> The only group, as Chesterton saw, in which you meet people you don't naturally like or understand to share interests with, is the larger family group. . . . I doubt if you can create in a town strong neighbourhood consciousness, though you can provide neighbourhood convenience. . . . People gravitate towards others of like social class and interest (*ibid.*, p. 245).

What, then, was Howard's and later Osborn's utopia? For both men it was very much the good life that they had been able to create for themselves. In it, a group of people would be able to get together in a framework supported and enabled – but not directed – by the state and found a settlement. Once a settlement was founded, the compelling advantages of an urban civilization in a rural setting would ensure economic development. Others would then be able to follow the pioneers to the town, build or rent a house and similarly take advantage of the better physical environment. Apart from this, family, social and political structures would be unaltered, except in so far as the improved situation would allow people to take more pleasure in them. The state's role, for Osborn and Howard, was limited to providing an orderly legal and economic context in which people could voluntarily decide to carry out their new town plans.

Inter-war housing and social problems

At the end of the First World War the national shortage of adequate housing was acknowledged to be a major problem, but as a result of government encouragement, and the extension of their powers through legislation, local authorities were increasingly enabled both to provide houses and to close and demolish old and unfit dwellings. The economic circumstances of the period made house-building a profitable venture, so that there came to be even greater activity in the private sector of building for sale and rent. (Indeed loan repayments were sometimes low enough to compete with public-housing rents, as T. R. Young (1934) records that they did on occasion in the Becontree and Dagenham areas.)

> By March 31st 1939 the grand total of houses built in England and Wales since the Armistice had reached the most gratifying figure of 3,998,366. Of these 1,112,544 were built by Local Authorities, 430,481 by private enterprise with State assist-ance and 2,455,341 by private enterprise without State assistance (Frazer, 1950, p. 445).

11

This furious activity was, however, largely unlimited by either negative or positive planning controls. Public housing was erected without the simultaneous development of employment, health, welfare, education, transport, shopping and social facilities. Private builders frequently took advantage of the infrastructure that the local authorities had provided by building on plots beside existing roads, thus creating the 'ribbon development' that came to characterize 1930s housing. In both the public and the private sectors, this large-scale provision of low-rise and relatively low-density housing led to a rapid increase in the physical size of urban centres. Hall *et al.* (1973, vol. 1, p. 83) record that by 1939 the built-up area of London grew to five times its size in 1919. For many people the journey to work became a wearying and costly business, as Young (1934) and Durant (1939) describe below. Industry, too, was expanding, at least in the prosperous Midlands and South East, but again unfettered by planning legislation and only randomly related to housing areas. Public concern was increasingly expressed not only at the cost of travel and its potential effect on health, but about the impact that the time lost would have on family life.

The birthrate in Britain had been declining since the end of the nineteenth century. By the mid 1930s the rate was well below replacement level and had come to be seen as an important social and political issue. The fears expressed at the prospect of a declining population ranged from the economic aspect – that there would be a lowering of demand and a contracting labour force unable to support an increasing dependent population – through military considerations to eugenics. It was suggested that the less healthy and intelligent lower orders would be over-represented in the population through their greater fecundity. In a pamphlet titled *Children for Britain*, the authors emphasized the public concern in the late 1930s and early 1940s. In a Lords debate it was claimed: 'There really is no other single political or economic problem that compares with this in fundamental importance' (Leybourne-White and White, 1945, p. 48).

'Rebuilding' family life became the focus of a social movement. Much effort was expended in trying to understand why the national trend to smaller families had occurred and how it might be reversed. Inadequate housing was advanced as a major cause and its improvement was therefore among the suggested solutions. Others included various fiscal measures as well as practical support in child care and education. Infant mortality and the health of children attracted particular attention. Frazer (1950, p. 438) records that Rowntree (1941) in *Poverty and Progress,* as well as numerous other studies of the circumstances of urban populations, had laid much emphasis on the consequences for later health, and even survival, of poverty and bad housing in childhood. Despite improvements in public health, epidemic diseases were still common. Many of these, particularly typhoid and TB, were directly linked to environmental quality, while others that took a large toll among children, especially diphtheria, scarlet fever, and measles, were exacerbated by overcrowding and poor nutrition. More and better housing was thus a public policy objective of continuing importance. By the 1930s, however, questions were being asked as to whether housing by itself was enough, especially given the unrelatedness of the new housing to other facilities described above. Two studies were done in that period which did much to hasten the search for comprehensive planning rather than merely housing solutions to redevelopment problems.

Social research on public housing estates

Terence Young's study *Becontree and Dagenham* was published in 1934 and Ruth Durant's *Watling* in 1939. The latter has become a minor classic and certainly has more 'sociological imagination', but the former is also fascinating. (Curiously Durant makes no mention of Young's study, despite the similarity of the situation he was examining, and the closeness of his conclusions to hers.) The study of Becontree and Dagenham were sponsored by the Pilgrim Trust, and Young carried out the work between 1931 and 1934, all based on secondary sources. There was no attempt to survey the attitudes or behaviour of residents. As is now well known, the London County Council developed the estates at Becontree and Dagenham, building houses for a staggering 103,000 people between 1921 and 1932. The housing was all of the cottage and garden type. No provision was made to attract additional industry to the area, nor was there the organization or the power to coordinate the provision of transport, education, welfare, health, shopping or recreational facilities. These were provided by other private and statutory undertakers in more or less *ad hoc* fashion, a situation not improved by the economic climate of the time and the fact that the vast estate fell into more than one local government area. Many of the problems that Young describes were reiterated in Durant's study and are still appearing today on peripheral estates and to some extent in new and expanded towns.

As both authors point out, the residents of the estates were not poor. Durant described the majority of Watling residents as of 'particularly prosperous forms and phases of working class life' (Durant, 1939, p. 4) with a sprinkling of clerical and professional residents. This was much the same situation as that in Becontree and Dagenham, where, as Young specifically explained (Young,

1934, pp. 25–6), 'slum' people could not afford the rents. He also emphasized that migration to the estate was entirely voluntary, and while it sometimes had to be stimulated by advertising at other times there was a waiting list. In terms of class and age structure, then, the estates were similar to the later new towns in their early stages of development.

Higher rents and the cost of furnishings, however, made for budget problems further complicated by high travel costs. Even in 1931, when the car industry was beginning to develop, many men were still travelling across London to work. 'Every morning a huge wave of workers gathered itself up upon the Becontree Estate and spread westwards over London . . .' (Young, 1934, p. 121).

Just under a third were able to work within five miles of the estate, but another third were travelling between ten and fifteen miles as the crow flies to places like Fulham and Wembley. It is hardly surprising that Young dwelt on the cost, both in cash and energy, of this kind of journey to work. At one point he casually defined the morning rush hour on the sketchy train service as 'from four a.m. to ten a.m.'. Ruth Durant takes up the effect on community life: 'Fatigue and worry keep the family at home' (Durant, 1939, p. 118).

How fine was the financial balance for many of the Becontree families is illustrated in Young's account of the circumstances of those who turned to statutory and voluntary welfare agencies. Other residents, observing that the repayment on local housing being built for sale was no more than the rent they were paying, had moved into owner-occupation, only to reapply to Becontree when they found that they could not afford the repairs and maintenance. This attention to the cost of living on the estate must be seen in the light of a contemporary controversy. In 1933 the Medical Officer of Health of Stockton-on-Tees, Dr McGonigle, had caused a *furor* by delivering a paper in which he claimed that people were dying at a higher rate on estates in his area through economizing on food. But, as Young pointed out (Young, 1934, p. 229), the people Dr McGonigle was concerned with were unemployed.

In many other respects, the Young and the Durant studies were similar. They both described the rise and fall of the 'pioneer' spirit with its accompanying local newspaper, and the dearth of all kinds of facility, from schools to community centres to cinemas. Young was more sanguine about their absence observing, for example, that running about wild in the country when there were no school facilities probably did the children no harm at all. When organizations and building did begin to appear he was as interested and painstaking in charting the development of pubs as of religious and political institutions. But while Young and Durant described much the same situation and process, their attitudes were subtly different.

When discussing the rate of turnover, Young recorded that rates ran at around 10 per cent, with a peak in 1928/9 of 17 per cent (Young, 1934, p. 210), a rate higher than that on other LCC cottage estates. He observed that this instability would slow down social development as it would lead to a lack of interest in voluntary associations and a loss of continuity of both members and officers. Against this, though, he recorded that living in Becontree brought major problems of rent and travel costs, especially compared with other LCC cottage estates with controlled rents. He also wondered what the removal rate would be in a 'typical London working class district' (*ibid.*, p. 210), with the clear implication that the Becontree situation was regrettable, but not disastrous. Such ebbs and flows were for him the outcome of individual families resolving their differences – or not. Durant, on the other hand, described the 10 per cent average annual rate of turnover in Watling as 'enormous' (Durant, 1939, p. 16), and dwelt at some length on how short a time most people lived there. In fact, much of the movement seems to have been unexceptional: people moving job, changing phases in the family cycle or buying their own home. In her now famous phrase, she describes the estate:

> In the long run Watling is not much more than a huge hotel without a roof; the constant turnover of its population is the greatest single handicap to its developing into a community (*ibid.*, p. 119).

Durant implied that the only worthwhile life is one of intensive communal activity and participation where, preferably, most people died in the same bed they had been born in. Like M. Young and Willmott (1957) later, she approved of the family but not of (nuclear) 'family-centredness': 'Nowadays domesticity predominates' (Durant, 1939, p. 89). Her prescriptions were the provision of more community buidings and that the estate should be a unitary local government area – which Young also recommended for Becontree and Dagenham.

Having analysed much the same kind of phenomenon and highlighted many of the same issues, Young and Durant differed fundamentally about the meaning that should be attached to their observations. Young saw a vast housing enterprise that displayed all the weaknesses of planning legislation and local government structure, but in which, nevertheless, thousands had better houses and stayed there. To Durant 'new estates are crucial instances of modern city life. They expose the loneliness of urban people and the paucity of their institutions' (Durant, 1939, p. 117).

The differences in the two situations did not, however, lie in the estates themselves, but in the authors' interpretation of them. Durant clearly embraced a collectivist perspective, and hers was the more influential study.

Garden cities and public policy

Inter-war governments were not, of course, unaware of the need to link housing, planning and industrial policies. The differential effects of the depression that began in the late 1920s and continued until the outbreak of the Second World War gave impetus to the search for coherent regional policies, most fully expressed in the 1940 'Barlow' commission on the distribution of the industrial population. Barlow was, however, the culmination of a series of committees that had started with the *Final Report* of Chamberlain's Unhealthy Areas Committee in 1921.

The Chamberlain committee saw two solutions to the problems of London: high-rise blocks and lower densities. Having rejected the high-rise solution in its *Interim Report,* the *Final Report* specifically recommended a policy of garden cities with state assistance in finance and in offering incentives to industry:

> That the development of self-contained garden cities, either around an existing nucleus or on new sites should be encouraged and hastened by state assistance in the early stages, such assistance to take the form of a loan secured as a first charge upon the land developed as a garden city (Unhealthy Areas Committee, 1921, p. 17).

The development agencies envisaged were local authorities and private groups. Such a state garden city policy suffered the same fate as much of the rest of inter-war permissive planning legislation, however, and the matter received little attention until ten years later when the Marley committee on garden cities and satellite towns was set up.

The remit of this committee was to 'examine the experience already gained in regard to the establishment of garden cities and villages and satellite towns' (Departmental Committee on Garden Cities and Satellite Towns, 1935, p. 3), and to make recommendations on whether they should form a part of government policy, how they should be financed and how industry should be stimulated.

These concerns were set, as we have seen, against a period of rapid house-building in the private sector and public housing on the massive scale of Becontree and Dagenham. There was much public concern about the haphazard destruction of the countryside and the growing tracts of housing without local jobs or other facilities. The committee assumed that there would have to be some central agency to formulate planning objectives and to control the location of industry. Instead of endorsing 'relatively isolated and detached new towns of the garden city type' (*ibid.*, p. 10), however, the committee advocated the development of 'more or less self-contained' satellite towns some distance from the original nucleus of the parent town. The intention, albeit not spelt out in detail, seems to have been that there should be housing with health, education, welfare and recreational facilities and some jobs but that commuting to the parent town would also take place.

The committee recommended that a non-political 'planning board' of about five worthies should be set up, answerable to the Ministry of Health, but that the actual development agency would be the local authorities, using section 35 of the Town and Country Planning Act 1932. Two members of the committee had reservations about this last recommendation. Theodore Chambers and Raymond Unwin wanted the local authorities to have power 'to delegate the duties to a suitable constituted board or commission' (*ibid.*, p. 23). (Two other members dissented from the committee's report entirely. Both felt the proposed planning board to be superfluous and one added that the whole notion of satellite towns was impractical and expensive in the current situation.)

The inter-war activities of the GCTPA

For most of the inter-war period the active members of the Garden City and Town Planning Association were preoccupied with the development of Letchworth and Welwyn. Starting the latter had been a decision taken by Ebenezer Howard alone. He had simply gone to the public auction and bought the land. Such were Howard's personal qualities that when he found that he had insufficient money for the deposit, the balance was put up by the surveyor acting for him (Purdom, 1949, p. 186)! Osborn later wrote of this development:

> I was speechless with admiration and baffled rage . . .
> because I knew that the initiation of another garden city by
> private enterprise was just the get-out that the authorities,
> slightly bothered by public response to our propaganda,
> would jump at (and they did) (Osborn, 1942, p. 9).

Osborn himself subsequently went to work and live at Welwyn. In 1936, as we have seen, he lost his job through reorganization and began his long career as virtually full-time propagandist of the GCTPA. During the same period, *Town and Country Planning*, the journal of the association, was revitalized under the editorship of

Gilbert Macallister, and became more concerned with wider planning issues, besides regular reports on the progress of Welwyn and Letchworth. It provided a platform for the pursuit of the garden city idea and for equally persistent crusades against the GCTPA's three horsemen of the apocalypse: high-density, high-rise and modernist architecture. The outbreak of war and the subsequent reconstruction period undoubtedly catalysed new town propaganda into policy, but without the foregoing years of work it is unlikely that those ideas would have been as much a part of the conventional wisdom of the time as they had become.

The flavour of the campaign comes vividly from the pages of *Town and Country Planning*. The Association was having to work defensively as well as offensively, of course, because, during the massive inter-war house-building, vulgarized garden city ideas had passed into common currency. Besides schemes like Hampstead Garden Suburb and Wythenshawe, any development with trees in the street and placed inconveniently far from urban facilities tended to be called a 'garden suburb'. A 1930 editorial reiterated garden-city principles: a garden city would be well-designed; healthy; of adequate size with adequate facilities; isolated and with the land held in trust (*Town and Country Planning*, February 1930). Later editions contained symposia of well-known public figures, (presumably) solicited testimonials to the need for garden cities and even shock reports on the perils of the city life! The March 1937 issue is a particularly vivid example. It contains an attack on the hypertrophy of London, a favourable review by F. J. Osborn of a Heath Robinson humorous book on flat-dwelling and an article by Norman MacFadyen entitled 'Thirteen Thousand Babies need not Die'. Dr MacFadyen, a passionate advocate of garden cities and biographer of Ebenezer Howard, inferred from comparing the infant mortality rate for England and Wales and that for garden cities, that 13,000 babies would have survived in a better environment. He also concluded that the total mortality rate would fall and the birthrate rise, thus emphasizing the link between the GCTPA's platform and wider public concerns.

Similar themes recurred throughout the late 1930s and into the early years of the war. In September 1937, Osborn was attacking the sentimental attachment of Le Corbusier and others to high-density living and a woman doctor was writing of children's need for gardens. Again in 1938, the journal described a report by the London Council of Social Service on the stresses caused by flat-dwelling, the main complaints being about noise and the lack of a garden. At this point concern about the vulnerability of big cities to air attack was beginning to be expressed too.

The GCTPA's evangelism did not, however, extend to endorsing the views of anyone who shared their belief in decentralization. A. Trystan Edwards had founded the Hundred New Towns Association in 1933 with the publication of his pamphlet *A Hundred New Towns for Britain,* under the pseudonym 'Ex-serviceman J 47485'. His plan was for five million Britons to be rehoused in towns of about 50,000 covering four square miles. The total cost he estimated at £10 million and the whole project would stand as a war memorial. Unlike in Ebenezer Howard's book there was no mention of what agency should be used to carry out the scheme. Both Purdom (1949, p. 493) and Simon (1945, p. 181) remark that Edwards specifically disliked aspects of the garden city idea, notably the green belt which he referred to as imposing a 'stranglehold' on the town, and low-density building which in his view destroyed the intrinsic sociability of high-density urban life. Instead he proposed 'green wedges' which would allow continued expansion of the town if so desired, and high-density terrace housing. The scheme was commended to the public in a letter to *The Times* (24 February 1934) signed by twelve notables. The GCTPA, however, was disdainful, describing his housing proposals as 'unacceptable' and concluding: 'Welcome as Mr Edwards's denunciation of the tenement flat system was, the TCPA could not embrace his Association as a valuable ally' (Osborn and Whittick, 1969, p. 98).

Edwards maintained his position, revising and republishing his proposals towards the end of the Second World War. So, too, did the GCTPA (renamed the Town and Country Planning Association in 1941). F. J. Osborn's 1918 *New Towns after the War* was republished in 1942, substantially unaltered, according to the preface. Again the dominant ideas of Howard and Osborn are rehearsed: 'The great city throughout history has been inimical to life and health' (Osborn, 1942, p. 27). The practicality of garden cities, the importance of providing jobs and facilities as well as housing, the voluntary nature of immigration, and the wish to enhance family life are all emphasized.

What a dramatic opening for the era of international reconstruction — Britain, which led the way to industrialism, now showing the way to a system in which industrial wealth is compatible with a sane, natural and cultured life for all! (*ibid.*, p. 70).

2 Wartime deliberation; post-war legislation

> We are informed that the development of this town is a
> matter of urgency . . . (New Towns Committee, 1964a, para.
> 16 (1)).

The report of the Barlow Royal Commission on the Distribution of
the Industrial Population (1940) has since been described as the
'essential basis of the post-war British planning system' (Hall, 1973,
vol. 1, p. 91). It established the principles of urban containment and
the decentralization of population and industry which underpinned
post-war new town legislation as part of a wider planning
philosophy.

The Commission was set up in 1937. Its analysis of social and economic process and the progress of planning legislation and of
'experiments in decentralization and dispersal' remains impressive,
even if its conclusions were, in the event, rather 'muted' (Hall,
1973, vol. 2, p. 47).

The Commission was concerned with the drift of population from
the country to the cities and from the north and west to the south-
east. The contrast in wealth and population density between
London and the rest of the country, though marked from at least the
Tudor period, was particularly acute in the 1930s. The hope was to
recommend means whereby the 'tide of forces' that was bringing
population to the large cities could be held back. After tracing the
decline of heavy and localized industries, the parallel growth of the
inter-related secondary and tertiary sectors of the economy and
changing transport patterns, the Commission turned to the effects
of the congestion of population. For this purpose a joint medical
committee had been set up, and its report clearly shows the effectiveness of Garden City and Town Planning Association lobbying.
It urges that overcrowding should be reduced by building houses at

twelve to the acre, that industry and housing should be zoned, that smoke pollution should be reduced and that people should be housed within easy reach of both their work and open countryside: 'the scheme of the Garden City is the model towards which the location of industry should work' (Barlow Commission, 1940, p. 65). The predominant theme, not only of the joint medical committee but of the rest of the Commission report, is physical health, not social disorganization.

The Barlow Commission weighed the dispersal-oriented medical evidence against both the problems of dispersal and the alternative solution of inner-city redevelopment. Their comments on suburban expansion are worth quoting in full, for their sad familiarity:

> Apart from the common absence of the correlation of housing and industry and the lag in the provision of community services, this suburban expansion is fed by the movement of men, women and children from the district and surroundings in which, more often than not they have been born and bred, in which their friends live and in which their interests are mainly centred. They may move miles from their old home to a large housing estate with little or no community life, lacking facilities conducive to the growth of a community life and, if the estate is composed of houses for one class only of the population, so constituted that the development of a full and healthy community life is next to impossible.
>
> The housewife finds that she has to pay higher prices for food and other family necessities than in her old district. The better housing accommodation which the family possesses may cost more in rent or similar payments (*ibid.*, pp. 68–9).

Turning to the problems of inner-city redevelopment, the Commission noted the unpopularity of flats but said that there are people for whom proximity to work in the inner city is paramount. The costs and benefits of continued urban concentration were examined and the Commission shrewdly observed that the piecemeal development of industry and the housing that follows it imposes costs on the community for infrastructure and facilities which had never been fully quantified (*ibid.*, p. 95). The growth of planning legislation to date was evaluated, and the Commission came to the unexceptionable conclusion, for that period, that the problems lay in the localized, piecemeal and permissive structure of the current legislation. Perhaps the greatest stumbling block to the extension of nationally unified comprehensive planning was the issue of compensation for loss of development rights and its corollary: the levying of betterment. (These important issues were

21

dealt with by an expert committee, the Uthwatt Committee, set up by Lord Reith in 1941; see below.)

Within their overall evaluation of urban growth and urban policy, the Barlow Commission's recommendations about garden-city development must be seen as crucial in the legitimation of these policies. Interestingly, the Commission sounded a note of caution about the potential of a dispersal policy which seemed to be over-looked in the framing of subsequent programmes. Their view as to the scale of urban growth at which a decentralization policy should be adopted was vague (*ibid.*, p. 132, para. 283) but there seemed to be an underlying assumption that some immanent process in city growth would force the adoption of decentralist policy. The Commission's prescriptions for garden cities and satellite towns were specific:

1   that they should be far enough away to make use of light, air and open space and should be surrounded by a green belt;
2   they should be off the main arterial roads . . . but should have good access to them and should be near enough to the big centre to enjoy its advantageous marketing facilities';
3   that they should provide diverse employment for a 'large, if not the greater, proportion of the inhabitants';
4   that local health, educational and recreational facilities should be provided but that the satellite town should be near enough to use the big centre sometimes.

> however well a suburban or satellite city may be equipped, its inhabitants will want to visit the centre in order to shop or see a good play or film or listen to a concert or a well-known speaker, or for many other purposes. But this is a very different thing from being forced to seek all their amusements and collective activities at a long distance from their place of residence' (*ibid.*, p. 133, para. 284).

Thus, while the Commission envisaged future garden-city developments as being relatively self-contained in employment terms and in the local facilities offered, they did not recommend the total self-sufficiency implied by much of the GCTPA propaganda and by the later New Towns Committee recommendations. Something of a hierarchy of urban centres was implied, rather than the ultimate redundancy of the great metropolitan centres.

Similar caution appeared in the Commission's discussion of the sponsorship and ultimate extent of a programme of garden cities, satellite towns, trading estates, etc. Such a programme mounted by local authorities with central government funds was endorsed, but:

> it is doubtful whether the policy of creating either garden

cities or trading estates is capable of very wide expansion and, indeed, it has been suggested to the Commission that something in the nature of competition is already arising in the case of the latter (*ibid.* p. 135, para. 289).

This reservation about the pool of mobile industry and the likely extent of economic growth has proved only too prescient in the light of events both immediately post-war and today. The new town lobby even came in for some gentle chiding:

in the view of many the ideal town should be limited to 50,000 to 100,000. The analyses . . . are often made without quite sufficient attention being given to the actual facts and causes of urban growth or to the diverse needs of modern civilization (*ibid.*, p. 154, para 323).

The central recommendation of the Committee, signed by the majority, was for a four-man 'National Industry Board' to formulate national economic and physical development strategies in conjunction with the relevant government departments. The co-ordination of local and regional planning schemes and the encouragement of a limited decentralist policy of garden cities was subsumed within this general function.

Three members of the Commission presented a minority report, and these included two influential members of the GCTPA, Patrick Abercrombie and Hermione Hichens. They urged the granting of the powers suggested for the NIB to a new government ministry with more executive power, based on the transfer of power from other ministries. The minister should have, they suggested, the power to control the location of industry, to formulate and impose a national development plan and the ability to offer financial inducements for 'desirable industrial location and proper planning' (*ibid.*, p. 204). The promotion of garden cities was especially urged. The proposed ministry was also to have research and advisory functions. Professor Abercrombie also contributed a further attack on the limitations of current planning powers.

The intimacy of the relationship between the Barlow Commission and the GCTPA emerges in a letter from F. J. Osborn to Lewis Mumford at the time of Abercrombie's death in 1957:

when he was a member of the Barlow Royal Commission I redrafted for him some of the key paragraphs of the majority report and drafted some of his own minority report − but it was all very 'hush-hush' and both of us were kept hard at this underground work by Mrs W. L. Hichens. . . . She and Abercrombie did get the wording of the main recommendations considerably strengthened, but not enough to avoid the necessity of the minority report (Mumford and Osborn, 1971, p. 271).

Undoubtedly the Commission had a profound influence on later planning policy, although its central recommendation was not adopted. Indeed the later changes in governmental organization that did occur were rather more like those suggested in the Minority Report. There remained, however, a crucial separation of power between planning and industrial location, originally between the Ministry of Town and Country Planning and the Board of Trade, and latterly between the Department of Industry and the Department of the Environment. Many of the oscillations of the new towns programme can still be traced to that situation.

Two issues that concerned the Royal Commission remained outstanding and were the subject of independent examination. In October 1941 Lord Reith appointed the Scott Committee on Land Utilization in Rural Areas. The Barlow Commission had made wry passing reference to the conflict of interest between the countryside lobby and the decentralists:

> While some planning enthusiasts advocate compulsory scattering of existing urban population by the million over unoccupied rural areas . . . the Ministry of Agriculture express a preference for the fringe extension of existing towns (Barlow Commission, 1940, p. 14, para. 34).

Fulminations about the romantic countryside lobby, represented by the Council for the Preservation of Rural England, appear several times in the Mumford/Osborn letters. The Scott Report (1942) could be interpreted as a photo-finish victory for the preservationists, despite the presence on the committee of the redoubtable Mrs Hichens and Professor Dudley Stamp, both members of the TCPA. Perhaps this was inevitable during the war, when agricultural productivity was of crucial importance. The committee's recommendations echo those of Barlow in their call for unified planning and effective legislation. On the other hand the 'onus of proof' formula was created, forcing planners and others to prove their need to use prime agricultural land for development (*ibid.*, p. 86, para. 233). Earlier passages seem to support a policy of high-density, high-rise housing in order to prevent urban sprawl and encroachment into agricultural land (*ibid.*, p. 71, para. 202). The sites of new towns should be chosen with care so as not to use top-quality land, and the committee even states: 'The country towns should be as compact as the requirements of healthy living permit' (*ibid.*, p. 72, para. 205). A minority report by Professor S. R. Dennison suggested that the majority was too committed to the *status quo.*

In the early years of the Second World War the major obstacle to large-scale development and redevelopment by public or private agencies was the liability of local authorities to pay compensation for the loss of the development rights, through public purchase of a person's land or loss of value as a result of a town-planning scheme. Provision for payment of compensation had been contained in the Town Planning Acts of 1909 and 1932. While the scope of planning was anyway limited even under the latter legislation, the liability of local authorities to pay compensation had acted as a further disincentive to the adoption of planning schemes. Parallel powers in both the 1909 and 1932 Act enabled local authorities to collect betterment from landowners, i.e. the rise in the value of their property brought about by the execution of a town-planning scheme. The 1932 Act was described by the Uthwatt Committee (1942) as 'largely ineffective' (p. 123, para. 291) and indeed hardly any betterment had been collected up to the outbreak of war (*ibid.*, para. 292).

Lord Reith appointed the Uthwatt Expert Committee on Compensation and Betterment in January 1941. Its deliberations were outstanding in two respects. First, the research and recommendations are exhaustive and highly specific. The *Final Report* amounts to a history and critique of the law on both compensation and betterment. Second, there was no member of the TCPA on the small (five-member) committee! It must be said, though, that its secretary was Frank Schaffer who subsequently became closely involved in the new towns programme.

The recommendations of the committee were not adopted in their entirety, although their work was used in the reformulation of compulsory-purchase powers and the legislation framed for acquiring and redeveloping war-damaged areas. Perhaps the committee demonstrated only too well the complexity of the issues involved. The 1947 Town and Country Planning Act's proposals on compensation and betterment were also doomed. Many involved in the planning debate then and now insist that the issue of land can only be solved by some form of community ownership, indeed this issue was a popular platform in Ebenezer Howard's youth, as we have seen.

Platforms into policy

By the outbreak of the Second World War it had become increasingly accepted that satisfactory standards of life could only be obtained by major intervention on the part of central and local government. National policies were being sought, not only in housing and education, but in health and welfare, town planning and the location of industry. Indeed 'planning' in a much wider sense had come to be seen as a legitimate concern of government. Even family life was defined as an area in which the state had an interest: 'because the family is the microcosm of the state, the state has gradually realized its responsibilities for the health and well-being of the family' (Marchant, ed., n.d., p. 68). An increasingly collectivist flavour had informed the social research and social policy of the 1930s. The outbreak of war transformed these ideas into institutional forms that were then consolidated and extended by the 1945 Labour victory. It has become a cliché that the Second World War gave people a sense of communal endeavour and comradeship unparalleled before or since. It also provided the opportunity for national planning − of manpower, industry and health services for example − giving both a logic and a framework for similarly centralized solutions to the problems of post-war reconstruction. In his history of war time social policy, Titmuss wrote:

> It would . . . be true to say that by the end of the Second World War the Government had, through the agency of newly established or existing services, assumed and developed a measure of direct concern for the health and well-being of the population which, by contrast with the role of Government in the nineteen-thirties, was little short of remarkable (1949, p. 506).

Even the 1941 Uthwatt Committee, which consisted entirely of prominent lawyers and surveyors, neither being professions in which radical ideas predominate, stated:

> The first assumption is that national planning is a reality and a permanent feature of the administration of the internal affairs of this country. We assume that it will be directed to ensuring the best use is made of land with a view to securing economic efficiency for the community and well-being for the individual, and it will be recognized that this involves the subordination in the public good of the personal wishes and interests of landowners (Uthwatt Committee, 1941, p. 11, para. 17).

Paradoxically, regionalism also received a fresh impetus, the assumption being that an overall planning strategy would be worked out centrally and administered at a regional level in areas large enough to have comprehensive powers but small enough to enable people to feel a sense of involvement. During the war, the country had been divided into twelve civil-defence regions with commissioners, to form the basis for provincial governments if need be, as well as to carry out civil-defence functions. In March 1942 one of the commissioners produced a Fabian pamphlet calling for the continuation of such regions after the war, governed by an elected body:

> Regional planning consists, first, of applying the principles of the national plan to the regional area. . . . On this plane would come the location of industry . . .; the provision of satellite towns and garden cities; the provision of large open spaces and green belts; major highways other than trunk roads; water supply; the siting of hospitals, clinics, libraries, swimming baths, secondary and technical schools and many other municipal institutions ('Regionaliter', 1942, p. 16).

Comprehensive planning solutions were gradually coming to be seen as self-evident, with a garden city programme an assumed part of them. The goal was not merely physical improvement, however. Many housing schemes were designed with the explicit aim of fostering community life. Reilly's (1947) plan for Birkenhead expressed the current conventional wisdom:

> The only new idea which has arrived since the garden city movement . . . is the return of the tradition of the village green and its inn, now called a community centre . . . it is necessary to work out some development of the physical form which will aid in establishing community life (p. 59).

Perhaps the most important outcome of war-time conditions, however, was the throwing together of lobbyists, academics and politicians in committees, conferences and boards that were intimate, overlapping and largely outside the normal framework of political accountability and horsetrading. They met often and developed a set of common assumptions and personal relationships that were to prove very powerful when some of the members were propelled into office in the 1945 Labour government. A typical example of the multiplex links of the policy-makers was the 1941 TCPA conference at Oxford which focused on the main recommendations of the Barlow Commission. (Its proceedings were published as Towndrow (ed.) 1941, *Replanning Britain.*) The speakers included Lord Harmsworth, Sir Montague Barlow, Professor Abercrombie, Dr Dudley Stamp, F. J. Osborn, Herbert Manzoni (City Engineer, Birmingham) and Lord Justice Scott. Much more important, however, was Sir John Reith's advisory panel on planning, appointed in 1941. The TCPA was well represented on this powerful body, with eight out of twenty-one members, including Abercrombie, Barlow, Dudley Stamp and F. J. Osborn. It is not surprising that the immediate post-war planning legislation was swift to appear and that the themes running through it were so well orchestrated. Even if the TCPA was not first violin, the motifs of urban containment and decentralization were clear.

Lord Reith's New Towns Committee and its philosophy

At the request of the Minister of Town and Country Planning, Patrick Abercrombie had prepared a plan for the post-war redevelopment of London (Abercrombie, 1945). The main theme of the *Greater London Plan 1944* was decentralization. The premise was asserted early and the whole plan followed from it.

> The need for decentralization arises from the twofold desire to improve housing conditions in those areas which are overcrowded and to reduce the concentration of industry in the London area which had caused the expansion of the metropolis to a size which had become quite unmanageable and one which has made of Londoners a race of straphangers (*ibid.*, p. 30).

By means of inner-area redevelopment, additions to existing towns within the greater London area, additions to towns outside the area, the building of satellite towns and the general encouragement of out-migration, the intention was to reduce the population of the county of London by 1·03 million people (*ibid.*, p. 33). The new housing would not be provided out of public funds alone; it was hoped that there would be extensive migration of professionals and small businessmen to private housing as well. Agencies for the infilling and for the proposed satellite towns were tentatively suggested as both private builders and consortia of local authorities:

> a number of authorities in the East London Area – e.g. East and West Ham, Leyton, etc. where problems of housing are more urgent than elsewhere and where large numbers need to be decentralized could combine to form a new East or West Ham in one of the Essex satellites. A certain measure of the existing community life could be transferred, the old and familiar faces of neighbours and friends would still be there, and settling down would be more easily undertaken (*ibid.*, p. 37).

(Doubtless it was exactly the spectre of a 'new Leyton' that haunted the burghers of Stevenage a couple of years later . . .) Ten specific sites were suggested for satellite towns, just outside the proposed greenbelt, about 20–25 miles from central London. Among the sites were Stevenage and Harlow.

After the Labour election victory of 1945, Lewis Silkin became

Minister of Town and Country Planning. In October 1945 he appointed a committee under the chairmanship of Sir John Reith. The latter, a Scot of strong religious and moral views and great organizational skill, had become a major public figure as General Manager of the BBC between 1922 and 1939. He had also been Minister of Works and Building from 1940 to 1942. The committee, which included F. J. Osborn and other members of the TCPA, seemed to have assumed that it would have a year to deliberate and report and that legislation would then be framed. In the event, however, matters were expedited with commendable − if not indecent − haste. The *Interim Report* on the choice of agency is dated 21 January 1946. It contains specific recommendations about temporary arrangements to allow Stevenage to be started in advance of the special legislation (New Towns Committee, 1946a, p. 15) and indeed the Stevenage project was announced in March 1946. The *Second Interim Report* appeared in April 1946. The introduction observes that the New Towns Bill, which had been expected in the autumn, was now to be 'very soon' because an 'unexpected opportunity for its earlier introduction had arisen' (New Towns Committee, 1946b, p. 3). The *Final Report* dated July 1946 preceded the passing of the New Towns Bill by only a week and there is, in the introduction, a hint of pique:

> The sequence of presentation is therefore not what we should have adopted had we been able to submit, before the introduction of the Bill, a single and complete report on the matters remitted to us (New Towns Committee, 1946c, p. 5).

The years of campaigning by the TCPA had suddenly borne fruit, almost to excess. Despite the apparent haste in preparation, the Reith committee made recommendations that were largely adopted in the New Towns Act 1946 and which remain, slightly extended but little altered, today. The British new towns programme has been arguably the most striking example yet seen of an attempt at comprehensive social and physical (and by implication economic) planning in this country or in most of the West. It is doubtful whether such a grandiose vision could have been contemplated at any other time than 1945−7, when socialism, optimism and national enterprise made the project seem attainable. The new towns reports and legislation are worth examination, not merely as pieces of radical legislation, but also as expressions of the social philosophy of that time − or at least that of the legislators.

New towns were to be an integral part of post-war planning strategy. They were also undoubtedly intended to bring about some sort of social change, although this, as will be shown later, was expressed in rhetoric and hope rather than in specific mechanisms in the legislation. Like Ebenezer Howard's, the deliberations of the New Towns Committee were primarily concerned with the 'how' rather than the 'why' of new towns. The much-discussed 'social goals' of the policy were asserted in the terms of reference and interpreted rather than evaluated in the text.

Lord Reith's committee was:

> To consider the general questions of the establishment, development organization and administration that will arise in the promotion of New Towns in furtherance of a policy of planned decentralization from congested urban areas; and in accordance therewith to suggest guiding principles on which such Towns should be established and developed as self-contained and balanced communities for working and living. (New Towns Committee, 1946a, p. 2).

Despite the lack of precision about how the new towns' social objectives were to be achieved in practice, the Reith committee's reports are quite specific about principles. After an initial recommendation that the optimum population target should fall in the range 20,000 to 60,000, the *Final Report* recommends a range of 30,000 to 50,000: 'Our conclusions have been reinforced by the replies received to a broadcast on 15th January, 1946' (New Towns Committee, 1946c, p. 9). (A timely corrective to those who might assume that phone-ins, etc. are a post-McLuhan phenomenon.) Similarly the definition of social balance is blunt:

> So far as the issue is an economic one balance can be attained by giving opportunity for many sorts of employment which will attract men and women up to a high income level. Beyond that point the problem is not economic at all, or even a vaguely social one; it is, to be frank, one of class distinction. So far as these distinctions are based on income, taxation and high costs of living are reducing them. We realize also that there are some who would have us ignore their existence. But the problem remains and must be faced; if the community is to be truly balanced, so long as classes exist, all must be represented in it. A contribution is needed from every type and class of person; the community will be poorer if all are not there, able and willing to make it (*ibid.*, p. 10).

The committee goes on to express the hope that administrative and research establishments would relocate in the new towns and that retired people and people of 'independent means' would choose to go to them. To bring this situation about two levers were to be used in conjunction with one another: the relocation of employment and the provision of a wide variety of housing both in

30

size and tenure. This should be attempted in the very earliest stages to avoid the town's becoming 'one-class', and the housing should be: 'provided by the agency, by housing associations, or by private builders for sale and letting as well as sites to be built to suit owner-occupiers' (*ibid.*, p. 10). The main meaning of 'balance' therefore is unequivocal: it is class balance, both in terms of income group and of status. (What the normal distribution of classes in a town would be, and how and at what stage of growth to assess it, has been extensively discussed in subsequent writing on the new towns. This literature will be reviewed in a later chapter.) Earlier in the report, the committee had also referred to the need for a 'well-balanced' provision of industry (*ibid.*, p. 9) to provide a variety of employment for men and women, presumably to avoid over-dependence on one type of industry or employer. Age balance is not discussed. The committee no doubt assumed that this would not be the problem that it had been on the inter-war estates, if sufficient choice of work opportunities was available. More detailed considerations of balancing the population in terms of the proportions of single people, the unemployed, unemployable, elderly and ethnic minority groups make no appearance.

'Self-containment', even more than balance, was central to the concept of a new town — to the extent that it is not singled out for explicit discussion by the Reith committee. Self-containment was to be achieved primarily by the provision of local job opportunities and thus the elimination of journeys to work except on foot or bicycle. This home/job link has of course been strengthened in practice by the use of the Industrial Selection Scheme or an equivalent in most new towns at some stage of their development. Under such a scheme, housing was offered on the one hand to key employees of relocating firms to encourage industry to settle, and on the other to individual migrants when they obtained a job in the new town. It is clear that the Reith committee did not envisage such a formal framework. Perhaps, like Howard and the TCPA, they took it for granted that the benefits of new town life would be so compelling as both to attract migrants and eliminate commuting. In the *Second Interim Report* they observe that the need for housing may at some stage 'outpace the transfer of industry' so that some arrangements for commuting will have to be made.

> This would be a regrettable necessity, since it makes the new town to some extent a dormitory for the time being. . . . But . . . a semi-dormitory which gradually becomes self-contained is better than a suburb which is a dormitory for all time (New Towns Committee, 1946b, p. 9).

A secondary meaning of self-containment was the evident intention that new towns should provide not only shopping, health, welfare and education facilities locally, but should also provide for recreational and cultural needs. The kind of urban hierarchy mentioned in the Barlow report is implicitly rejected.

As well as being examined independently, self-containment and balance – themselves interdependent ideas – can be subsumed under the more fundamental assumptions that the Reith committee were making about the importance of community life.

> Of all the groups and societies to which men and women are attached, perhaps the most important, next to the family, is the local and geographical community. In great cities the sense of community membership is weak and this is one of the most serious of modern urban ills. In a true community, everybody feels, directly or through some group, that he has a place and a part, belonging and counting (New Towns Committee, 1946c, p. 42).

The function of new towns was not to recreate this quality of life, however, but to provide the medium for its renaissance in a new and egalitarian form; a process brought on in part by the war years. Social class, the Reith committee assumed, and hoped, was breaking down, as is clear from their discussion of balance. Their goal was a 'socially homogeneous community' (*ibid.*, p. 10), brought about by communal facilities, and by mixing housing types and tenure plot by plot. Neighbourhoods, beloved of later new town designers, are specifically rejected. It is a convenience: 'a natural and useful conception –, but it should not be thought of as a self-contained community of which the inhabitants are more conscious than they are of the town as a whole' (*ibid.*, p. 16). There would be more leisure in the new environment to enable people to play a part in civic life, especially the women. To this end the Reith committee recommends the provision both of day and night nurseries (*ibid.*, p. 42) and restaurants:

> War-time experiences have strengthened the impulse to escape from the necessity of preparing and clearing up every meal in the week. . . . Hired domestic labour is unlikely ever to become as plentiful as it once was, and women naturally want to take what respite they can afford from work in the home (*ibid.*, p. 46).

An ideological rift appears in the pages of the *Final Report* in respect of the good life. It is almost as if the struggle to avoid paternalism has been lost. Discussing social life and recreation Lord Reith and his colleagues stoutly assert:

It is not possible, and even if it were it would not be wise, to prescribe the social and cultural pattern of a new town. The interests, groupings and cultural activities of citizens must grow of themselves. . . . It is this variety that gives character to towns, and any thought of standardizing the pattern, or even of standardizing the equipment, must be dismissed (*ibid.*, p. 43).

Yet, on the following page the committee suggests that a town of 40−60,000 would require two theatres, a concert hall and an art gallery. 'Indeed, if the cultural standard of the population is high, this range of buildings may be required by the time the town reaches 25,000 to 30,000' (*ibid.*, p. 44). As for the cinema:

the programmes shown in commercial cinemas have a limited cultural range and American productions dominate. There may be room for a civic cinema . . . where documentary, scientific and other films of all countries which rarely appear on commercial screens, could be shown (*ibid.*, p. 45).

The committee makes the admirable suggestion that licensed cafés serving meals on the continental model should be encouraged, but commercial dance-halls are not mentioned, horse racing is thought unlikely and greyhound racing is positively spurned: 'while there may be a demand, it would bring in its train consequences likely to be specially objectionable in a new town because displeasing to a large proportion of the residents' (*ibid.*, p. 51). Clearly no 'new East or West Ham' was envisaged by the Reith committee.

The intention of this discussion of the social and cultural goals implicit and explicit in the New Towns Committee's reports is not merely to draw attention to their Reithian prescriptions about the good and wholesome life. It is to illustrate the more paternal quality of those reports and subsequent practice than that envisaged earlier by Howard and the TCPA. For the pioneers and propagandists the cultural life of the new towns would be developed by collective but voluntary effort, not by statutory agency. Both Terence Young in his study of Dagenham and F. J. Osborn writing to Lewis Mumford drew attention to the fact that most people's social relationships are made with people similar to themselves, rather than those with widely different life experience, income and life-style. It is not clear whether the assumption from which the remit and recommendations of the Reith report sprang was that the mass of the population needed re-educating or merely that in a new and better environment more 'worthwhile' pursuits would automatically become ascendent. Certainly the wish for a middle-class element in the new towns seemed to spring from the assumed need for an example rather than from the benefits that such a group's higher disposable incomes might bring. One of the most fascinating aspects of the development of new towns policy is that a vision of the good life was interwoven with the hard practicalities of what was primarily a housing/industrial location policy. More interesting still is the taken-for-granted quality of this vision. The reader does not suspect the members of the committee of wilfully imposing their views on others, but only of being unaware of the possibility of divergence from their valued way of life.

Reith on ownership and management

The development of the new towns policy has been characterized by a trend towards centralized provision and an element of cultural paternalism. To put the considerable achievement of the Reith committee in a fair perspective it must be said that many of their recommendations were interpreted in a way that took this tendency much further than seems to have been intended by the committee. The two issues of agency and house ownership illustrate the trend.

The outcome of the *Interim Report* of the New Towns Committee (1946a) was a recommendation that new town development should be carried out by a body set up for this purpose and with no other responsibilities. The committee rejected the possibility of this being done by commercial enterprise or a housing association and endorsed: 'a government sponsored public corporation financed by the Exchequer' (1946a, p. 16). Public corporations 'sponsored and financed by interested local authorities' are not ruled out, however, nor are 'authorized associations'. In the event, all the central-government-funded new town development has been carried out via development corporations with no direct representation of local interests, or local finance. Despite the committee's statement that: 'it is essential that there should be only one local authority for the whole site' (New Towns Committee, 1946b, p. 19), and their consequent recommendation of referring the matter to the Boundary Commission, the new towns in England and Wales retained their piecemeal local government status until local government reorganization in 1974. (An unkind interpretation would be that the *status quo* benefited the development corporations because it reduced the unity of any local opposition, and by implication increased central control over the new town programme.)

Consistent with the spirit of Ebenezer Howard and the garden city experiments at Letchworth and Welwyn, it was recommended that the development corporation should hold the freehold of the whole site, except for a small number of private houses. This is indeed what has occurred until recently. The New Towns Committee also anticipated some of the issues of later stages of development. Foreshadowing later debates, a majority of the committee felt that: 'it may prove unwise to combine the functions of land-owner and local authority in a single body' (1946b, p. 21). Accordingly they recommended that either the government should buy out an 'authorized association', or in the case of a corporation, it should be modified to carry out the functions of 'land-owner and estate manager'. Their suggestion is, however, different in two crucial ways from the Commission for the New Towns as subsequently set up. First, the local corporation was to be as decentralized as its parent development corporation, and to include a minority of members elected by direct local vote. Second, when the town came to the stage where a profit was being made on its holdings, the profit should: 'go to benefit the town generally, for example by provision of amenities' (*ibid.*, p. 20). The Commission for the New Towns, which will be discussed more fully later, consists of a central body plus local appointed committees, and its profits are subject to recall by the Treasury.

Housing in the new towns was envisaged by the Reith committee as being as varied as possible. There was to be public building for rent, housing association building for rent, and private building for rent and sale. National economic circumstances overtook the new towns programme, however, and from 1946 until the mid-1960s nearly all the housing in new towns was built for rent by the development corporations, with none by local authorities dispersing population and very little housing for owner-occupation. (This issue will also be discussed more fully in a later chapter. An exhaustive history of early new town housing policy can be found in Cullingworth and Karn, 1968.)

Thus by a mixture of design and accident, the new towns programme became more subject to central control than was envisaged even by the Reith committee, with their hopes for a new egalitarian world of 'third-programme' standards. Ironically their recommendation that there should be a central advisory commission (New Towns Committee, 1946a, p. 12) to co-ordinate research and experience was not taken up.

The New Towns Act 1946

The New Towns Bill was presented to the House of Commons on 17 April 1946. Introducing the second reading debate, Lewis Silkin set the legislation in the context of utopias from Sir Thomas More's onward. The new towns, as he envisaged them, were to be a large-scale but relatively short-term effort by central government. The use of local-government-sponsored agencies was at that stage rejected, as were authorized associations. Later in the debates doubts were raised about the wisdom of excluding the latter group. The minister outlined the structure and powers of the proposed development corporations and added: 'I should like the development corporations to be daring and courageous in their efforts to discover the best way of living' (HC Debates, vol. 422, col. 1090). But the development corporations were clearly expected to be short-lived. The assumption that local government boundaries should be altered to match those of the designated area has been mentioned. The minister also assumed that the local authority would quickly apply to become a municipal borough. When the winding up of the corporation was discussed in the committee stage of the debate, all were agreed that the corporations should be wound up as soon as possible, primarily because of their non-democratic structure. The only argument hinged on who should be empowered to decide when the 'purposes of the corporation have been substantially achieved' (*ibid.*, vol. 424, col. 2369) and whether the Treasury should have a central place in the taking of the decision.

Lewis Silkin's commitment to the measure went beyond that appropriate to a major innovation in comprehensive planning.

> Our aim must be to combine in the new town the friendly spirit of the former slum with the vastly improved health conditions of the new estate, but it must be a broadened spirit, embracing all classes of society. . . . We may well produce in the new towns a new type of citizen, a healthy, self-respecting dignified person with a sense of beauty, culture and civic pride (*ibid.*, vol. 422, col. 1091).

The new towns were clearly seen not merely as a means towards meeting housing need. Euphoria permeated the whole passage of the bill, which received almost unanimous support. At the third-reading stage a member described it as: 'one of the greatest measures which the Government have attempted to place on the Statute Book' (*ibid.*, vol. 424, col. 2518), and no one dissented except Viscount Hinchingbrooke (Dorset Southern) whose lone voice against the bill received no support at all.

During its parliamentary passage the bill underwent only minor amendment, perhaps the most important being the introduction of the possibility of a public inquiry at the designation stage. There were divisions on only two of the many amendments. The degree of accord prompted the member for Oswestry to comment, during the fulsome compliments directed at Lewis Silkin from all sides:

> If I have any complaint at all to make, it is only that, because the co-operation between him and our own Front Bench has

been so complete, it has been very difficult for us on the back bench sometimes to hear the confidential whisperings which have taken place during our deliberations (*ibid.*, vol. 424, col. 2549).

Thus the new towns policy became virtually apolitical, a tradition which continues and is annually reinforced in the debates on new towns money. The New Towns Bill completed its parliamentary passage without a division on 5 July 1946.

The structure and powers of development corporations

There have been four major acts laying down the legislative status of new towns. Those of 1959 and 1976, dealing with the Commission for the New Towns and with the transfer of new town housing assets respectively, are described in later chapters. The 1965 Act updated the 1946 legislation (and consolidated the 1959 Act) for England and Wales. It is upon this act that the following outline of new town development procedures is based. The framework is in most important respects the same as that enacted in 1946. (There was a parallel act for Scotland in 1968.)

The site for a new town is decided by the Secretary of State (for the Environment in England, the Secretary of State for Scotland and since 1965 the Secretary of State for Wales) 'in the national interest' after consultation with 'any local authorities who appear to him to be interested' (New Towns Act 1965, section 1(1)) and others. Latterly, planning consultants have sometimes been employed to carry out feasibility studies on the choice of site, but the decision is ultimately the Secretary of State's. A draft designation order is then published. If there are objections the Secretary of State will appoint an inspector to carry out a public inquiry, and will then decide to proceed with, modify or abandon the project on the basis of the inspector's report. If the designation order is confirmed, objectors can then appeal to the courts, or, in the case of the local planning authority, can apply to the House of Lords or Commons for its annulment within forty sitting days (Schaffer, 1972, p. 45).

The Secretary of State appoints a board of not more than thirteen part-time paid members of whom two will be chairman and deputy chairman:

in appointing members of the corporation the Minister shall have regard to the desirability of securing the services of one or more persons resident in or having special knowledge of the locality in which the town will be situated (New Towns Act 1965, schedule 2(1)).

In its turn the board will appoint a general manager and chief officers and their full-time staff. There is no prescribed departmental structure. The goal of the new public corporation is the 'laying out and development of the new town' (*ibid.*, section 3(1)). Money to do this must all be borrowed from the Treasury, via the (now) National Loans Fund over sixty years at the rate of interest in force at the time of the loan. Funds for the new towns programme are subject to parliamentary approval, so there have been annual (latterly biennial) money bills laid before parliament to raise the total sum allowable, which is currently £2,750 million with the option to raise to £3,250 million as a result of the 1977 bill.

For a period in the 1960s it seemed likely that all the new towns would, in the foreseeable future, come into surplus, i.e. they would have repaid both the principal and interest on their advances. By 1973 all the Commission new towns (Crawley, Hemel Hempstead, Hatfield and Welwyn Garden City) were in this position, as were Bracknell, Corby, Harlow and Stevenage. Subsequent inflation and the steep upward trend of the interest rate, which peaked (to date) on 4 January 1975 at 17⅜ per cent and continues to alter about once a fortnight, have made break-even dates for the new towns both more distant and more unpredictable. Obviously, recent designations have suffered most. The cumulative average rate of interest for Stevenage at 31 March 1977 was 6·38 per cent, for Peterborough 13·25 per cent and CLNT 14·19 per cent (*Town and Country Planning,* February 1978 − summary data on the new towns may be found in the journal every February).

Development corporations have the crucial power, once the designated area is determined, to buy the land they need by a simplified form of compulsory purchase. The procedure still derives from the Town Planning Act 1944 and the compensation payable depends upon the prevailing legislation and case law which applies to compulsory purchase. Broadly, the price that a development corporation must pay excludes any rise in the value of the land brought about by the building of the new town. This does, however, raise the issue of what could reasonably have been expected to have occurred in the future if there had been no new town scheme. A Lands Tribunal Case (*Estates Gazette,* 1973) explored the matter in great detail. The claimants declared that future population growth and public policy would inevitably have produced a demand for residential development in the Bletchley area of Buckinghamshire. This could have led to permission to develop under normal planning powers (i.e. not by compulsory purchase). Milton Keynes Development Corporation replied that there was no such likelihood and that the land was therefore worth only existing use-value in terms of future events, as well as the circumstances at designation in 1970. The decision favoured the development corporation and the compensation was valued at £230,700, instead of £636,070, a 'question therefore of more than academic interest' as the judgment observed! (Fuller discussion of this issue can be found in *Estates Gazette*, 1973, and Schaffer, 1972, ch. 7.)

The corporation has a duty to acquire land from any owner in the designated area who wishes to sell and whose property has not yet been bought, seven years after designation (New Towns Act 1965, section 11). It must also look favourably upon requests from displaced owners to obtain accommodation on other corporation-owned land − unless the person sells intoxicating liquor (*ibid.,* section 18)!

New town development has usually been based on a master plan prepared by the corporation or delegated by them to consultants. All such plans and major projects have to be submitted to the (now) Department of Environment for approval (*ibid.,* section 6(1)) so that in a very real sense the new towns are under the control of central government − albeit negatively. In this, the new town planning and execution procedures bear more resemblance to the 'blueprint' style of planning enshrined in the 1947 Town and Country Planning Act than the more flexible and conceptually sophisticated − but as yet unproven − controls of the 1971 Act. Once approval is given for a project, which may be as small as a housing estate or as large as a township, then the development corporation has planning permission and becomes, in effect, the planning authority for the area of the project.

The governing criterion of consent for projects was laid down in the 1965 Act as those 'being likely to secure for the corporation a return which is reasonable, having regard to all the circumstances, when compared with the cost of carrying out these proposals' (*ibid.,* section 42(3)). The definition of 'reasonable' has inevitably been the subject of continuing political debate and the subject of significant shifts of policy.

The corporation has the duty to prepare for the Secretary of State an annual report and audited statement of account, which are subsequently laid before parliament and published (*ibid.,* section 46). In turn, the Secretary of State is answerable to the Comptroller and Auditor General for new towns expenditure (*ibid.*).

Many people who have had dealings with development corporations, whether as residents or otherwise, gain the impression that they are omnipotent. In reality their powers are limited to providing some housing and commercial and industrial premises with the appropriate infrastructure of water, sewerage, drainage, minor roads and some community facilities (the 1965 Act provides for development corporations to become sewerage authorities if necessary), although there are extensive powers for corporations to contribute to the expenditure of other local authorities' or statutory undertakers' projects relevant to the new town (*ibid.,* section 3(3)). The structure and powers of the local authorities and other bodies providing, for example, gas, electricity, water, telephones and local health services remain unaltered. Nor, of course, does the development corporation have any power of compulsion over potential residents, employers or suppliers of retail or leisure facilities. These have to be courted and cajoled to contribute to the new town's development. More surprisingly, there is no formal mechanism to co-ordinate those policies of other central government departments controlling, for example, industrial relocation, major health and transport expenditure, which will be critical to the success or otherwise of new towns. This paradox and its outcome is one of the dominant themes of the rest of the book. (Note: more detailed accounts of new town designation procedures in principle and in practice can be found in Levin, 1976 and Schaffer, 1972.)

3 The end of the beginning: the Mark One new towns

> On the one hand there is a sense of achievement that so much has been accomplished; on the other there is an appreciation that not all the high hopes held in 1947 have been fulfilled (Hemel Hempstead DC, 1957, p. 285).

Stevenage was, as expected, the first new town to be designated under the New Towns Act 1946. The Act received the Royal Assent in August and was followed within a few days by a draft designation order which was the subject of a public inquiry in October. So great was the enthusiasm of the Ministry of Town and Country Planning to embark on the new towns programme that land acquisition had begun in April of 1946 under section 35 of the 1932 Town and Country Planning Act 'with a view to the development of the area as a garden city' (Orlans, 1952, p. 59). A lack of consultation of local people, combined with residents' fears for their own property, produced a *furor* that became a national issue. Clearly the minister was caught between his commitment to 'the people' and people locally. On 6 May 1947 he visited Stevenage and made a speech during which he drew attention to the likelihood of unplanned development in the area anyway and contrasted it with 'a daring exercise in town planning' (*ibid.*, p. 65) calling upon the residents' idealism. His mind seemed to be made up: 'It is no good your jeering: it is going to be done' (*ibid.*). The obvious determination of central government catalysed the opposition. A local referendum showed 52·4 per cent of respondents to be 'entirely against' the new town.

The designation order was published in December 1946, whereupon three local residents, representing the Residents' Protection Association and the National Farmers' Union jointly, brought a high court action to have the order annulled on the basis that the minister was too committed to the project fairly to evaluate the findings of the public inquiry. This view was upheld, but the quashing of the order was itself reversed, when the minister appealed, in March 1947 (Orlans, 1952, p. 70). The designation orders at Crawley and Hemel Hempstead were the subject of similar litigation. Thereafter, whether as a result of increased subtlety by central government, or resignation by the residents of projected new town areas, designation proceeded without major ideological or legal battles. Crawley, Hemel Hempstead, Harlow, Newton Aycliffe and East Kilbride were designated in 1947. The remaining towns in what has come to be called the Mark One phase – Peterlee, Welwyn Garden City and Hatfield, Glenrothes, Basildon, Bracknell and finally Corby – were designated by April 1950.

Both those who hoped for a tidal wave of houses and industry and those who dreaded it were to have their expectations unfulfilled. In December 1947 the worsening national economy forced public expenditure cuts which limited new town development to planning and the provision of infrastructure during 1948, except in the case of those towns meeting industrial needs (defined as Aycliffe, Peterlee and East Kilbride). The new towns intended to decentralize population and meet housing need (which included all the London new towns at that date – Stevenage, Hemel Hempstead, Crawley and Harlow) were reduced to apparent inaction and their housing programmes seemed doomed never to meet the original targets. For many people the spectacle of new towns as consisting only of highly paid staff, equipped with rare and precious motor cars, apparently concerned only with providing themselves with homes and offices, vindicated all their fears of socialism and its *apparatchiki*. The financial squeeze even meant that land acquisition could not be carried out for other than immediate needs. Orlans records, in his painstaking study of this period in Stevenage, that the planned house-building programme was intended to reach 3,000 houses by 1951. On 31 December 1950, 28 permanent houses were complete and 306 were under construction. 'The first London family to move to Stevenage New Town occupied their home on February 2nd, 1951' (Orlans, 1952, p. 75).

Meanwhile, even in those new towns which were favoured by government policy, progress was also slow. In its first three annual reports, to 31 March 1950, the Aycliffe Development Corporation commented on problems with labour shortage and the potential burdens on the local authorities in the area responsible for infrastructure. Peterlee was currently locked in battle with the National Coal Board over compensation for the coal seams under proposed built-up areas. Only East Kilbride showed visible progress, and its 1950 annual report mentioned labour shortages (East Kilbride DC, 1950).

The first four years of the new towns programme saw the replacement of idealism with disillusion about its feasibility and some ill-
will about the mechanism for carrying it out. Within that brief
period constraints were placed on, and appeared from within, the
concept of new towns which deflected them from some of their early
goals and which have determined their subsequent development.

New towns were to be 'balanced and self-contained communities
for working and living' (New Towns Committee, 1946c, p. 2).
Whatever the intrinsic merits and feasibility of this aim, development corporations were from the start concerned to attract employment, to build houses for all income groups and to provide, or
encourage the provision of, publicly and privately funded facilities
for education, health and recreation. It quickly became clear that all
these goals were interlinked and that their achievement required
the commitment and co-operation of a large number of statutory,
voluntary and private bodies, and a reliable flow of cash.

Housing

The Reith report had laid much emphasis on the representation of
all income groups in new towns. Latterly the new towns have been
interpreted as being intended as an instrument of the redistribution
of wealth, so that after thirty years of new towns it is being said that
they have not done enough for the poor. The income levels and
age structure of the early new towns population quickly moved outside the control of the local policy-makers, however. In the period
immediately after the war, not only finance but labour and building
materials were short. Building itself was controlled and licensed by
the Ministry of Supply. When these restrictions were slackened, the
major effort was put into public housing. This had always been intended at East Kilbride, which was geared to meeting Glasgow's
appalling housing problems, and in Cwmbran, Corby, Peterlee and
Aycliffe, all of which were aimed largely at providing housing and a
good standard of public and private facilities for centres of employment that already existed. In the event, the London new towns were
under considerable pressure to rehouse Londoners in need as
quickly as possible. In the case of Stevenage and Hemel Hempstead
there was direct pressure from the Metropolitan boroughs which
had had hopes of specific links with new towns, and the right of
direct nomination into the new houses from their own waiting list.
The issue of the expense of accommodating and staffing the
development corporations was raised in parliament by members for
the inner areas needing housing for residents (HC Debates, vol.
468, col. 1651). At Hemel Hempstead, which had a formal, though
ambiguous, link with the boroughs of Wembley, Willesden, Acton,

Harrow and Hendon until 1953, there had been some ill-feeling with the local authority, too, which wanted access to new town houses for tenants from within the designated area (Hemel Hempstead DC, 1948, p. 66).

From about 1950 house-building in the new towns accelerated, but the absence of houses was replaced by a new problem: that of rents. Like local authorities responsible for housing, the new town development corporations had to build housing to minimum standards of space and finish – and indeed most were keen to build to as high a standard as possible. Similarly, they were constrained by having to seek central approval of the cost of their schemes. (According to the architect at Hatfield there were six other hurdles for housing schemes as well, all tending to produce 'signs of compromise' (Brett, 1953).) In a number of other respects, however, the new town development corporations were at a disadvantage compared with local authorities when they fixed rent levels. The rents were supposed to be economic, i.e. to reflect accurately the cost of building and maintaining the house. In the early days of new towns, the development corporations were covered, unlike local authorities, by the Rent Restrictions Acts (this group of acts was finally repealed in 1968), which prevented the raising of the rents of houses once occupied. Future rises in the cost of maintenance had to be anticipated and the rent set accordingly.

The finance advanced to development corporations was limited to that from the Public Works Loan Board, provided over sixty years at a commensurately high interest rate, which was inevitably reflected in the rents. The possibility of other sources of finance and shorter-term borrowing appears frequently in early new towns annual reports. In 1953, for example, the chairman of Bracknell observed:

> It is hoped that the Minister will consider making advances to the Development Corporations for a period of 15 years or less i.e. the approximate life of the corporation . . . the resultant saving on loan charges of ½ per cent would enable the corporation to reduce its rents by approximately 3/6 per week (Bracknell DC, 1953, p. 88).

It should be noted that 3s. 6d. (17½p) was at the time nearly 10 per cent of the lowest rent (*ibid.*, p. 85).

In addition, most local authorities had a stock of older property, with lower outgoings, with which they could form a rent 'pool' and thus subsidize the rents of more recent building. For local authorities other components of housing costs – staffing, infrastructure and maintenance – could be 'lost' in other accounts or subsidized from the rates. Early new town rents were therefore set above the levels of similar local authority housing in the area. As building costs and interest charges rose (which they did at an unprecedented rate in the early 1950s) this, too, had to be passed on to the tenants of the new houses, so that there were disparities in rents between development corporation tenants. The Report of the Cwmbran development corporation for 1953 outlined their position and continued:

> The general public do not always appreciate the factors which give rise to the higher rents charged by the Development Corporations as compared with the rents of council houses. (Cwmbran DC, 1953, p. 204).

Gradually the corporations were able to create a rent pool, sometimes in conjunction with a rebate scheme, to try to reduce discrepancies between new town and local authority rents and those within the new town itself. Stevenage did so in 1956–7:

> A Development Corporation is not allowed to make good a loss on new house-building, except from the pool of income produced from house rents. . . . Reluctantly it was decided that in order to create the pool of income necessary to keep down new rents, the rents of all existing housing must be raised . . . considerable public feeling was aroused. . . . The corporation tried to meet the difficulties of the lowest paid tenants by means of a limited rent rebate scheme, but in spite of this, there was undoubtedly some hardship due to the high level of rents (Stevenage DC, 1957, p. 362).

Similar themes had appeared in the reports of other new towns, sometimes every year, as from Cwmbran, where the corporation had the additional handicap of being in an area of traditionally low rents. New towns' complaints about the financing of their housing understandably focused on the problems that resulted for their current tenants, and those actively contemplating a move. The high rents in new towns produced two other linked trends. One was that in order to consider a move to a new town, a family had to be on a relatively high and secure wage. Most of them were: 'At present average family incomes are comparatively good, and no problem in letting has been experienced so far' (Cwmbran DC, 1953, p. 204). What, though, of those with low family incomes? Presumably individual families would be discouraged or even effectively debarred from new town houses, especially if they had any hope of local authority homes. More importantly, rent levels may well have influenced certain employers from moving to the new town if substantial numbers of their key workers could not contemplate the transfer on financial grounds. The new towns have been characterized as having discriminated in favour of nice, clean, modern, capital-intensive and thus high-wage industries. It is not at all clear, however, that they were able to be selective, especially when there was so much pressure to show results in housing. What part did rent levels play in the alleged under-representation of labour-intensive employers of unskilled workers?

Ironically, housing for higher income levels was also affected. Most new towns had hoped to let some more luxurious 'middle-class' housing, but the fully economic rent seemed unattractive: 'there is already some evidence of resistance in the case of rents for better-class houses, without which the ideal of a balanced community cannot be achieved, (Basildon DC, 1952, p. 56). Housing for sale, too, had been an integral part of the Reith committee's vision of new towns. From the start the development corporations tried to attract owner-occupiers by selling plots to individuals or developers. Some were permitted to build for sale themselves. The high costs of building discouraged individual buyers, especially in the non-London new towns. Corby reported in 1954 that six middle-income homes had been sold (Corby DC, 1954, p. 125) and that they planned to build some more in addition to twenty-four building plots already made available. By 1955, however, the response had been 'disappointing' (Corby DC, 1955, p. 109). Even Bracknell, which was expecting in 1953 that people would buy plots, by 1957 remarked that despite interest being shown, few plots had been sold. In the same year they reported that houses already built for sale by the corporation were going well (Bracknell DC, 1957, p. 88). Hatfield corporation had been selling houses and building plots briskly since 1953. The progress of Basildon in private housing is illustrative of the interaction between government policy and market forces that produced disparities in the levels of private housing between new towns and thus undermined at least one interpretation of 'balance'.

In 1952 Basildon corporation observed to the minister that there was a need for higher-standard housing for rent (Basildon, DC, 1952, p. 57). By 1957 there was no progress on higher-rented housing, nor on sales to sitting tenants because of the considerable gap between the rent and mortgage repayments, nor much response from speculative builders. The corporation: 'are hopeful therefore, that they may be permitted themselves to erect, speculatively, more higher income group houses' (Basildon DC, 1957, p. 48). By 1959 two private developers had schemes under way (1959., p. 49).

The garden city movement and even the Reith committee and the minister for town and country planning had assumed that the advantages of new towns would be so luminous as to need mere enabling rather than positive intervention. In the housing sphere, as in a number of others, the movements of the economy had a fundamental impact.

Relations with statutory bodies

Compared with the circumscription of local authorities by political accountability, the rates, their departmental structure and the principle of *ultra vires*, development corporations are often seen as omnicompetent by academics, residents and local politicians alike. In fact their strength has been their flexibility, not in providing services and facilities where their powers are limited, but in planning and then exhorting other bodies to provide services. Much of the literature on the pioneering days of new towns has tended to gloss over the conflicts that occurred between new town development corporations and the other bodies, both public and private, with whom liaison was necessary to produce a town.

All development corporations had to negotiate with at least one county council (the Crawley designated area was within three county areas for a period, and in two until 1954) and with a small or large number of parish, rural and urban district councils. Many of these were anyway hostile both to the imposition of a development corporation and to the incipient urban hordes. They also had real fears about how they would be able to fund their increased statutory responsibilities before the new town enhanced their rate income. In some areas even street cleansing and lighting would not have been supportable. These fears were compounded by the consistent refusal of the ministry to have any formal representation of local authorities on the boards of development corporations. In a parliamentary written answer in 1950, a questioner was assured that all the new towns had people who were or had been locally elected representatives on the board, but that they would continue to be ministerially appointed (HC Debates, vol. 476, col. 208). A joint committee on the financial arrangements between new towns and development corporations failed to agree in that year, and negotiations had to continue in a local and *ad hoc* fashion.

Relations between local authorities and the Mark One new town corporations thus varied widely both in structure and cordiality. In some places, of course, the new town had been welcomed or even instigated by local authorities, as in Corby and Peterlee. Yet even there problems sometimes arose, often because of general economic difficulties of spending limitations imposed by central government.

From reading the new town annual reports, it quickly becomes clear how crucial is the provision of infrastructure to the success, or even possibility, of building a new town. The slowness, unremunerative expense and invisibility of the product at this stage clearly contributed to the disillusion in the early years of the new towns. All three factors seem to have been underestimated by those responsible for the programme. The New Towns Act 1946 had anticipated that the new town corporations might have to become both water and sewerage undertakers on a temporary basis. Section 9 of the 1946 Act provided for the corporations to deal with sewerage. Most operations ran without disagreement, although the major project at Rye Meads, operated by the Harlow and Stevenage corporations to serve Harlow, Stevenage, Welwyn, Hatfield and many existing towns, was a cumbersome and expensive operation with a loss amounting to £½ million until 1963 (Schaffer, 1972, p. 151). Some new towns found difficulty in persuading the local authorities concerned with sewerage schemes to make a contribution from the rates. Aycliffe had to ask the ministry to make an arbitration award between itself and Darlington RDC (Aycliffe DC, 1958, p. 10). In 1957 the Basildon Report remarked wryly:

It will be observed that the Basildon Council have made no contribution from the rates this year towards this expenditure, which is maintaining an essential service for every rateable property on which rates are payable to the Council (p. 53).

In 1959 negotiations were still continuing.

Similar difficulties arouse between some new town corporations and the county councils over roads, involving the sharing of construction costs of both minor and classified roads, their maintenance and adoption. The 1957 and 1959 reports from Basildon refer to negotiations with Essex County Council, while Harlow wrangled with the same authority for years on end. A lack of agreement first appeared in 1949 (Harlow DC, 1949, p. 67):

Attention must again be drawn to the difficulties arising from the construction and adoption of New Town roads . . . the standards and specifications required by the Highway Authority as a condition of takeover are extravagant in present circumstances (*ibid.*, 1952, p. 239).

After prolonged negotiations, the Highway Authority have taken over the majority of the roads in [the completed neighbourhood] . . . The Highway Authority (and consequently the Ministry of Transport) are consequently bearing no share in the costs of roads which are scheduled for potential classification (*ibid.*, 1954, p. 251).

Unfortunately there is nothing favourable to report on the longstanding dispute with Essex County Council (*ibid.*, 1955, p. 224).

An agreed set of procedures, or even the central information and research co-ordination envisaged by Reith would have saved time, money and reduced inequities. The same must be said *a fortiori* of the interpretation of section 11 of the 1946 Act:

> any such corporation may, with the consent of the Minister, contribute such sums as the Minister, with the concurrence of the Treasury, may determine towards expenditure incurred or to be incurred by any local authority or statutory undertakers in the performance, in relation to the new town of any of their statutory functions.

The development corporations appear to have wished to interpret this clause as liberally as possible, but in respect of community facilities, especially for leisure and recreation, limitations on spending imposed by the minister brought adverse comment from the corporations. In their 1953 *Reports,* for example, Cwmbran, Harlow, Stevenage and Welwyn Garden City all commented on the shortfall of this type of facility. In many cases, of course, the problem was not the tight-fistedness of the local authority, but that the cash was only made available to them by other central government departments, as in the case of many services classified as educational. On other occasions they could not obtain loan sanctions, either to contribute their share of the cost of a project, or to take it over when complete. Economic boom and slump had immediate effects on government policy about spending on just the sort of 'frills' that the new town corporations needed to provide to live up to the vision, to satisfy their new residents, most of whom had urban standards as regards leisure, recreation and other facilities, and to attract future residents and industrialists. Writing in 1957, the Harlow chairman illustrated a number of these issues:

> The demand for playing fields is just being met − but the future is precarious because of the general limitation on public expenditure on playing fields which has accentuated the difficulties of the local authority in finding the necessary money to lay out the sites that the corporation has reserved . . . It is hoped that the necessary approvals will be forth-coming to enable the council to complete this work and to supplement the existing facilities to meet the needs of the incoming population. . . . For the time being the local authority has also not felt able to take over any functions in relation to the Town Park (Harlow DC, 1957, p. 248).

These difficulties must be seen in perspective, however. Many development corporations had almost no recorded disputes with the 'host' local authorities during their build-up − and some of these apparent failures to agree finance may have been tactical devices. Many essential services were introduced relatively smoothly and in step with the population build-up even where, as in the case of education, the age structure of the new towns produced disproportionate demands and the possibility of complaints about the share of the education authority's total budget that was committed to them.

In its 1957 report the Crawley Board took the opportunity of reviewing the previous ten years and paid very warm tribute to the co-operation that it had received from all the local authorities:

> The county had a very considerable burden to carry. This council had to ensure that at the right time the police and fire services were operating, that the health clinics were expanded, that the library facilities were available and above all that education facilities were available for the children. . . .
>
> The corporation considers that the County Council have carried this [education] programme out magnificently . . . [it] is necessary to bear in mind that when the County Councils made most of their decisions to build these schools, they considered that Crawley would be a financial burden on the rest of the county. . . .
>
> The corporation has throughout the past ten years received the utmost co-operation from the County Council and its officials (Crawley DC, 1957, p. 153—4).

The review continues in a similar vein about relations with the district councils and other statutory undertakers: the Thames Conservancy, gas boards, etc.

Unfortunately, not all new towns enjoyed the same mutual admiration with the local authorities in the designated area, and with hindsight it must be questioned whether the apparent policy of letting development corporations and local councils fight it out was necessary for the corporation's autonomy and to assuage local political sensibilities, or whether the process of developing a *modus operandi,* learning from your own mistakes and rumours of other people's was needlessly repeated by each development corporation in turn.

Relations with central government

The new towns programme, although directed and controlled by the Ministry of Town and Country Planning and its successors, involved other departments of central government, notably the Treasury, Board of Trade, Ministry of Education, Ministry of Health and Ministry of Housing. Other arms of government, for example the General Post Office and the National Coal Board, were also concerned. After the initial problems of expenditure cuts and general shortages, coupled with controls over building and labour, most ministries seem to have given some special consideration to new towns. This was confirmed in the response to questions in the 1953/4 parliament. The GPO was earmarking funds for new towns (HC Debates, vol. 531, col. 1910), and unfavourable comparisons were made between Ministry of Health policies and the approach of other ministries concerned (HC Debates, vol. 522, col. 561). Hospital provision was slow to come to those new towns not fortunate in having one nearby, no doubt because of the contemporary trend to bigger hospitals and away from local cottage hospitals. Stevenage and Peterlee, in particular, both complained vigorously in the late 1950s about their seeming lack of consideration by the hospital authorities. It appears that capital-expenditure cuts combined with the regional structure were at the root of the problem.

> The corporation continues to press the authorities concerned to expedite the commencement of (hospital) building operations (Peterlee, DC, 1957, p. 333).

> it would appear that no tangible results are likely in the near future (*ibid.,* 1958, p. 321).

> a special sub-committee to consider the question of hospital provision in the new town, and arrangements are being made for a meeting . . . to discuss this important project (*ibid.,* 1959, p. 325).

> It is . . . extremely frustrating to find, after a period of years that no hospital is to be built in the New Town in the foreseeable future (*ibid.,* 1960, p. 311).

In 1960 Stevenage sent a deputation to see the Minister of Health on the subject (Stevenage DC, 1960, p. 354).

Relations with the National Coal Board were limited to Peterlee and Glenrothes. In both cases there was considerable conflict, resulting in the development corporations concerned feeling that their own objectives and *raison d'être* were being given short shrift by the Board (Peterlee DC, 1949, 1950, 1951, 1952; Glenrothes DC, 1954, 1955, 1956, 1957).

Apart from the Treasury, the department of government most centrally connected with the idea of new towns was the Board of Trade, which was (and is) concerned with the direction of industry through a frequently changing set of positive incentives and negative controls, principally Industrial Development Certificates. (New towns and regional policy will be discussed more extensively in chapter 7. For a detailed history of government intervention in the location of industry and employment, see McCrone, 1969.) Bearing in mind the crucial importance of the Barlow Commission (1940) in the formulation of all post-war planning policy and legis-lation, it should be remembered that the Commission's view of planning took economic policy and physical planning as inseparable and assumed that the National Industrial Board it recommended would be responsible for industrial location. This was not done and could be said to be an emasculation of the potential of new towns. An apparent lack of co-operation between the Board of Trade and the ministry responsible for new towns was remarked on by Rodwin in 1956 and continues to be an issue up to the present day. New towns outside the development areas (in their various manifes-tations) have had to struggle to attract industry on the scale necessary to be other than dormitories. The most striking example of recent years is Telford (formerly Dawley) which, though in a depressed and declining area, has been subject to the same re-strictions as the prosperous West Midlands conurbation which is nearby, but too far to be useful.

Rodwin's study could only draw on the earliest days of the new towns, but already the pattern was emerging:

> There would have been some advantages in making the development corporation responsible to the Board of Trade . . . [it] is a Senior Ministry. . . . Final decisions on location of sites for new towns are made by the Ministry of Housing and Local Government. Such decisions should be based on economic as well as other factors, but there are scarcely any trained economists in the Ministry. . . . New town proponents have charged that the policy of the Board of Trade has not been helpful to the new towns, or conducive to the policy of dispersal. This accusation may be true, but it is less a reflection of hostile attitudes than of inconsistent policy commitments (Rodwin, 1956, pp. 58–9).

Rodwin's very pertinent questioning continued by asking whether there was any real financial analysis of the outlay on new towns in terms of their being a better investment than other forms of development, as opposed to merely being a better focus for spend-ing money that would somehow have been spent anyway (ibid., p. 62). These questions did not receive a public airing until 1974 (Expenditure Committee, 1974, and 1974–5a).

The lack of central co-ordination sometimes took curious forms. Aycliffe New Town was specifically intended to provide housing and services for workers on a nearby ex-ordnance depot that had become a trading estate – and was owned by the Board of Trade itself. The town was in a development area, yet in 1956 the chairman wrote:

Recently . . . there has been some hesitation by the Board of Trade in financing the provision of new factories in the Aycliffe industrial area. This could restrict the growth of industry and adversely affect the county council's policy of encouraging the flow of labour from other parts of the country to Aycliffe . . . as one of the few points in the county where interrelated industrial and housing expansion are taking place . . . your decision . . . is awaited with great interest, tinged with anxiety (Aycliffe DC, 1956, p. 6).

New towns in the London area also suffered from the departmental division of responsibilities. Basildon, in many ways the 'poor relation' among the group of Mark One towns, having been saddled with complex and expensive problems of land acquisition and the installation of infrastructure, was perhaps even keener than most new towns to start getting some visible progress and return on the investment. The Report for 1951 complains with barely suppressed fury that a would-be migrant firm had got as far as designing the factory:

when it was learned that a building licence was not likely to be granted in the near future. The reasons for the present restrictions on capital investment are appreciated, but changes in policy and the apparent impossibility of obtaining any firm indication whether a building licence is likely to be granted for any particular project inevitably prejudices the corporation's relations with prospective industrialists, to the detriment of the new town (Basildon DC, 1951, p. 45).

In 1952 Basildon observed that all the necessary paperwork for a factory development took 'two years or more', and obliquely asked for an assurance of support over the issue. By 1953:

the outlook . . . for 1954 is far from satisfactory. . . . Inquiries are still numerous but the obtaining of Industrial Development Certificates and Building Licences presents the major barrier to the establishment of new industry (*ibid.*, 1953, p. 53).

Relations with industry and commerce

As the Basildon report quoted implies, the post-war period, at least until 1960, was a time of industrial expansion. Despite gloomy prognostications at the end of the war that there would not be enough mobile industry to support dispersal and decentralization (*Planning,* 1944), the development corporations seem to have had little trouble in attracting industry. Employment was crucial to the new towns concept because of the rejection of commuting and the consequent aim of 'self-containment'. All new towns aimed to keep a fairly tight rein on the link between homes and jobs through the Industrial Selection Scheme and similar procedures, although this was not a central directive (HC Debates, vol. 523, col. 826). Only relatively small numbers of new town residents came through other routes, for example housing for elderly parents or higher-income housing for sale or rent. Occasional parliamentary questions reveal a reluctance on the part of the Ministry of Housing to say how many new town residents worked locally (e.g. HC Debates, vol. 504, col. 107 written). Presumably this was another consequence of the lack of either central government or development corporation research capacity to deal with this and other 'theoretical' issues which nevertheless should have been a part of monitoring and evaluating the new town policy. (Such research was done outside later on: Cresswell and Thomas, 1972; Ogilvy, 1968 and 1971.) It must be admitted that part of the function of new town Annual Reports is to whistle a happy tune, because their industrial and commercial success demands at least a superficial air of confidence. The absence of explicit references to difficulties in attracting industry should, therefore, probably be treated with some caution.

Crucial though a good range of shops is to a complete town, the Mark One new towns seem to have accepted that building the town centre would have to follow the population rather than precede it, because of the understandable reluctance of traders to spend an indeterminate period with no turnover. What were sometimes referred to as 'pantry' shops were provided in the neighbourhoods as they were built − and were indeed a part of the definition of neighbourhood which was seen more as a collection of facilities rather than necessarily a social unit. The Crawley review of progress, referred to above, reads almost like a pocket guide to new town planning. It places 'the Town Centre' tenth out of ten in a list of the order of development (Crawley DC, 1957, p. 155). Somewhat fortuitously the new towns were poised to build their town centres as the economic optimism of the 1950s accelerated. The projects came to fruition at around the same time. Six development corporations mentioned progress on the planning or execution of their town centres in their 1955 Reports although some of them had to record a slowing down of the project in 1958−9, when a minor recession affected investment.

New towns were particularly fortunate in being able to cash in on post-war changes in shopping habits, with the growth of multiple stores, self-service and an ever-increasing demand for parking. Some of them, like Stevenage, were pioneers of pedestrian-only shopping in this country. Others quickly followed, as Schaffer described (1972, ch. 10). Private developers, too, were quick to see the potential of new town shopping. The corporation entered into some arrangement with private developers in at least six new towns in the mid-1950s. (In four places the company was Ravenseft − Aycliffe, Harlow, Peterlee and East Kilbride − a fact that attracted several parliamentary questions in 1956 and 1957.) The government's argument was that to introduce private capital was to spread the risks (HC Debates, vol. 560, col. 167). It is instructive to observe, however, that several of the development corporations that clearly considered themselves to be successful undertook the town centre themselves: Crawley, Hemel Hempstead and Stevenage. In 1960 the Glenrothes report remarked that, despite offers, it had decided to do its own town-centre development: 'After a careful consideration . . . of the return likely to be obtained on the development, (Glenrothes DC, 1960, p. 108). Sharing the risks is also sharing the profits.

Both Ebenezer Howard and Reith's committee had plans for recreational and cultural activities which now seem absurdly grandiose, reflecting changes in the economics of such facilities in terms of the necessary catchment area, as well as the paternal and uplifting element that was undoubtedly present in the early policy. By the mid-1950s not only had concert halls, theatres and greyhound racing vanished from new town plans, but even cinemas, which had reached the acme of their popularity during the war. East Kilbride, which must have had a board and/or staff weaned on the silver screen, campaigned for a cinema for several years (East Kilbride DC, 1951, 1952, 1953, and 1955) and finally failed to secure one. Although one or two towns recorded regret at the problem with hotel facilities, there seemed to be little difficulty in attracting public houses to the new estates − especially after that other legacy of Reith, the proposal for state-owned pubs in new towns, was scrapped by the 1951 Conservative government.

Perhaps F. J. Osborn was right to attack the café-lounging élite and their ideas of the good life, but, whether new town residents wanted it or not, they certainly did not get a high level of public entertainment in the early new towns − except for sports facilities which were generous and well-patronized. Young and Willmott in their famous study (1957) assumed that home-centredness was a necessity forced on the people of 'Greenleigh'. New town inhabitants were more voluntary migrants, however, and still demonstrated the same emphasis on the family as a focus of leisure, with the shops and that mid-century palace of culture, the sports hall, as their only other venue. They demonstrated their priorities with their feet.

The aesthetes versus the missionaries

What 'the people' wanted continued to be asserted both by new town propagandists, and by their opponents, usually with little subtle analysis or even examination of the limited evidence to hand. In July 1953 the *Architectural Review* opened up a controversy which attacked the whole rationale of the new towns policy. Despite some searching questions about the achievement of the social and economic goals of the new towns, the fundamental focus was symbolic and aesthetic. Sadly the rejoinders were confined to similar topics, so the opportunity for a thorough-going debate and review of the policy was lost. The social and economic questions dealt with by the writer (Richards, 1953) can be reduced to his regret that although the new towns had set out to be complete towns, they had, by force of circumstance, become mere housing estates, and not very inspiring ones at that. He was not concerned with the effectiveness or desirability of the dispersal policy, the income or life-style of the migrants, nor whether they were fundamentally disadvantaged by the current shortfall of public and private amenity. Similarly he mentioned the crucial role of the Board of Trade, but suggested no solution, as with his other scapegoats: economic problems and unwieldy bureaucratic machinery. (With hindsight, less than eight years from the Act's becoming law was an absurdly short time to write off the programme as a social and economic venture.)

The centre of Richards's polemic was architectural. He complained that new towns were low density 'prairie-planning', in Cullen's phrase: 'it was justly said that the Englishman had forgotten how to build towns, he built garden suburbs instead. Today he goes on building suburbs which he dignifies by the name of towns.' Urbanity, for Richards, should be expressed in the physical symbolism of compactness:

> It is a sociable place, for people who want to live close together, and expresses itself as such through the compactness of its layout, through the sense of enclosure experienced within it and through being composed of *streets*. The new towns, by and large have none of these attributes. They consist for the most part of scattered two-storey dwellings . . . in a desert of grass verges (*ibid.*, emphasis in original).

And so on. The correspondence that followed centred upon Richards's use of density figures and indulged in a good deal of sophistry about the difference between gross and net residential density and overall town density, etc. Even the *Architectural Review* referred to these arguments as 'gamesmanship' in a later edition, but wider issues about new towns as a government policy and a social and economic system were left alone.

Even taken at its own level the *Architectural Review*'s attack lacked credibility. The development corporations were aware of the monotony of their skylines. Aycliffe reported in 1951:

> we found it difficult to find any purpose for which tall build-
> ings would be needed, and yet some variation in height of
> buildings is needed if the town is to have character and con-
> trasts, and not look like a large housing estate (Aycliffe DC,
> 1951, p. 9).

Several towns shared this concern, but felt that this 'variation' and urbanity would have to be at the town centre. Most centres were not even started by 1954, not only because of failures of government will, but because of the realities of private finance. The root problem was that 'the people' wanted a two-storey house and garden, just as *Town and Country Planning* has said in the 1930s. Many new towns had to reduce their already small planned proportion of flats.

Richards also overlooked the fact that new town residents were voluntary migrants, less in housing need than those who stayed behind, often to sample the LCC's more effective housing programme and visionary architecture. While it must be admitted that private speculative building has an inherently conservative bias, compounded by the sensitivity of building societies, it should also be noted that private estates are built to the lowest density that the market will bear. The more grass the higher the income levels. Suburbanization has, after all, been proceeding apace since the late nineteenth century.

Some responsibility for the narrow focus of the debate on the Mark One new towns programme must be laid at the door of the Town and Country Planning Association. Since they were the pressure group for garden cities and then the new towns, it is not surprising that the tone of their publications was 'new towns, right or wrong', especially as the organization has always been run on a shoestring. In the absence of central government collection and collation of new towns research data, experience and procedures, the TCPA came to be seen as having this function when it could not possibly have fulfilled it. Some more analytical approaches to issues could have been adopted, even so. Over the issue of high rents, for example, the TCPA response, in an article by F. J. Osborn (1954) was only to assert that rent levels elsewhere were too low. The garden city movement was always populist rather than concerned with redistribution, but this lack of interest in who might be able to enjoy the new towns, as opposed to who already was doing so, was unnecessarily blinkered. The same lack of a detached approach was visible over the general issue of decentralization. Repeatedly during the 1950s, the TCPA, through executive statements and editorials, asserted that the weakness of the policy was due to lack of stronger controls over office and factory development in the inner city and the absence of money or powers to buy out and demolish the properties vacated by firms migrating. There was no analysis of actual population movement, of the relative growth and location of manufacturing employment, or of the inner city as a system necessary to a complex society.

These are issues that have come to prominence recently. Maybe there was neither the need nor the resources to examine them before 1960, but some of them perhaps could have been approached, had not the TCPA tended to polarize the world into those unequivocally for the new towns and those against them. It was under their auspices that the debates took place, in the absence of Ministry of Housing commitment to full-scale – or even partial – monitoring and evaluation. A more curious inconsistency of the TCPA platform was the striking contrast between, on the one hand, its emphasis on the voluntariness of migration and local effort that characterized Letchworth, and, on the other, its prescription for a successful dispersal policy, reiterated in an executive statement in 1960 (TCPA executive, 1960), involving Draconian controls over employment, urban renewal and greenbelts. Elsewhere the association restated its belief in total development corporation (in effect central government) ownership of the freehold of designated areas. In any other context, this would have raised howls of fury at the extent of centralized socialism – or at least corporatism – it implied. This arm of public policy remained comfortably apolitical.

For the rest, the TCPA in the 1950s continued, via F. J. Osborn, to battle against the architects, with periodic ridicule of Le Corbusier and his Unité d'Habitation in particular. The two major campaigns in the pages of *Town and Country Planning* were against the supposed alliance of the farmers, land-owners, preservationists and the idle rich and their continuing fears about the extent of first-class agricultural land lost by new town and other development. The TCPA retaliated with numerous tracts on the food yield of urban gardens and allotments. (The debate died down with peace time and increased agricultural yields, but looks set for a renaissance.) During the 1950s, public housing subsidies began increasing to favour high-density and high-rise development. F. J. Osborn railed against this constantly, and never missed an opportunity to point out in the Association's journal that a saving on subsidies made it cheaper to rehouse people at low density in the new towns – even including the initial infrastructure and other unremunerative costs (e.g. Osborn, 1955a, b, c, d). As the Mark One new towns began to show a profit, his arguments must have found more receptive listeners.

The policy of government in the 1950s

It has been argued that the visionary quality of the new towns quickly disappeared, at least in terms of their priority as an expensive and risky project of a junior ministry. The Labour administration that had instigated the programme had been defeated before there was any visible progress in most of the towns – let alone any indication that they would ever be other than a drain on local and central government money. Apart from Cumbernauld, which was designated in 1955 directly in response to the housing problems of Glasgow, there appears to have been no positive element in government policy towards the new towns throughout the 1950s. In 1952 the Town Development Act was passed, and although it was accepted as part of a Labour strategy towards dispersal and meeting housing needs, the Conservative government intended to make it the central tool, rather than subsidiary to the New Towns Act 1946. There were regular debates in parliament, arising from the need to vote for more money for the new towns programme. New towns were not a political hot potato, however. In the fourth of these finance bill debates, in 1957/8, the member for Wellingborough, a stalwart of such occasions and indefatigable proponent of new towns, observed gloomily how few members were present (HC Debates, vol. 578, col. 1377). The debate had been opened by the minister's saying that it might well be the last such occasion. After persistent rumours of plans to hold and not disaggregate some of the assets of the development corporations, there were hints of the proposals that subsequently became the New Towns Act 1959, setting up the Commission for the New Towns (*ibid.*, vol. 578, col. 1347). Ownership had been broadened by the involvement of private capital in town-centre sites and the gradual build-up of private housing for sale. The freehold sale of some of the industrial sites was also being 'favourably considered' (*ibid.*, vol. 580, col. 148 written).

The Royal Address opening the 1958–9 parliament announced the substance of the 1959 Act. Not long afterwards, the then Minister of Housing, Henry Brooke, reaffirmed the policy of using the Town Development Act (*ibid.*, vol. 618, col. 33 written), instead of the New Towns Act for major development. (The procedures of this Act, and its most successful manifestation at Swindon, are described by Harloe, 1975). The new towns, it seemed, despite the international acclaim, the polyglot crowds of visitors and the intimations of financial self-sufficiency, or even profitability, were an experiment that was not to be continued.

4 Renaissance and redirection 1960–74

Overspill from London must be faced as a continuing process – as indeed it has been from the sixteenth century onwards (Powell, 1960, p. 81).

The first phase of the new towns programme had embodied what might be called the 'Abercrombie model' of decentralization and regional balance. It was assumed that regional inequalities of population and prosperity could be controlled by a national industrial location policy, and that once the drift southwards and eastwards was controlled, enough of the newly stabilized population could then be redirected to self-contained new settlements to permit the redevelopment of the inner city at more acceptable levels of density and amenity. This model depended implicitly on the assumption of a stable or only slowly growing population – a reasonable inference from the low birthrates of the 1930s, which formed the statistical information available to the Barlow Commission and subsequently to Abercrombie for his plans for London (1945) and Clydeside (1949). By the time that the unprecedented birthrate for 1947 had been assimilated, the trend in live births was again moving downwards steadily. It continued to do so until 1955.

In 1960, however, came the first public acknowledgment that this model of population and employment trends might have become inadequate, especially in the formulation of policies for the South East. A paper was read to the British Association for the Advancement of Science (and subsequently published) by a research officer at the Ministry of Housing and Local Government (Powell, 1960). It demonstrated that the expansion of high-technology industry and the tertiary section of the economy was centred on London, uncontrolled by IDC policy and in fact benefiting from the vacation of premises by migrating manufacturing industry. The structure of industry, the improvement of transport facilities and the geographical location of London in relation to Europe and world markets were producing a continuing (and, Powell claimed, inevitable) expansion of industry and population in a conurbation

> stretching in an almost continuous Thames-side belt from Reading to Southend, which provides a base for an even greater fan of development extending to the north, north-west and north-east along every artery leading outwards from the heart of this new industrial Britain (*ibid.,* p. 84).

While population was declining in the old metropolitan area it was increasing rapidly in the outer area of the London region. Employment was increasing both in the central area, as office jobs expanded, and by the 'steady evolution' of factory development on the periphery of the built-up area and in new centres like Chertsey, Debden and Harold Hill. Powell also identified two other crucial trends: first, that the population growth was largely by means of natural increase, and not net immigration. The attraction of the London areas for young workers was nearly balanced by the loss of the region by retirement. Nevertheless, the area was attracting an above-average ratio of employed persons and of people in the family-formation stage of the life-cycle. Second, Powell drew attention to the increased demand for separate households, with its implications for housing policy and targets.

The redirection of policy implied in the Powell paper was in fact taking place within the Ministry of Housing, and elsewhere in the Conservative administration. In 1961 Skelmersdale was designated specifically to provide housing land for Liverpool. The site was originally put forward in the 1956 Lancashire development plan (Lancashire County Council, 1956). Three White Papers presented to parliament in 1963 led directly or indirectly to more new town designations. *Central Scotland: a programme for development and growth* (Cmnd 2188, 1963) recommended a new development at Irvine. It was subsequently designated a new town in 1966, becoming the fifth new town in Scotland, joining East Kilbride, Glenrothes, Cumbernauld and Livingston, the last having been designated in 1962 with the objective of taking 80 per cent of its new population from Glasgow. *The North East: a programme for development and growth* (Cmnd 2206, 1963) was the outcome of the appointment of Lord Hailsham as Minister for the North East in January 1963. Thomas describes the document as 'distinctly thin', but the package of measures as 'a creditable shot at regional planning – the first in Britain for a couple of decades' (Thomas, 1969b, p. 890). Washington new town was proposed in the White Paper and subsequently designated in 1964 specifically as a stimulus for regional growth. The population target of Aycliffe, too, was more than doubled, as the study recommended.

The White Paper on the London region *London – Employment: Housing: Land* (Cmnd 1952, 1963) was overshadowed by its off-spring, *The South East Study* (MHLG, 1964), which was set up to examine, among other things: 'The need for a second generation of new and expanded towns which would provide both houses and work for Londoners, well away from London itself, and draw off some of the pressure on the capital'.

It appeared in March 1964, causing 'a shock with its central premise: that in the twenty years from 1961–81 the South-East would have to house some 3½ million extra people' (Hall, 1973, vol. 1, p. 470). Essentially the *Study* (MHLG, 1964) confirmed the processes that Powell had identified, although amplified by further increases in the birthrate. After assessing the population trends, the need for housing and the land available in the region, the report concluded that there would be a shortfall of 350,000 houses for a million people. A programme of alternative centres of growth was proposed: 'Towns which are themselves centres of commerce and industry could make a large contribution to national prosperity and rising standards of living' (MHLG, 1964, p. 53).

It was concluded that it would be most economical to concentrate on a relatively small number of sites which could grow by at least 30,000 and would be cheaper to administer than a larger number of small-scale schemes. In 1962 consultants appointed to examine the feasibility of expanding Ipswich, Peterborough and Worcester to meet London's and Birmingham's housing needs, had concluded that it would be cheaper per person to double the population than to add 50 per cent (MHLG, 1964, p. 67). Accordingly, the search was on for sites which could accommodate at least 150,000 with room for further growth if the need arose, and which presented no major problems of water supply, drainage and communications, while not occupying first-class agricultural land.

Finally, a list of recommended sites was put forward, classified as 'new cities, big new expansions and other expansions' (*ibid.*, p. 73). The new cities were in the Southampton/Portsmouth area, the Bletchley area and the Newbury area. The first and biggest of these was later the subject of a consultant's report, but was ultimately left as the responsibility of the local authorities. Newbury was dropped, despite its particularly good location because of local opposition and the doubts being expressed about its being too close to London to be a 'counter magnet'. The 'Bletchley area' project was designated in 1967 as Milton Keynes, with a planned population of 250,000.

The 'big' expansions were similarly thinned in the course of events. Stansted (Essex) and Ashford (Kent) were quietly abandoned and Swindon was left as a scheme under the Town Development Act 1952. Ipswich, Peterborough and Northampton were the subject of draft designation orders, but only the latter two were confirmed in 1967 and 1968. Ipswich was rejected after the public inquiry in 1969. Local farmers had mounted a campaign against designation, on the basis of the loss of high-quality land. Their case was stiffened by yet further changes in demographic statistics, which by that stage suggested that population growth would fall short of that predicted in *The South East Study*. A further outcome of the study was the recommendation of large increases in the target populations of Harlow and Stevenage. In both cases a situation of uncertainty was created that was to drag on for over ten years. Two significant general recommendations were also made: that there should be more emphasis on office employment, as against manufacturing, in the new schemes, and that the principle of a rigid metropolitan greenbelt should be maintained.

Labour was returned in the general election of 1964, but since the new towns programme was dearer to the Labour than to the Conservative heart, the programme of proposals and designations was uninterrupted – as the chronology above implies. Redditch and Runcorn had been designated in 1964, to meet Birmingham's and Liverpool's need for more housing land. In 1965 another Birmingham new town, Dawley in Shropshire (originally designated in 1963), was recommended for expansion to a target population of 225,000 after the report of the West Midlands Economic Planning Council (WMEPC, 1965) in the light of contemporary population trends. In 1968 the designated area was doubled and the town renamed Telford. Economic Associates had produced a report in 1965, recommending a new town in Mid-Wales with a population of about 70,000 as a focus for regional regeneration. Local interests killed the scheme, but in 1968 Newtown, near the original site of Caersws, was designated as a new town to double its population – from 5,500 to 11,000. The scheme was to be administered by the Mid-Wales Industrial Development Association, using staff from Cwmbran Development Corporation, with the aim of introducing new industry to arrest the drift of population away from the area.

The 'second generation' of new towns was completed by four more designated proposals. Warrington was confirmed to take Manchester overspill in 1968. Central Lancashire new town was announced in 1965, but only designated in 1970 in the face of local opposition. Its purpose, to house Manchester overspill and to revitalize the northern part of Lancashire, was the subject of much argument at Cabinet level. George Brown and Richard Crossman supported the notion of a 'growth point' in the Chorley/Leyland

area. They were opposed by Douglas Jay, who did not want investment diverted from the areas in need of economic assistance.

> I said in reply . . . if we don't allow the growth areas to grow
> and if we divert all the industry from them into the old
> development areas, we shall have a terrible situation where
> growth is penalized and failure is encouraged . . . I got my
> way (Crossman, 1975, p. 149).

The future of Central Lancashire new town remained the subject of
rumour and speculation until 1977, when the project was curtailed,
but not abandoned.

For the sake of completeness, it should be said that the two new
towns designated most recently were Llantrisant in South East
Wales in 1972 and Stonehouse in 1973. At Llantrisant, the designation order was dropped after the public inquiry because of local
fears about the proposed town's economic consequences. (The
Royal Mint, however, continued with its planned move to
Llantrisant, giving rise to the unkind jibe that the area is 'the hole
with the Mint in it'!) In an unprecedented decision, which must have
struck a chill into the hearts of many new town staff elsewhere, it
was announced on 12 May 1976 that Stonehouse new town was to be
stopped. The town was being developed by staff of the East Kilbride
Development Corporation to take Glasgow overspill. The funds are
to be redirected to inner-city renewal schemes. (The rationale for
this reversal is discussed in chapters 7−9.)

The appointment of Richard Crossman as Minister of Housing in
1964, an appointment that he held for two years, was obviously
significant for the new towns programme. His keen interest in
housing, which he made clear in his published diary (Crossman,
1975) ensured the government's commitment to new towns. The
administration was anyway dedicated to economic planning and the
development of integrated regional policies. It appeared from
Crossman's comment about new towns, however, that he viewed
them almost solely in the light of their potentialities for meeting
housing need. Their economic and financial possibilities and complexities he seems either to have been uninterested in or not to have
appreciated. This was no doubt as much a source of fury to his
Permanent Secretary, Evelyn Sharp, as some of her attitudes were
to him.

> She sees the new towns as the great creation of her Ministry
> and she loves them because they have been created auto-
> cratically from above. She is determined to keep that tradi-
> tion, although it is high time some of them were turned over
> to their local authorities (*ibid.*, p. 66).

Crossman's judgment on the new towns tended towards the visceral rather than the rational. He described Risley, a new town site selected under Keith Joseph's ministry and subsequently part of Warrington, as 'a ghastly flat area. . . . I took one look at it and came to my conclusions' (*ibid.*, p. 125), and the Central Lancashire designated area: 'an area with, at one end a really ghastly town called Chorley and at the other end a slightly less ghastly expanded village called Leyland' (*ibid.*, p. 171).

Despite his occasional feeling of ineffectiveness 'I am always discovering great segments of the department where my policies have not impacted. New Towns is one of them' (*ibid.*, p. 463), he concluded at the end of his ministry that he had been effective on new towns. With hindsight, however, Crossman's ministry was marked neither by any fundamental policy review nor by distinctive changes in policy.

During the 1960s changes in the new towns programme continued to occur incrementally, with little divergence in party policies. The only major political confrontation over new towns had occurred in 1958–9 when the Conservative government had introduced legislation to create the Commission for the New Towns, thus interpolating a new stage in the ownership and management of new town assets. This major policy change and its aftermath deserves a chapter to itself (chapter 5), but some indication of the subsequent all-party support for (or indifference to) the general trajectory of the new towns programme can be gained from Richard Crossman's response to a parliamentary question soon after he took office. Labour had sworn to dismantle the Commission for the New Towns as soon as the opportunity arose. Asked about this, however, Crossman referred rather circumspectly to the distinction between ownership and management, and the problems that might arise if the local authority were to become monopoly landlords (HC Debates, vol. 709, col. 296). Thus the matter rested until 1976.

In 1965 a fresh New Towns Bill was put before parliament. It was merely a consolidating bill, bringing relevant acts of 1944, 1946, 1959 and 1962 into orderly form. One of the few substantive changes was to devolve responsibility for the Welsh new towns to the Secretary of State for Wales. It was not a controversial procedure. The bill progressed from second reading to Royal Assent in seven days, the third reading being passed with neither division nor amendment. At one stage the members present had to be counted, to confirm that there were the required forty for the bill to continue its parliamentary passage!

During the whole period 1960–74 no major changes were made in legislation determining the liaison between government departments in relation to new towns, between development corporations and central government or to that between local authorities, development corporations and central government. Cumulatively, however, adjustments were made within the existing framework which profoundly altered the rationale of the new towns programme.

Relations within central government

There had never been any formal mechanism for integrating the policies and expenditure plans of central government departments in respect of new town developments. Members of the select committee on new towns seemed to expect that there would be:

> As soon as you have a new town in mind . . . and know it's going to need a new hospital for example, then presumably you would put in a bid to the DHSS for the DHSS to include in its P.E.S.C. forecasts the money for the hospital. That is the case, is it not? – That is not usually the way it works. The development corporation is the body responsible for securing the development and the laying out of the new town and it is they who usually make the first approach to these other departments (Expenditure Committee, 1974, p. 82).

In fact, as later questioning revealed, the New Towns Division of the Department of the Environment does not move amongst other central departments pleading the new towns' case when, for example, expenditure cuts are proposed. Central departments continue to vary, as they did at the inception of the new towns, in their willingness to earmark funds for new town projects. A memorandum from the DHSS later in the hearing spelled this out:

> it will be the responsibility of the Regional Health Authority to develop strategic plans and priorities based on a review of needs and its judgement of the right balance between claims on resources. In doing so, it cannot lose sight of the claims of other parts of the region, such as old established industrial towns (*ibid.*, p. 545).

There is little evidence of discrimination towards new towns, as many continued to complain of their hospital provision, or rather non-provision, in the 1960s and 1970s as they had done in the 1950s. The 1975 Report of the Milton Keynes Development Corporation, untypically forthright for the *genre,* asserted that the town is 'disgracefully under-provided with health facilities'. 'We should not be asked to build houses without a guarantee of jobs for those who come to live in them and without the assurance of proper supporting services' (Milton Keynes DC, 1975, pp. 186, 189).

Road provision, too, continued to lack clear central direction and co-operation. Harlow was left in suspense for several years while the then Ministry of Transport pondered the line of the M11, the Norwich radial road.

> The Corporation recognises that new considerations may have arisen which would make a major change in the line of the M11 road desirable. But it feels bound to point out that such a change might well destroy the fundamental traffic basis of the carefully executed Town Plan (Harlow DC, 1964, p. 210).

> A fundamental part of the town's design was its relationship with the line of the Norwich Radial. . . . In 1964 the Ministry of Transport decided to reposition the Motorway. . . . This vitally affected the Harlow Plan, but the corporation had no alternative but to accept the new routing . . . the motorway proposals have now been published and the Corporation has two main objections to them (*ibid.*, 1969, p. 179).

Harlow was also in dispute with the county council over payment for new town roads. The disagreement here, and elsewhere, was to what extent, if at all, the local authority should contribute to 'main' roads in the town. (Trunk roads were anyway a county responsibility and estate roads fell to the development corporation.) Various formulae were adopted, the most common, according to Schaffer's succinct history of the issue (1972, p. 152), was that adopted by Stevenage and Hertfordshire County Council. The corporation paid the cost of providing the road to 'ordinary' new town standards, while the county paid the extra necessary to bring the road up to the standard to carry through-traffic, aided by the usual Exchequer grants.

This situation remained unresolved from 1946 to 1967 and as Schaffer points out 'Eventually the money has to come from public funds of one sort or another but the quibbling about which pocket it should come from can take a lot of time' (*ibid.*, p. 152). It reflects the apparent lack of central commitment to a well-integrated new town programme that this wasting of manpower should have gone on for so long.

In 1967 all other than principal roads were absorbed into the Rate Support Grant system, a situation which seemed likely to increase the volume of 'who should pay for what' debates until a separate programme of roads for new and expanded towns was announced at the end of 1968 (HC Debates, vol. 775, col. 1688). Another major change in road financing occurred in 1975.

A similar lack of co-ordination continued in industrial location policies. A later chapter will explore the place of the new towns in regional policy, but a couple of illustrations will serve to show that the new towns continued to suffer from the separation of the ministry responsible for new towns from that issuing Industrial Development Certificates. Corby new town had been designated primarily to provide housing for the steel plant which was the dominant employer in the area. Despite curtailment of expansion plans in the steel industry, of dramatic importance in what was virtually a 'company town' (and a government-controlled company at that) the development corporation found difficulty in diversifying local employment, as they had been instructed to do.

> There would be little difficulty in obtaining as much industry of the right type as is needed for diversification and development provided firms were allowed to move to the town . . . the efforts of the corporation have been frustrated by refusal of applications for Industrial Development Certificates, even for firms wanting to move from the East Midlands and from London, both areas for which Corby is recognised as a reception area (Corby DC, 1971, p. 113).

The corporation went so far as to write to the minister in December 1970, asking for a 'directive as to how they were to carry out their task in view of the difficulty of obtaining Industrial Development Certificates' (Corby DC, 1972, p. 125). The 1973 Report detected more sympathy from the Department of Trade and Industry. Speakers in a debate on new towns in 1968 voiced similar complaints about the situation of Redditch and Peterborough (HC Debates, vol. 777, cols 513 and 516).

Relations between development corporations and local authorities

Two major issues – apart from the ultimate ownership of new town assets – have come to the forefront of relations between new town corporations and their 'host' local authorities since 1960: the non-elective nature of new town boards, and the gap in time between the demand for local authority services in new towns and their yielding substantial rateable value.

New town development corporation boards were, and are, appointed by the Secretaries of State for the Environment and for Scotland and for Wales. The lack of direct democracy in new town corporations had been debated with some acrimony when the 1959 New Towns Act was before parliament. Despite Labour's criticism of board structure while in opposition, they were not, in the event, to alter the system. Richard Crossman was certainly aware of the political sensitivity of the issue in the new town areas. Visiting Corby in 1965 he described the UDC as 'very excitable' and continued:

Corby makes pretty clear the psychological and political problems created by plonking a development corporation next door to a disgruntled, competitive U.D.C. I tried to make the corporation see that it was *their* duty to make the running in friendly co-operation (Crossman, 1975, p. 354).

Basildon UDC was 'very militant' (*ibid.*, p. 463) and at Runcorn 'The UDC felt the usual hate of the development corporation with their brand new offices, their big salaries and their air of being the feudal masters' (*ibid.*, p. 460). He concluded that in future the development corporation would have to play a 'much more political role' (*ibid.*, p. 496), but no legislative changes were made to the composition of new town boards. In 1966−7 the Parliamentary Under-Secretary to the Minister was again refusing to commit the department to appointing members of the local authority to new town boards (HC Debates, vol. 734, col. 1585).

In 1968−9 the situation was modified by an undertaking that until the assets were disposed of there would be local members on the board − but still appointed, not elected. In the debate a member referred to a forthcoming 'explosion' at Basildon (HC Debates, vol. 775, cols 1641 and 1652). In 1968 the ministry 'suggested' that development corporations should set up a formal channel of communication with local authorities in their area, and thereafter there are references to such meetings in most annual reports of the development corporations. Arrangements varied, but some seem to have been lacking in intimacy. The Aycliffe Report for 1971 records one meeting of members (p. 11), but it should be said that later reports made it clear that officers were meeting more regularly. Elsewhere comments on such arrangements betray a sense of scepticism: 'The Liaison Committee . . . provides a forum for a continuing dialogue with mutual advantages' (Basildon DC, 1973, p. 41).

At Skelmersdale the lack of communication was revealed in 1973. A motion was put to the UDC saying that 'no useful purpose' was served by attending the joint meetings with the development corporation.

> We often put forward strong, and we think constructive, views but the corporation officials and board members usually either disagree with them or are non-committal . . . The meetings really do amount to a charade . . . it looks to the ratepayers as if we are subservient to the development corporation (*The Times*, 20 March 1973, p. 3).

The development corporation on the other hand described the meetings as 'very useful' (*ibid.*), but the issue was not mentioned in the annual report of the corporation.

Resistance to direct nomination or election to new town boards was confirmed in 1974 in answer to a written question in the Commons (HC Debates, vol. 876, col. 277 written), but the scope of appointment has been extended under the New Towns (Amendment) Act 1976. The boards will now have eleven members, plus chairman and deputy chairman. Recent new town annual reports show that local councillors figure prominently on new town boards especially in the latest designations. There will, presumably, have to be a more rapid turnover of board membership than used to be the case, to keep up with electoral ebbs and flows.

No doubt charges of a political bias in the appointment of board members will continue to be made. Crossman wrote in 1965 that:

One of the problems is the personnel of the corporations after thirteen years of Tory selection. They are certain standard types. There is nearly always a colonial governor. There is nearly always a woman from the W.R.V.S. and a surveyor with strong Tory sympathies . . . (Crossman, 1975, p. 182).

Conversely, in 1968–9 there was a complaint of the Bracknell board's being 'packed' with Labour sympathizers where the local council was Tory (HC Debates, vol. 775, col. 1672). Some readjustments must have been made in 1970-4, because in 1976 the Secretary of State was accused of a 'flush of political appointments' (HC Debates, vol. 913, col. 644)!

Where the New Towns Act was to be used to expand and redevelop an area with a substantial population and political infrastructure, like Peterborough, the ministry had come to realize that some concession had to be made to the local authority. Thus the concept of the 'partnership' new town was born, the inspiration, according to Crossman, of Keith Joseph and Dame Evelyn Sharp (Crossman, 1975, p. 554). Such was the flexibility of the Act that this arrangement needed no legislative change. It consisted solely of an 'agreed memorandum' between the ministry and the local authority.

'Partnership' agreements have been made with the local authorities of Peterborough, Northampton – both of which claim to be the first (Peterborough DC, 1969, p. 279; Northampton DC, 1970, p. 275) – and Warrington. Close relations with the ministry followed, but did not precede, designation, according to Crossman (1975, p. 565) who writes that the Northants County Council was not consulted at that stage.

The 'agreed memorandum' dealt with four main issues: political accountability; joint action; paying for amenities and paying for local authority services. Elective boards were still resisted but concessions were to be made:

the Minister would think it appropriate that the personnel of the corporation should be agreed between himself and the County Borough Council, and that there should be adequate representation of the Council on the development corporation (Expenditure Committee, 1974—5a, p. 808).

Planning proposals would come from the local authority, as the planning authority, based on consultants' reports and supported by the development corporation. Similarly the development corporation would make 'proposals first to the County Borough in the manner of the normal planning applicant' (*ibid.*). In Northampton co-operation has extended to the use of each other's staff. There, the borough was to do engineering and legal work for the corporation, while the Chief Estates Officer was to 'act for both parties in attracting industry and office employment to the town' (Northampton DC, 1970, p. 275).

The memorandum between the ministry and the Northampton County Borough Council further agreed on the provision of services and facilities. The development corporation was to provide infrastructure, housing and employment in the new areas, while the borough undertook

a   the redevelopment of the town centre
b   the provision of leisure an: ameni*t*v facilities and
c   the provision of the normal distric. council services in the expanding area (Expenditure Committee, 1974—5a, p. 805).

A major administrative change was made in respect of the third heading. It had previously been the conventional wisdom that although there would be an additional financial burden on new town local authorities at all levels because of the need to provide services for the new population in advance of its arrival, this would be short-lived and there would quickly be a net gain through the enhanced rateable values of the area. The 'agreed memorandum' acknowledged that this stage might be problematic and made the general statement that:

it seems appropriate that the corporation's share of the costs of expansion bear roughly the same proportion to the share borne by the County Borough Council as the intake of planning overspill bears to the population increase arising from other causes. Further discussion of this matter will be necessary (*ibid.*, p. 809).

This formula was further explained in a debate in parliament. Contributions from central government to the local authority via the development corporation were intended not to 'insulate' ratepayers from general rises in costs, but so that they would not 'bear more than their fair share of the costs of expansion' (HC Debates, vol. 734, col. 1582).

Northampton Development Corporation reported to the Select Committee in 1975 that, as well as their customary contributions towards sewerage, sewage disposal, water supply, amenities and roads, they had contributed a total of £716,000 to the local authorities towards the 'undue burden' on the ratepayers (Expenditure Committee, 1974–5a, p. 798). This total was based upon a complex calculation of the costs attributable to the immigrant population minus new rate income, and the part of the Rate Support Grant generated by the new population. All was not well, nevertheless. The borough also submitted a memorandum to the Expenditure Committee (*ibid.*, p. 805) describing its financial predicament. The rapidly rising costs of both the town-centre redevelopment and the provision of other facilities were accounting for most of the cash available for 'locally determined' capital projects, thus widening the gap in the standard and extent or provision between the old and new areas — with predictable reactions from existing ratepayers. 'Revenue' services like public transport, refuse collection and street cleaning were being similarly affected:

> because of the design of the expanded areas [the] unit cost of providing the services in the new areas is higher as compared with the existing town. . . . These additional services are having to be provided as new commitments when we are being asked by the D.O.E. to restrict growth . . . it is impossible to do this unless it is prepared to reduce existing standards in the old Borough areas (*ibid.*, p. 805).

The situation in non-'partnership' new towns was worse still. The issue had been raised in 1966 when a new towns money bill came before parliament, but the government response was that outside the 'partnership' schemes the issue of contributions to local authority expenditure was too complex for rules to be laid down (HC Debates, vol. 735, cols 1717–27). No agreement was reached on the issue of contributions to statutory local-authority services. Feeling in some areas was running high enough to provoke an adjournment debate in 1974, when the financial and political problems of Redditch were used as an illustration. The need to provide facilities and services in advance of the population, and thus in advance both of the rate product and the element in the Rate Support Grant attributable to the new population was summarized:

population up 24%
rate product up 45%

expenditure up 201%
levy up 125% (HC Debates, vol. 871, col. 770).

Again the insult to existing residents was being compounded as the increased levy went to produce a higher standard of local authority service in the new areas.

The eruption of local-authority services as a problem in new towns has been caused directly by cuts in central government spending. Although there was a similar shortage of resources early in the new towns programme, it was less a case of abrupt cutback on ambitious schemes than of a slower build-up to what then had been hoped for. The standard and extent of local authority services has vastly increased since the 1950s – and in the most recent new towns there is a much larger indigenous population to make the invidious comparisons.

During the early 1960s the disputes between local authorities and development corporations were less to do with statutory services and more to do with 'amenities'. Development corporations have had two funds to provide amenities, an amenity having been defined in 1974 as: 'anything that makes the town an attractive place to live and work in, including facilities for the enjoyment of leisure' (HC Debates, vol. 865, col. 452 written).

The minor-amenity fund was a relatively small amount, which the corporation could disburse as it wished. The major-amenity fund consisted of a much larger figure, based on the incoming population, which the corporation could spend on or contribute to projects, subject to ministry approval. The corporation could, in addition, provide tenants' meeting rooms on the housing account. The minor-amenity fund stood at £2,000 and the major-amenity fund at £4 per head of incoming population from 1963 to 1971. The sums were not princely, but were enough perhaps to make a small local authority envious, so that it reacted, at least in one case, as if the development corporation was a 'milch cow'. Reading the annual reports for the 1960s and 1970s, sports and leisure facilities are a recurrent theme, as the early new towns became able to improve their social provision and later new towns started with more ambitious standards. Joint projects between the local authority and the corporation appear to have been the most common arrangement for sports facilities, while private enterprise provided pubs, dance halls, and less frequently bowling, skating and cinemas. (East Kilbride's cinema was at last agreed in 1966 and completed in 1969 crowning 'many years of patient negotiation' (East Kilbride DC, 1966, p. 73)!)

By the end of the 1960s the amenity funds had been overtaken by inflation. In 1971 the minor-amenity fund was 'topped up' by £100 per thousand completed dwellings. The major-amenity fund was also increased by £5,000 in the smaller, and £10,000 in larger new towns. A further ministry circular of 1972 announced, however, that a by-product of the Housing Finance Act, 1972 was that henceforth meeting halls would have to come out of the major-amenity fund. In 1973 the major-amenity fund was again revised to a figure of £11 per head for uncompleted towns and £6.50 per head of new town population for commission towns, minus past expenditure based on the old formula. Northampton, at least, reported with chagrin that the outcome was an 'effective reduction of £900,000' now that meeting halls had to be paid for (Northampton DC, 1974, p. 244).

The costs and benefits to local authorities in new town areas have become a major debate in the current economic climate, and formed a central issue in the deliberations of the Select Committee's hearings on new towns. They will be explored further in chapter 8.

Relations between local authorities and development corporations were not eased by changes in their respective powers over land assembly. Between 1952 and 1959 local authorities had been able compulsorily to purchase land for fulfilling statutory functions at 'existing use value'. After the 1959 Planning Act, however, they had to pay market price for it, i.e. a price reflecting its value with planning permission. Development corporations have had, since 1946, the power to buy at a figure nearer existing use value. This was not affected by the 1959 Act and has come to be a central legitimation of their effectiveness – or even existence. Until 1962 they were free to transfer land to local authorities and other public bodies at whatever terms were agreed, and these were often very advantageous to the local authority. The ministry then issued a circular, known as M199, which dictated that the land must be sold to the local authority at a price midway between existing use value and its market value, both to be determined by the District Valuer. There were some exceptions. Land for roads was transferred at purchase price, plus development costs. That for open space was sold under the M199 formula, but subject to restrictive covenants which depressed the market price and thus the ultimate price to the buyer. There were also concessions to, for example, religious bodies (Expenditure Committee, 1974–5a, p. 953). The development corporation was thus collecting 50 per cent of the 'betterment', which must have become increasingly galling to local authorities as development values accelerated later in the 1960s. In many ways the M199 ruling typifies the shift in new town policies towards a logic based on financial goals.

Relations with the private sector

Until 1960 the principal involvement of the private sector in new towns had been via manufacturing industry and the slow expansion of retail facilities. Attracting industry remains both a primary means and end of new town development. It continues, of course, to boom and slump with the national economy, and there is little sign of regional disparities between southern and northern new towns being reduced, despite the multiplication of incentives (see chapter 7).

The effect of the expanding tertiary sector was particularly visible in the development of the new towns during the 1960s. At the start of the decade, the London-ring new towns were anxious to attract office employment, both to diversify the employment and social class composition of the population and to provide employment for the 'second generation'. 'The national campaign to encourage office tenants to move from London has not resulted so far in any exceptional demand for office accommodation in Harlow. . . . The corporation continues to make strenuous efforts . . .' (Harlow DC, 1963, p. 186). By 1971, however, 'All existing office accommodation is occupied and the demand remains unabated' (Harlow DC, 1971, p. 179).

A similar process occurred in other towns, particularly in the south-eastern new towns, but also in Runcorn, which was 'unexpected' (Runcorn DC, 1967, p. 307). *The South East Study* (MHLG, 1964) recognized this trend. Northampton, Peterborough and Milton Keynes were expected to draw a significant amount of employment from the relocation of head offices, etc. Despite contraction of the national economy these three, at least, continue to attract employment to the extent that a chairman could write in 1974: 'The location of Milton Keynes continues to create a demand for housing and employment which, even amid present economic difficulties, seems insatiable' (Milton Keynes DC, 1974, p. 189).

There was for the new towns a happy coincidence between the government's announcement, in 1968, that half the capital for commercial and industrial development should come from the private sector and the growing interest of institutional funds in property as a secure investment at a time of instability in other markets. In July 1969 an Advisory Panel on Institutional Finance in New Towns was set up to provide 'more specialized expertise and greater knowledge of the day-to-day state of the institutional market' (Expenditure Committee, 1974-5a, p. 815).

The particular brief to the panel was to enable development corporations to make arrangements that enabled private capital to be used, while still providing the corporation with revenue, usually by means of 'lease and lease-back'. A circular to corporations in 1969, 'When it seemed that the Treasury tap for finance was being turned off' (*ibid.*, p. 818), explained the principle. The development corporation leases the site to the developer who designs and builds the project. The development corporation then takes a long lease back so that the corporation can then allocate tenancies and collect rent. It meanwhile pays the institution rent in turn, so that the institution has a hedge against inflation plus funds to cover the wasting asset. As Schaffer points out, it enables the mobilization of private capital, but at the cost of a loss of revenue to the development corporation and thus the public sector (Schaffer, 1972, p. 206). If, though, the investor should be the Post Office Pension Fund, which is investing £24 million in the Milton Keynes city centre, the boundaries between public and private finance become hard to discern.

New town development corporations quickly became more adept at making such financial arrangements and were described as 'very much more sophisticated than they were in the early days' when the Panel gave evidence to the Select Committee (Expenditure Committee, 1975-5a, p. 819). In those 'early days', however, the Panel had to give basic advice about the possible lack of scruples of middle men and other problems in drawing up a viable and attractive project. In 1970 they drew the attention of the corporations to the greater interest of institutions in shops and offices than neighbourhood centres, cinemas and car parks – and more tellingly to their preference for the home counties versus the development areas. Northern new towns would therefore have to rely more on limited government finance, but would also be able to collect all the revenue.

The Panel made it clear to the Select Committee that their task was not to test the viability of commercial schemes, and had recommended that development corporations consider whether they should appoint economic consultants. In 1971 the minimum acceptable rate of return on private housing, industrial and commercial development was specified at 10 per cent, where previously it had merely been required to be 'reasonable' (New Towns Act 1965, section 42(3)), so a still greater degree of financial acumen was demanded of development corporations.

From the mid-1960s onward joint office projects with insurance companies and major development companies appeared increasingly frequently in the new town annual reports. Town-centre developments, which were apparently not considered viable for at least ten years in the early new towns, began sooner after designation. In part this must be the consequence of the larger existing population and especially the much larger target populations and populations within the catchment areas of recent towns. It seems certain, however, that investors have also come to regard new towns as a good risk, as opposed to the completely unpredictable venture that they were considered in the 1950s. The Advisory Panel on Institutional Finance also observed in a circular that the young and fecund population of the new towns, and the ability of the development corporation rigidly to control against over-investment, added to their attractions. Such was the shortening of the time-scale of investment that Irvine, designated in 1966, announced, in the 1971 Annual Report, an agreement with Ravenseft to develop an ambitious town-centre scheme (p. 141), and was then able to write that the offices and shops were pre-let in 1975 (Irvine DC, 1975, p. 125). The centre was open by 1977 (*ibid.,* 1977, p. 121).

It should not be thought, however, that the impetus for town-centre schemes came entirely from investors. During the 1960s new town development corporations were becoming increasingly aware of the central role of attractive shopping facilities both for confirming that the town was established, and for providing the assurance that it would be. As wooing footloose industry and skilled labour became more and more competitive, the pressure to develop good facilities increased. Marks and Spencer changed its policy and began to build in the London new towns after 1968 (Schaffer, 1972, p. 144), much to the evident pride of the towns concerned. Woolworth's have opened Woolco superstores in Cwmbran, Washington, Cumbernauld and Livingston, among others, and Carrefour are opening a hypermarket, conventionally expected to be 'out of town', in the new central area of Telford. A Savacentre store, operated by a consortium of Sainsbury's and British Home Stores, has opened at Basildon. Perhaps the apotheosis of the rush to attract popular retailers came at Peterborough. Sainsbury's and Boots opened in the Bretton township when there were only a few houses completed. It was incongruous for a time – a little retail island lapped by cars in the open country – but it was well-patronized from the start. The official imprimatur on the symbolic and economic significance of new town-centre development came from Frank Price, writing in a TCPA sponsored publication, where he compared the hypermarket at Telford with the pioneering of pedestrian shopping precincts at Stevenage (Price, 1972, p. 122).

Recently new towns, with some infamous exceptions like Telford, have been sited largely because of existing communications. Unsurprisingly, the office and retail and also the distributive elements of the tertiary sector have developed an interest in new towns. Harlow, Northampton, Warrington and others have found an increasing demand for warehouse facilities. This has had paradoxical consequences. On the one hand, warehousing is clean and relatively cheap to erect and service. It is therefore a pleasant and profitable way for the development corporation either to build and let space, or to lease or sell the site. On the other hand, the ratio of jobs to square metres is much lower than for office or factory employment, so that the earlier calculations of the population/ houses to jobs/industry formula, made in planning the size of the designated area and its subdivision, have become redundant in many towns. Extensions to the designated area have been called for in some places. Then again, warehousing does provide some un-skilled work, which is another issue that has taxed new towns recently.

Development corporations and commercial viability

Neither the Reith committee, nor legislators of 1946, were much concerned about the ultimate financial status of the new towns. It was hoped that the development corporations would be able to balance their books and it was assumed that 'Any profit, after meet-ing interest and amortisation, would go to benefit the town generally, for example by provision of amenities' (New Towns Committee, 1946b, p. 20), but 'the matter will be unlikely to need decision for some twenty years' (*ibid.*, p. 21).

For a long period the issue was more of accounting for loss than distributing profit, but by the early 1960s a small annual profit was appearing in some towns (HC Debates, vol. 687, col. 723), arising mostly from commercial and industrial investment. Deficits were largest in those towns where the corporation owned little other than housing, as in Cwmbran, and in Scotland, where the historically low level of house rents kept the housing-revenue accounts in large and apparently intractable deficit.

As the potential for new towns to yield substantial profits — sooner or later — was realized, so too the Treasury baulked at pro-viding all the capital for development. The pressure on develop-ment corporations to programme their work so as to aim for finan-cial 'break-even' at a forseeable date increased. There appears to have been little difference in policy between the two main political parties over this. Labour encouraged the increase of owner-occupation and set up the Advisory Panel on Institutional Finance. When government changed hands in 1970 little change occurred except the setting of more specific financial targets for the develop-ment corporations. Latterly there has been a falling out about the sale of new town houses to their tenants, but this is more a spill-over of a rather stylized confrontation over housing policy than a genuine difference about new town goals. As a member remarked in a 1969 Commons debate: '[New towns] are not, and never have been, a party matter' (HC Debates, vol. 777, col. 532). The internal consistency of the programme might have been subject to more rigorous examination if they had been.

Concurrent with the new emphasis on profitability of individual projects and overall objectives, and the search for private funds, two further constraints faced corporation staff. The first was the lack of mobile industry, which has dogged the new towns since they began. This was not unrecognized by the ministry. The parliamentary Under-Secretary, speaking in a 1971 adjournment debate on Aycliffe remarked: 'It is a sad fact of life that at the moment there is too little mobile industry to go around' (HC Debates, vol. 818, col. 546). In 1972 a circular from the Advisory Panel on Institutional Finance reinforced the point by reminding the northern new towns that they would have to 'sell' themselves. All new towns have had increasing programmes of publicity, aimed primarily at industrial investors, as regular reading of *The Times*'s or the *Guardian*'s advertising features will confirm, but references to really aggressive selling of the town appeared more in the northern, Scottish and newer towns.

In 1973 Northampton was strenuously campaigning for contacts in Europe (*ibid.*, 1973, p. 320). Livingston was publishing promotional literature in German (Livingston DC, 1972, p. 187), and many corporations wrote of advertising campaigns, attendance at trade fairs and similar exercises. Both the Scottish and the north-eastern new towns (Aycliffe, Peterlee and Washington) had established joint offices in London for promotional purposes (Livingston DC, 1977, p. 159; Washington DC, 1976, p. 477). When a 1972 ministry circular notified general managers that they would no longer need specific permission to make trips abroad, many took the hint, most notably at East Kilbride. According to the corporation's Reports, staff made trips in 1969, 1971, 1972, 1973 and 1974, visiting the United States, Japan and Germany amongst others. In 1970 East Kilbride was 'paying its way' and claimed to have attracted more industry than any other new town (East Kilbride DC, 1970, p. 49), so these efforts could be said to have been effective. The contrast with Glenrothes is striking. The latter had passed through desperate times since its designation in 1948, having suffered the closure of the colliery that had formed its main justification, the Cadco affair (see Thomas, 1969b, p. 931) and the continued absence of major road links. Yet in 1974 the annual report remarked that 'no major promotional campaign is necessary' (Glenrothes DC, 1974, p. 83). The following year, however, the rate of industrial development was only 'fairly satisfactory' (*ibid.*, 1975, p. 87). Given the anodyne language of this literature, such a phrase can be translated as 'poor'.

The second severe limitation on new town management from the mid 1960s was the level of their loan charges. Complaints at the rising rate of interest were frequent enough in the early 1950s, but the rate has moved relentlessly upward. The consequences of this have been several. Since 1971 the rate has been changed about once a fortnight, making financial planning very difficult and destroying the initial forecasts of 'break-even' in the more recent towns. 'High interest rates and inflation make speculation on our break-even point an academic exercise' (Milton Keynes DC, 1975, p. 197). The need not to have capital tied up in unremunerative projects or stages of projects has thus become a constant preoccupation, pushing commercial viability to the top of the list of justifications for any project. Whether and in what way this affects the 'social' justifications of new towns remains to be seen. The system of National Loans Fund borrowing has been described by the Advisory Panel on Institutional Finance as 'an anachronism' (Expenditure Committee, 1974−5a, p. 823). This conflict between using the logic of the private sector in conjunction with the mechanisms (including detailed central control) of the public sector reflects either a lack of direction or schizophrenia within central government about what the new towns are supposed to be for.

The increasing emphasis on new towns as business enterprises has been, predictably, reflected in their structure and staffing. Originally, corporations had tended to be modelled rather on the lines of local government, with departments based on professional skills like engineering, architecture and estate management, working to chief officers with direct access to the general manager. In the early new towns these men frequently had military rank − naturally enough. Some of this ethic remained, provoking Willie Hamilton to ask a parliamentary question on the subject. He was told that of the five Scottish new towns, three had general managers who had been in the regular army. He then inquired whether the towns were seen as a 'military exercise' (HC Debates, vol. 704, col. 375)! Recently there has been a shift to general managers with backgrounds in law, local government and colonial administration, or some combination of the three. Interestingly, though, three of the towns that are often characterized as the *dernier cri* of new town thought do not fit this mould. At Milton Keynes the general manager is an architect, at Peterborough the ex-director of the Town and Country Planning Association and at Northampton an ex-senior member of the Scientific Civil Service, until his retirement.

Matching the shift in personnel, there seems to have been a recasting of departments, with Finance and Estate Management occupying a more central position, and greater emphasis on both project- or area-based teams and on monitoring and evaluation. The impression is that there has been a move towards a production-oriented, rather than an administration-oriented model of organization.

When the demand for financial and economic effectiveness began to tighten, it was suggested that one of the first aspects of the development corporation's functions to be curtailed might be social development (Horrocks, 1974) but so far this does not appear to be happening except in some of the earlier towns. In Stevenage social development work has been absorbed into the general manager's department (Stevenage DC, 1978, p. 387), and Aycliffe and Peterlee have amalgamated their staff (Peterlee DC, 1976, p. 281). More recent research (Baer, 1976; Wirz, 1975) does not reveal any reluctance to appoint social development staff either in the research and policy monitoring, the community organization or the arrivals functions. In at least some towns, the inadequacy of resources in the county social services department, despite their 1972 reorganiz-ation into a supposedly more family-oriented and area-based service, is forcing a social work role on to development corporation community workers. It may also be that the sheer scale and 'profes-sionalism' of post-1960 new towns has resulted in the professional-ization of the job of integrating newly arrived residents and mobilizing community resources. Many senior staff in small, usually older, schemes told the Birmingham research team that 'social development' was something that all corporation staff did, not only as part of their job, but in their capacity as citizens (Horrocks, 1974, p. 38). In one of these places, at least, a community worker has now been appointed. This personal and informal style has perhaps been made not only impracticable but even incongruous in the present ethos of new towns. It may also have made the corporation's board and officers seem more remote and thus maintained the pressure for more political accountability, when the sheer effectiveness of the operation might otherwise have won the day.

Membership of the board, which should be the interface between the corporation and the policy, both locally and nationally, seems to be pulled in two incompatible directions. The pressure for local elective representation has been described above, but there has, at the same time, been a call for business experience to be put into the service of the corporation. Is there room for such persons as well as the statutory professor and local councillor (to paraphrase Crossman)? Dame Evelyn Sharp wrote a very telling passage on her views on the subject, after retirement:

> Sometimes it seems that boards are chosen rather as advisory committees are chosen; on the basis of the interests they represent, instead of the skills and experience they can bring to the job. . . . New towns . . . ought to be seen as commercial enterprises for all that their purpose is social; unless they are the towns will not prosper. The people chosen to run them — in particular the chairmen — ought ideally to have a proved capacity to run such enterprises (Sharp, 1972, p. 43).

This implicit rejection of political accountability in favour of effectiveness is echoed by Wyndham Thomas, general manager of Peterborough, elsewhere in the same publication. He rejects the new conventional wisdoms of public participation and the accusation that development corporations are unresponsive to the public.

> It is far more important, in my view, for us to be accessible and approachable, to give the best and fullest information we can. If you do this well . . . you will give the overwhelming majority all the participation they want (Thomas, 1972, pp. 51—2).

Both writers appear to share a fundamental conviction that the goals and methods of the new towns policy are not only outside politics, but somehow self-evident. Indeed, the reaction of both the ministry and the Town and Country Planning Association to criticism conveys the deep shock that such an attitude would engender.

Housing, however, is unequivocally a political issue, and the 1960s saw a continuing debate about how much owner-occupation there should be in new towns, provided for whom by whom, and also what body should own and manage the rented housing.

5 The ownership and management of new town assets

in brief to be an enlightened landlord with a social conscience (Expenditure Committee, 1974, p. 294).

Little detailed consideration was given to the ultimate disposal of new town assets when the 1946 New Towns Act was drafted and debated. The New Towns Committee had expressed some reservations about the local authority's being monopoly land-owner (New Towns Committee, 1946c, p. 21), but the 1946 act simply provided for the minister to make an order to dissolve the development corporation when

> the purposes for which a development corporation was established under this Act have been substantially achieved and . . . that the circumstances are not such as to render it expedient on financial grounds to defer the disposal of the undertaking of the corporation (New Towns Act 1946, para. 15(1)).

The assets were to be transferred to the local authority and statutory undertakers, although the basis of transfer was not specified. In the parliamentary discussion of the Act, the Conservative opposition, in particular, wished to see the early withering away of the development corporations and a return to the usual framework of local democracy.

There the matter rested for some years, not least because, as Cullingworth and Karn observed, 'The discussions in 1946 were frequently based on an assumption of deficits rather than profits . . .' (Cullingworth and Karn, 1968, p. 21). In the mid-1950s, however, the issue was rekindled, as profitability became a possibility and some local authorities chafed at the apparently interminable presence of the development corporation in their area. Cullingworth and Karn (1968) describe this period in the preamble to their review of housing assets in the new towns: from 1954 onwards the debate intensified, with the local authorities and the Labour opposition ranged against the Conservative administration. The Town and Country Planning Association discussed the issue within its ranks and with outside experts. In 1958 the association finally committed itself to the continuation of development corporations until the stage of accommodating 'natural increase' was over (i.e. when the children and the first new town migrants had themselves set up households). 'They considered that the proposals for handing over the assets to a central agency or to the local authorities were premature and could see no advantage in creating a central agency' (*ibid.*, p. 24). They felt that after a few more years the economic context and financial future of new towns could be more reliably assessed. The TCPA position was, however, interpreted as that of supporting the Commission in the subsequent debates on the bill to create the new body – when issues 'became over-simplified' (*ibid.*).

The Commission for the New Towns was intended to hold and manage the land, housing, industrial and commercial assets of the new towns in England and Wales and although it was described as an interim and not a terminal stage of development, no provision for ending the life of the Commission in its turn was included in the bill. Support for the legislation was justified on both moral and pragmatic grounds – although the distinction was not always clear. It was claimed that the investment in new towns had been made by taxpayers at large and that the advantages of the possible profits should not accrue to local residents in addition to their higher-quality environment. Conservative members also voiced fears about the problems that could arise when the local authority was landlord of all the land, most of the housing, and the industrial and commercial property – including the local newspaper. Tenancies and rents policy could be used to buy votes. More mundanely it was also claimed that many of the local authorities concerned were too small to have the necessary expertise among their staff to manage the assets. Much was made of local councillors' naïvety. At Crawley the UDC discussed 'everything but the local affairs of Crawley' including disarmament (HC Debates, vol. 596, col. 890).

Labour speakers took a diametrically opposed view on almost all points. If the local authorities were small and inexperienced the approaching county reviews could be used to reorganize them (HC Debates, vol. 596, col. 868). The members' stature would grow to meet their new responsibilities. Any fear of local corruption was secondary to the undesirability of the non-democratic development corporation's being replaced by a similarly non-elective body. The real reason for the Commission, it was claimed, was that all the new town local authorities would be Labour (HC Debates, vol. 596, col. 938)! Contrary to the government's view, Labour asserted that since much of new town social and financial investment had come from the local ratepayers, they should be able to enjoy at least some of the consequent profit. It was considered quite unjustified that the Treasury should apparently want to reclaim not only the original advances, plus interest, but the profits, too. It was suggested that the Treasury would not allow the Commission to use any of the surplus to provide amenities (HC Debates, vol. 608, col. 314ff.), or worse, that the Commission could become a 'disposals board', which was denied by the government (*ibid.*, vol. 596, col. 850). Attempts to limit the Treasury's claim on any surplus accumulation by the Commission were defeated (HC Debates, vol. 608, cols 327 and 363), as were clauses to prevent the Commission from raising rents and to safeguard new town staff (*ibid.*, cols 294 and 310).

Opposition centred on the apparent shift of emphasis to financial considerations, and it was suggested that the minister (Henry Brooke) was viewing the matter entirely from the perspective of his former position as Financial Secretary to the Treasury (*ibid.*, col. 322). The Labour member for Wellingborough summarized the hostility:

> Tory governments have persistently stinted the new towns. . . . The primary purpose of the new body is to be a financial one, to enhance the value of the asset, while the comfort, welfare and convenience of the inhabitants, which used to be the primary object of the new towns, is now relegated to second place . . . merely something to which the Commission is to 'have regard' (HC Debates, vol. 596, col. 869).

The bill was passed without a division, nevertheless, since the Labour party supported some of the other provisions contained in it. A last stand on the issue was made in 1961. Labour moved amendment of the order setting up the Commission. The same arguments were rehearsed as in 1958, with the new minister, Keith Joseph, also assuring the House that there was not to be a disposal of the assets. The motion was defeated (HC Debates, vol. 645, cols. 349ff.). A novel situation had been created. The Conservative government had set up a small nationalized industry which had been attacked by Labour for its centralization and bureaucracy (HC Debates, vol. 608, col. 377). Labour swore to dismantle it at the first opportunity.

The structure and work of the Commission for the New Towns

The remit of the Commission for the New Towns was laid down in

paragraph 2 of the 1959 New Towns Act (and subsequently consolidated in section 36 of the 1965 New Towns Act):

> taking over, managing and turning to account the property
> previously vested in the development corporation. . . . It shall
> be the general duty of the Commission to maintain and
> enhance the value of the land held by them and the return
> obtained by them from it, but in discharging their functions in
> relation to any town the Commission shall have regard to the
> purpose for which the town was developed under the New
> Towns Act 1946 and to the convenience and welfare of
> persons residing, working or carrying on business there.

The Commission is primarily a management rather than a development agency. It holds the unbuilt-up land that had been acquired
by the development corporation and, until 1978, it also held the
freehold of the housing, commercial and industrial assets formerly
held by the corporation, but has no compulsory purchase powers
and is subject to the local planning authority in the usual way. It can
acquire land, contribute to local amenities and services under the
formulae outlined in chapter 4, offer mortgages and dispose of property. Development and redevelopment of land and the freehold
sale of land, or its disposal or leases for longer than ninety-nine
years are subject to specific permission of the minister. Like the
development corporations, the Commission can only raise money
by central government loans, but it can also invest any surpluses
until their recall by the Treasury.

There are two levels in the Commission structure. First, there is a
board of not more than fifteen members, based in London. (In 1977
there was a chairman, deputy chairman and six other members.) It
is appointed by the Secretary of State for a term informally expected
to be three years (Expenditure Committee, 1974, p. 307). The
board is served by a secretary and a small headquarters staff. In
addition there are local committees in each new town, consisting
'partly of persons who are not members or servants of the Commission . . . for any part of [the] business to be conducted on behalf
of the Commission' (New Towns Act 1965, schedule 9, para. 3(1)).
Again in 1977, these committees consisted of a chairman and eight
others at Crawley, eight at Hemel Hempstead and eleven at Welwyn
Garden City and Hatfield (CNT, 1977, p. v). The business of the
committees is confined to the local application of policy, including
building houses and other facilities, their maintenance, contributing to local amenities and lending mortgage finance. They are in
turn served by a general manager, chief officers and a substantial
staff, many of whom transferred from the development cor-
portation on dissolution. Members of the local committees are

hired and fired, and their delegated functions controlled, by the board. As with current development corporation practice: 'The Commission aims at including at least two members of the local authority on the local committee, but as individuals, not delegates' (Expenditure Committee, 1974, p. 296). The chairmen of local committees are appointed by the board, and have always then been appointed to the board itself by the Secretary of State. Although the Commission, in evidence to the Select Committee (1974, p. 310), emphasized that the minister does not have to do this, there have been no exceptions to date, so there is an element of self-selection that is a little cosy, not to say incestuous. Wyndham Thomas was chairman of Hemel Hempstead Committee for a period (and hence a member of the board). He left to become general manager of Peterborough. The first general manager of Northampton, John Weston, was for a period on the committee at Welwyn.

The first two new towns to be transferred to the Commission were Hemel Hempstead and Crawley on 1 April 1962. Welwyn Garden City and Hatfield followed in 1966. Thereafter the Commission existed in a state of insecurity for several years. It had only published two annual reports when a Labour government was returned in 1964. During that period it had started building houses and factories for sale (on long leasehold) and rent, as well as leasing land for offices and contributing to local amenities, and was attempting a revival of the old high street in Hemel Hempstead (CNT, 1963, and 1964). In reply to a question in 1965, Richard Crossman described the Commission as 'a temporary form of government of which we do not approve' (HC Debates, vol. 720, col. 910). This attitude was reiterated by the 1966 Labour Manifesto which specifically promised the abolition of the Commission, but a distinction was beginning to be made between management of the assets and their ownership. According to Cullingworth and Karn (1968, p. 29) the minister was 'dissatisfied with the current arrangements under the Commission but felt that further investigation was needed before a decision was taken about ultimate ownership' (*ibid*).

For the duration of the Labour government, the Commission expected the axe to fall, but although a new housing policy was implemented (see below) no further move was made to wind up the Commission until 1970, when the government announced that a policy statement on the future of new town assets would be made that summer (HC Debates, vol. 799, col. 225). Then the axe did fall, but on the Labour government instead. The new administration quickly announced its wish to retain the Commission (HC Debates, vol. 809, col. 1058). Ironically, its existence for the forseeable future was secured by the Labour government which succeeded in turn in 1974. Changed economic and demographic circumstances provoked a review of new towns policy (described more fully in chapters 7 and 8), which resulted in the decision to wind up eight more development corporations (Basildon, Bracknell, Corby, Harlow, Runcorn, Redditch, Stevenage and Washington) between 1980 and 1983. Although their housing and related assets will be transferred to the local authority under the New Towns (Amendment) Act 1976 – as were those of Crawley, Hemel Hempstead, Hatfield and Welwyn Garden City on 1 April 1978 – the Commission will have the task of managing and developing their commercial and industrial properties.

Giving evidence to the Select Committee, the Commission described its task as being 'an enlightened landlord with a social conscience' (Expenditure Committee, 1974, p. 294). Its remit had at that stage already become rather narrower, as its building of housing for rent and sale had been curtailed by degrees between 1968 and 1971 (CNT, 1968, p. 34; 1970, p. 5 and 1971, p. 7). Until that time its concern had been to help to provide for both the growing children and ageing parents of the migrant generation, but by 1974 building was limited to that for the elderly – although the demand for this outstripped supply (Expenditure Committee, 1974, pp. 295, 303). It was still selling land to the local authority for housing purposes to meet natural increase, and itself organized the provision of employment, offices, shops and other facilities, primarily by using institutional finance. An interesting paragraph in the evidence remarks 'roads, sewerage and water installations, parks, playing fields, etc. used for the statutory purposes of a local authority will be transferred to the appropriate authority long before the Commission takes over' (*ibid.*, p. 294), drawing attention to the fact that the arguments since 1958 have not been about new town *assets*, but about *remunerative* assets, which rather undermines the position of those who justify their case for transfer solely on the issue of democratic control.

The claimed skill of the Commission in the management and 'turning to account' of the new town assets has certainly been vindicated, although doubtless assisted by economic trends since the war and the fact that all the early Commission towns are very close to London. In 1974 the Commission had not needed a Treasury advance for 'several years' (*ibid.*, 1974, p. 296) and there was an accumulated surplus of £23 million after provision for maintenance, loan debt repayment, administration, corporation tax, etc. The Commission had, at that time, £30 million on loan to various public authorities, so that the surplus was being further swelled by interest (*ibid.*, p. 306). In 1975 the Treasury claimed its right to the golden egg. The Commission repaid £25·786 million of the surplus to central government (CNT, 1977, p. 14). In its first fifteen years of existence, up to 1977, the total surplus amounted to £65·76 million (CNT, 1977, p. 12).

The Commission for the New Towns, during those first fifteen years, could be said to symbolize all the contradictions of the new towns policy. Claimed by many to be the most dramatic evidence of the switch from a social to a financial rationale for new town development, it was staffed by people with a long history of involvement in new towns and with an intense belief in the concept. Although more centralized than the structures envisaged by Howard and Osborn, the Commission could be interpreted as potentially fulfilling the early intention to plough betterment and revenue surplus back into the creation of more new towns and the raising of standards of provision in the earlier towns. The fact that the Commission was not permitted to do this is less to do with its rationale and structure than the limitation of its potential by central government. In its evidence to the Expenditure Committee, the Town and Country Planning Association − guardian of the new town ideal − advocated that

> surpluses from new towns (as they arise) should be put into a special fund from which contributions would be made towards the cost of social facilities in *all* the new towns, made at the most useful stage of their development (Expenditure Committee, 1974, p. 135).

The government 'line' conversely, is expressed by Evelyn Sharp:

> there is no real logic in this. The right doctrine, I am sure, is that for better or worse, every town must stand on its own feet . . . a town should never be started where it looks as if it will never stand on its own feet. . . . Unfortunately it is in just such places that political pressures for a town are apt to be greatest (Sharp, 1972, p. 42).

It is understandable that central government should not pour money into hopeless ventures and even that there should be a wish to see new towns 'pay their way'. If the site and targets are well chosen, however, it is less easy to see why the surplus from 'certainties' like Welwyn earlier and later Milton Keynes, for example, should not be redirected to those towns where circumstances are less favourable. Not to do so certainly accords with the position expressed by Richard Crossman and reproduced in chapter 4: that it is bad policy everlastingly to reward failure, but it is very difficult to see how this position can be integrated with the aim of using towns for regional regeneration. Does the resistance lie in the fear that new towns will become too autonomous an operation or that their accounting, already muddled by grants and subsidies, will become even less effective in assessing the costs and benefits of development? Perhaps it is merely a lack of one set of coherent policy objectives. Several of the decisions on new towns taken in the 1960s served to amplify the process of to him 'that hath shall be given' between new towns and their inhabitants. The constraint placed upon the Commission was one.

Alongside its success in the financial world, the Commission at the same time seemed to be attempting to maintain the early objectives of new towns. The 1965 Annual Report of the Commission expressed considerable concern to maintain self-containment. Although they were selling housing, it was only on leasehold so that 'the Commission can keep some control over the occupancy of houses as and when they become vacant, and ensure that the dwellings continue to be used to accommodate people working in the town, (CNT, 1965, p. 6). With the same end in view, they were also attempting to confine sales to those 'living or working or about to work in the town' (*ibid.*) and imposed a fifteen-year pre-emption clause on sales, giving the Commission the right to buy back at market price for that period. When leasehold reform was introduced in 1967, the Commission attempted to limit its effect by getting approval for 'schemes of management', but only succeeded in respect of part of Welwyn Garden City. The Commission's regret at the loss of control over occupancy is clear in the 1969 Report (p. 7).

The Commission also dragged its feet on implementing government recommendations to sell commercial and industrial freeholds, although the reason seems to have been a mixture of attachment to the principle of unified land ownership in the new towns and financial considerations:

> it is the policy of the Government that they would not object to the sale of freeholds of industrial sites but it is the New Towns Commission which in fact has not sold any at all? Is this a matter of policy or just of co-incidence? − No, it is not a co-incidence . . . we have not sold the freehold of developed and commercial properties except on very rare occasions (Expenditure Committee, 1974, p. 301).

The chairman of the Commission went on to explain that because of the possibilities of lease and lease-back and the historically low rents of the Commission new towns they saw no reason to part with freeholds. There may also have been an element of benevolent paternalism and a desire for order and logic. The Commission's annual reports stress its capacity for effective management of assets centrally (this function was not delegated to local committees) and also take pride in its systematic letting policies and the programmes of maintenance and improvement of both houses and their landscape. Some of the resistance to leasehold reform stemmed from fears that covenants in freeholds, designed to maintain the aesthetic unity of the neighbourhoods, would not be effective.

The financial possibilities of the Commission did not escape notice even in the 1960s, despite the then government's expressed dislike of the actual structure of the Commission. A 1968 motion to the Labour Party Conference called for transfer of housing and neighbourhood shops to the relevant local authority, but that the commercial and industrial assets, including town-centre shops, should be held by a New Towns Industrial Corporation (Schaffer, 1972, p. 238). Significantly, when Richard Crossman commissioned Professor J. B. Cullingworth's survey of attitudes to ownership and management in new towns, the remit was limited to housing.

Housing assets and the move to owner-occupation

The report that Cullingworth and Karn produced (1968) repays close attention, not least because its central conclusions have been frequently misused and over-simplified. It is now often asserted that the report was responsible for the switch of Labour-party thinking towards owner-occupation. There are, however, three quite distinct issues in the ownership of new town housing: building for sale by public or private agency; building for rent and the question of the ownership and management of this stock; and the selling of houses originally built for rent either to tenants or other people when they fall vacant. The researchers' brief originally concerned only the second of these topics, but extended into the third. The desire to raise owner-occupation in new towns involved all three and the political controversy has centred on the second and third elements. Sadly the issues have frequently been conflated, which has not benefited the consistency of policies.

Cullingworth and Karn carried out their research between September 1966 and October 1967, seeking evidence from central and local public agencies and from new town tenants and residents (a neglected group in new town policy-making). Their work included surveys of administrative practice and local opinion in Crawley, Stevenage, Aycliffe and East Kilbride.

The broad positions taken up by development corporations and the Commission for the New Towns, on the one hand, and local authorities, on the other, were predictable. The local authorities were in favour of their both owning and managing new town rented housing (Cullingworth and Karn, 1968, pp. 37ff.). They argued that the control of the housing would become more accessible and accountable, that the life of the town would be unified and enriched by a new sense of common identity. Most dismissed the doubts about the powers of, and pressures on, tenant councillors in a near-monopoly position and also the claims that the local authorities concerned could not carry the increased administrative burden. Cullingworth and Karn wryly drew attention to the fact that where misgivings on local authority control were expressed, it tended to come from respondents who were officers, rather than members, of the local authority!

The development corporations and the Commission claimed as virtues (*ibid.*, pp. 44ff.) the very characteristics that had been condemned by the local authorities. Their non-elective structure ensured efficiency, the careful blending of skills and experience and, above all, continuity. The Commission recommended a switch in the other direction: the creation of a national rent-pool of new town housing that would enable the equalization of rent levels between rents for older and recent new town houses and thus the lessening of disparities between new town corporation/Commission and local authority rent levels (this argument has been made partly redundant by the 1972 Housing Finance Act and subsequent legislation) as well as contributing to amenities. The Commission stressed their skills in management and the economies of scale in their organization, but were nevertheless willing to contemplate transferring the management of the housing to the local authority while leaving the freehold ownership in central government hands, thus retaining the value of the land and the possibility of comprehensive development when it fell due (*ibid.*, p. 58).

Allocation of new town tenancies has been linked traditionally with a policy of local employment and, to some extent, regional housing needs. Some doubts were expressed by local authorities about whether these objectives could be met alongside their more usual criteria of need and local residence (*ibid.*, p. 38). Development corporations did not see this as a major problem however, since they expected the housing to be transferred, if at all, when the target population had been reached and the homes/jobs link was therefore declining in importance.

There was found to be a measure of agreement between corporations and councils on two issues. Firstly, all the local authorities and several new town corporations wanted transfer to be on the basis of outstanding loan debts and charges. The parallel of the transfer of hospitals at the inception of the National Health Service was used.

Any transfer would have to be on the basis that the new body merely stood in the shoes of the commission or the appropriate development corporation. . . . Any basis that involved revaluation and re-financing at present borrowing rates would mean a sharp and unjustified increase in rents (*ibid.*, p. 50).

It would also lead to an increase in rates, which led to the local authorities' rejection of transfer at market value. The only group in favour of the latter arrangement were 'some of the development corporations with the greatest financial problems' (*ibid.*) who had visions of thus realizing their assets and wiping out both deficits and loan charges!

Secondly, all agreed that the Scottish new towns would present a problem. The tradition of very low rent levels had resulted in all the Scottish new towns having, at the time of the study, a large and growing deficit on their housing revenue account. Cullingworth and Karn wrote (*ibid.*, p. 104) that the issue of transfer 'Given current attitudes and rent levels . . . will . . . be a difficult operation', since either of the methods of transfer discussed above would result in a burden being placed upon the local authority.

The attitude of residents to the ownership of rented housing turned out to be much less decisive. Surveys both of all residents and of tenants alone in the sample towns showed broadly the same response: two-fifths for transfer, two-fifths for the *status quo* and one-fifth 'don't know'. The main reason for wanting transfer was political accountability, which emerged most strongly in the Aycliffe sample. The response to questions about whether new town houses should be offered for sale to their tenants was much more unequivocal: of the 'whole town' sample in all four towns, 88 per cent said 'yes' or 'qualified yes', and 86 per cent of the 'tenants' sample gave a similar answer (*ibid.*, p. 65). Respondents were not, however, asked whether they thought that all the houses in the town should be sold.

It is this finding that naturally attracted much attention, but people using it in later political arguments rarely went on to qualify the finding as Cullingworth and Karn did. Tenants' wishes to buy were very different from whether they could buy, and if they could, whether they would want to buy the house they occupied. In a later chapter (pp. 107ff.) Cullingworth and Karn explored the relationship between new town incomes and the price of new town houses. They found that while those who wanted to buy had incomes similar to the distribution of income of those who had bought houses throughout the country in the period 1960–4, the level was lower than that of existing new town owner-occupiers. A detailed examination of the actual capacity of tenants to buy their homes revealed that the average head of household could only barely afford the loan on the lowest priced new town house. Many people come into owner-occupation through buying older, cheaper houses, or inheriting outright ownership. National figures for ownership by income also include the retired who have become outright owners and also have a very low income, thus disguising the much higher income needed to enter the housing market for the first time. New town corporation houses were — and are — usually built to higher minimum standards than those at the lower end of the private building market, thus reducing still further the pool of potential buyers. In addition, many of those questioned may well have been in middle life, so that the length of mortgage available would be reduced and the payments increased.

A final and crucial element in the translation of an abstract wish to be an owner-occupier into reality is one of attitudes and aspirations. With hindsight it is particularly striking that few respondents in the Cullingworth and Karn study mentioned the 'investment' or 'saving' element in house ownership, which has come to the fore since about 1970. Many said that renting was 'cheaper', or that they had 'never thought of buying', especially in East Kilbride (*ibid.*, p. 132). There are regional, as well as class, income and age variations in the propensity to buy houses, as became increasingly clear when a policy of owner-occupation was being pursued in the new towns after 1966. Cullingworth and Karn concluded that, leaving aside those who rightly assumed that they were too old to buy and/or that they could not afford to do so, there would have to be incentives to overcome inertia.

Both development corporations and local authorities wanted to see an increase in owner-occupation. The councils, in particular, were concerned that it should *not* be by means of sales to tenants, because of the loss of older, cheaper housing stock and the effect on their rent pools. The same problem was raised by one development corporation, which observed that it would depend whether the profits from the sales could be used to defray the loss to the housing revenue account (*ibid.*, p. 117). Hindsight again emphasizes the fact that only the Commission and one corporation mentioned that sales (of rented housing and land for housing) would enable corporations to realize and 'roll-over' their assets (*ibid.*, p. 112). The stability and 'leadership' that owner-occupation would bring and its importance in bringing new towns to 'normality' received greater emphasis.

Doubts were expressed by both development corporations and local authorities about the effect of a major shift to owner-occupation on both the new towns' obligations towards the housing of overspill and the use of housing for key workers as bait for industrialists and their labour force. Some respondents wondered whether people would want to buy in 'rented' areas and what problems of organization and cost of maintenance would emerge from such 'pepperpot' sales. These reservations were not strongly expressed, however, which is hardly surprising since the government had already committed itself to a policy of 50:50 rented to owner-occupied housing in England and Wales new towns, and 75:25 in Scotland. Richard Crossman was thinking along these lines in 1965, as his diaries show (Crossman, 1975, p. 376). The policy was announced in November 1966 (HC Debates, vol. 735, col. 1757) and detailed in a circular in mid-1967. The objective was that the post-1961 generation of new towns should provide half owner-occupied and half public-rented housing during their period of 'planned intake', of which two-thirds should be built by private enterprise. The towns in the natural increase stage should raise their proportion of owner-occupiers by selling to sitting tenants, but 'overspill' towns in both cases should keep a stock of moderately rented housing – and should sell with pre-emption clauses.

The major departure in policy was not the selling of houses, but the scale on which it was being proposed. During the strict post-war control on private building some development corporations, like Harlow (Harlow DC, 1968, p. 206) had been forbidden to build houses for sale. Others, however, had been doing so from the start. 'There was already in 1948 a considerable demand from people who wished to own their houses. . . . The first group of 36 houses for this purpose . . . was occupied in 1953/55 on 999 year leases . . .' (Hatfield DC, 1966, p. 466). Most new towns were willing to make individual plots available for owner-occupiers, but take-up was very limited. By 1960, private developers had schemes in at least eight towns, including East Kilbride. The development corporation was building for sale in six, and three – Aycliffe, Harlow and Hemel Hempstead – were selling to tenants. Only Cumbernauld, designated in 1955, made no mention of private housing, although activity seems to have been very limited in Peterlee and Glenrothes. The provision of private housing, mainly by developers and the corporation building for sale, gathered momentum after 1960 in the first generation of towns. The 'second generation' designated from 1961 onwards were either barely under way or not yet designated when the announcement of the 50:50 split was made in 1966, and thus had it as an objective from the first.

Cullingworth and Karn's doubts that, whatever their wish for owner-occupation, people would not actually be able to buy in large numbers were quickly vindicated. Sales of all kinds were highest in the towns nearest London where a tradition of relatively large numbers of sales had already established itself, as in Bracknell, which had a waiting list to buy in 1962 (Bracknell DC, 1962, p. 86), Hemel Hempstead, Welwyn Garden City and Hatfield. Elsewhere the complex interaction of low wages, the high price of development corporation housing and a local tradition of renting led to a slow response from corporation tenants offered the chance to buy. Those who could afford to buy sometimes rejected corporation housing even when it was built for sale (Corby DC, 1967, p. 108; Cwmbran DC, 1970, p. 149).

Sales were further frustrated by an apparent reluctance of the building societies to grant mortgages, particularly in some of the towns outside London and the West Midlands. Their caution was based on the unorthodox construction and layout of some of the houses, and the lack of certainty that there would be a ready market for their resale. Despite a meeting of new town chairmen with the Building Societies Association in October 1967 (Corby DC, 1968, p. 107), corporations had to start to provide mortgages themselves. For some at least, this came to be a valued source of additional income (Basildon DC, 1972, p. 44).

In a further effort to boost sales, a ministry circular of 1968 suggested that corporations should try to provide housing for lower-income groups, by competitive tender amongst small local builders and by building 'simple' housing that could later be improved by owners themselves. This was of course a hint to build at less than Parker Morris standards for selling, but was not popular with corporations, largely because the possible savings were marginal and reduced the attractiveness of the housing to buyers. Another attempt to increase sales by making mortgages available was made in early 1970, when the government had to acknowledge that the policy of owner-occupation had got off to a slow start (HC Debates, vol. 783, col. 243). The gap between the expressed and effective demand was emphasized by the response to two parliamentary written questions in 1969 and 1970. These revealed that an average of only 6 per cent of the housing stock was actually available for sale and even then that in some towns houses for sale were standing empty (HC, Debates, vol. 778, col. 185 written; vol. 800, col. 40 written). The matter was the source of some political embarrassment for the Labour government, given the waiting lists for new town rented housing and much longer lists in the cities.

The situation was transformed during the period 1970–2. When the Conservatives were returned, the new minister, Peter Walker, quickly announced that new town houses would be on sale to their tenants at discounts of up to 20 per cent off the market price. The announcement, in October 1970, declared that not only was owner-occupation a worthy objective in itself, but that it would serve to erode the monopoly position of the development corporations and the Commission for the New Towns. All dwellings should be on offer, except for flats and old people's dwellings, and, although there should be no pre-emptive clauses, the buyer should pay back a reducing proportion of the discount if the house were resold in the first five years. To build up confidence in the marketability of new town houses, the development corporation should itself undertake to buy back the house within that period at market price less the discount still outstanding. The only major limitation was that the discounted price should not be less than the cost of the house to the corporation, including land and development expenses. Skelmersdale, at least, found itself in this position (Skelmersdale DC, 1972, p. 487), but the restriction was removed in 1971. Still tenants in some towns were slow to take advantage of the chance to buy their houses. Corby found sales of houses to tenants slow and of land to builders equally discouraging in 1971 (Corby DC, 1971, p. 115), while Peterlee wrote of having to 'persuade tenants to buy' in the same year (Peterlee DC, 1971, p. 343)!

If the 'pull' of discounts failed, the 'push' of the Housing Finance Act 1972 certainly succeeded. For many people, in the new towns and elsewhere, the transfer of housing subsidy from the dwelling in the form of a low rent to persons in the form of rebates, narrowed or even eliminated the gap between rent and mortgage repayments. Mortgage finance became freely available and there was a national explosion of demand for houses. It was, naturally, closely followed by an explosion of house and housing land prices, since the building industry, organized as it is mostly in small firms with perennial cash-flow problems, will respond to demand, but cannot afford to anticipate it. Ironically, this was the very problem that convinced many people that home-ownership was an attractive investment and not a costly responsibility. The annual reports of many development corporations outside the London area reflected this realization. Corby, Cwmbran and Livingston, areas where owner-occupation had been slow to get established, all reported a rapid expansion in 1973, while at East Kilbride house sales had 'doubled' to over 13 per cent during the year (East Kilbride Development Corporation, 1973, p. 51). Given that the Housing Finance Act did not apply in Scotland, the incentive must rather have been a widespread awakening that owner-occupation was not something available only to other people.

For new towns in the Midlands and the South the upsurge of interest in owner-occupation convinced them that they would achieve the 50:50 target. Northampton thought that it might even exceed it (Northampton DC, 1972, p. 300). The high rate of selling was to be achieved by sales to tenants and private building. A circular in 1971 had instructed development corporations to concentrate their own building on providing for unmet needs. Land should be made available to developers to build, and they should not be 'hedged about with restrictions' on the design of the houses, or on the categories of people to whom they could be sold, which would be 'incompatible with a free market economy'. Later that year a 10 per cent return was laid down as the minimum acceptable for housing and housing land.

As the move to owner-occupation had started earlier in the south where wage levels were higher, so too it showed signs of slowing down in the south first. Rises in house prices were greater in the London area than elsewhere and passed first beyond the reach of the average industrial wage earner and then beyond higher-paid groups, exacerbated by rises in the mortgage interest rate. Milton Keynes had been particularly concerned to provide housing for sale to average-income earners and it was their Report of 1972 (p. 241) that was one of the first to suggest that the equilibrium between wages and house prices had been upset. A similar process was also occurring elsewhere and was followed by the abrupt decline of private developers' building for sale. This 'virtual collapse' (Telford DC, 1975, p. 398) of private housing in 1974 was accompanied by a rapid rise in demand for rented housing in the new towns – even in Bracknell (Bracknell DC, 1974, p. 68) – which the development corporations were completely unprepared to meet. Waiting lists lengthened, despite corporations' being reminded of a 1970 circular enabling them to buy and let unsold private developments. Warrington, which had started with the goal of a 70:30 split of private to rented housing revised its target to 25:75 (Warrington DC, 1975, p. 436). In a small number of cases, corporations bought houses back from tenants for whom costs of maintenance and rising interest had proved unsupportable (for example, Basildon DC, 1975, p. 37), a reminder that the financial balance is as delicate for some as it was for the inhabitants of Becontree in the 1930s.

Labour won the election of March 1974, and one of John Silkin's first acts as minister was to send a letter to the new towns 'advising' them to stop selling houses to tenants and sales of housing land without central consent. The request was followed by an instruction in September 1974 that confirmed the ending of sales to tenants and the confining of freehold sales of housing land to voluntary housing associations and to individuals. For the time being the new towns were to concentrate their attention on building up their rented stock.

The issue continued to attract debate as part of the larger controversy over the sale of public housing, which has achieved the status of a symbolic party political division. Two attempts were made by the Conservative opposition to get sales restarted: a technical amendment to the New Towns (Amendment) Bill tabled by the leader of the opposition, and a Private Member's Bill (defeated by an amendment in the name of the prime minister).

The government position, in regard to new town houses, was that the concentration on house sales between 1970 and 1974 and the accompanying rise in prices had resulted in long waiting lists for rented houses. Selling the rented stock would, under the circumstances, be irresponsible, at least until waiting lists had shortened. The opposition advocated a renewed policy of sales to tenants at 20 per cent below market value with five years' pre-emption, and brought a number of diverse arguments to bear. It was claimed that apart from home ownership being *ipso facto* desirable, tenants would be either buying the house they occupied or would continue to rent it. They were unlikely to leave it, so that selling it would not deplete the housing stock or affect the waiting list, because these houses would not anyway be available for re-letting (HC Debates, vol. 908, col. 251). It was also claimed that in some cases the costs of retaining the house in loan servicing, rent collection, maintenance and administration was as much as three times the revenue coming in from rent (*ibid.*, col. 250), so that selling would be a saving. It would, in addition, end the housing subsidies being paid and release revenue for the development corporation. It was for this last reason that the development corporations, through the New Towns Association, had pressed the DOE to reconsider its policies on sales (*Guardian,* 27 February 1975), and their views were used by Conservative speakers in support of their case.

During the debate on the Private Member's Bill, the minister was able to announce a modification in the government's policies. The objective of reducing waiting lists had, he said, been achieved at least in part, so that a review of the situation in each new town was possible.

In August 1976 a circular was issued to the development corporations informing them that they could apply to the DOE for permission to sell to sitting tenants providing that they consulted the local authorities in their area, and that the waiting list for rented housing was less than three months. The cost to tenants was to be full market value minus 20 per cent for those of more than four years' standing − although this discount had to be repaid if the house was resold within five years, on the formula 5/5 in the first year, 4/5 in the second year and so on. Dwellings specifically adapted for the elderly or disabled were not to be sold. By the summer of 1977, all of the fourteen new towns which had applied to sell had been given permission to do so (HC Debates, vol. 933, col. 395).

Comment has been made elsewhere in the book about the remarkable lack of summary data available about the new towns. This is nowhere more vividly illustrated than by the issue of housing. Replying to a written question by the MP for Nottingham

North, William Whitlock, the minister was able to supply figures on owner-occupation in the new towns for 1972 and 1978, but not for 1966: 'To obtain it would involve a costly and quite disproportionate amount of research', implying that basic factual information was not to hand when the new emphasis on owner-occupation was decided upon.

Table 1 shows that the new towns in 1978 fall into two broad groupings in respect of owner-occupation. In Mark One towns and some of the greenfield Mark Two towns like Skelmersdale, the proportion rose between 1972 and 1978, quite dramatically in some cases, as in Basildon, Harlow, Crawley and particularly Stevenage. Where there was already a considerable existing population, as in

TABLE 1 *Percentage of owner-occupied dwellings in British new towns (figures supplied by DOE, 21 March 1978)*

	New town	1972	1978
ENGLAND	Aycliffe	8·7	21·4
	Basildon	17·8	27·0
	Bracknell	25·6	29·3
	Central Lancashire	62·5	62·3
	Corby	11·0	20·6
	Crawley	37·5	42·8
	Harlow	13·1	23·9
	Hatfield	29·8	32·6
	Hemel Hempstead	31·7	40·0
	Milton Keynes	57·3	43·4
	Northampton	59·2	55·6
	Peterborough	54·8	48·2
	Peterlee	4·2	11·3
	Redditch	59·4	49·8
	Runcorn	36·1	29·3
	Skelmersdale	20·7	21·9
	Stevenage	16·1	37·8
	Telford	35·5	35·7
	Warrington	55·1	56·8
	Washington	24·8	28·2
	Welwyn Garden City	27·2	28·3
SCOTLAND	East Kilbride	12·0	17·5
	Glenrothes	8·1	13·8
	Cumbernauld	9·0	18·4
	Livingston	3·4	8·1
	Irvine	26·1	18·3
WALES	Cwmbran	18·6	21·2
	New Town	31·7	40·0

Runcorn, Redditch and Peterborough, the effect of the development corporation's output of rented housing has been to reduce the proportion of the total housing stock in the designated area in owner-occupation.

The policies about owner-occupation are unusual in the history of the new towns programme in the sense that they have been explicit and applied to the programme as a whole. We have seen, however, there must be more than a suspicion that the targets produced in 1967 were plucked out of the air, unrelated to any coherent view of the goal or goals of the new towns. As will be argued in later chapters, expediency and expenditure remain the moving forces in this as in other aspects of the policy.

Land and other assets

As earlier chapters have suggested, the ownership of the industrial and commercial assets of the new towns has become the subject of tacit agreement between the two main political parties. Neither, by the end of the 1960s, was willing to see this complex and remunerative property pass into either local-authority ownership or local-authority management. Latterly, of course, the ownership of these properties, or at least the income from them, has been distributed amongst institutional funds and property developers as well. Few recent industrial and commercial properties are wholly owned by development corporations. Among the exceptions are the advance 'nursery' factories, which are to be found in the towns serving London and the Midlands as well as in the regions where various incentives apply.

The land and buildings for local authority services and those of other statutory undertakers are now usually owned by those agencies themselves, who provide the building on a site sold to them by the development corporation. Where facilities were provided by the corporation, there has been a long standing and uncontroversial tradition of transfer to the local authority. Annual reports for the 1950s frequently refer to the sale of parks, recreation grounds and even public conveniences (Aycliffe DC, 1955, p. 8). Difficulties have, however, arisen more recently, not over the principle of ownership, but the practice. Some over-extended local authorities have not been able to afford to maintain their new asset, as was the case at least for a period at Northampton (Expenditure Committee, 1974–5a, p. 802). Water and sewerage undertakings, which had been the subject of possible debate or dispute between new towns and their local authorities, have been transferred to the new regional water authorities under the Water Act 1973. Corporations will still be able to provide sewers (but not disposal works) themselves or for the water authority as agent if necessary. Relationships and finance have been simplified.

Since leasehold reform in 1967, the sales of houses in new towns had largely been on a freehold basis. This was confirmed in a ministry circular of 1971. Until that year sites for commercial and industrial building too had always been leased, for periods of varying length. Early in 1971 the ministry let it be known that free-hold sales of such sites would be considered. The Commission for the New Towns resisted this (see above). The incoming Labour government stopped the practice in the 1974 letter and circular. In the intervening time, disposals (including housing) were sufficiently lucrative for some new towns to become self-financing (see, for example, Basildon DC, 1975, p. 40 and Bracknell DC, 1973, p. 75, and 1974, p. 73) or to show a surplus (Corby DC, 1973, p. 138, Cwmbran DC, 1974, p. 13, and Peterlee DC, 1973, p. 380), which is the more interesting because among the towns concerned some had had persistent economic difficulties in their unglamorous early years. Arguments about whether unified land ownership should be retained have come, for the most part, to be based upon purely pragmatic arguments about the realizing and recycling of new town assets. As Schaffer's comments about lease and lease-back illustrate, the question of short- versus long-run considerations is crucial. The policies of governments have, since 1969, moved towards shorter-run considerations, which is probably inevitable in a climate of inflation and soaring loan charges.

A major feature of policies since the late 1960s has been the increasing importance of land acquisition as trends in land values and rents led to a situation where the development corporations' largest sources of revenue were the sale of houses and the collection of betterment. Government policy on development corporations' programmes of acquisition has been erratic. The credit squeeze, which nearly ended the new towns before they had begun, included curtailing the assembly of land in the designated area. These restrictions were gradually eased, to the later benefit of the development corporations. In 1966 public expenditure cuts again led to an instruction that most development corporations should not buy land in advance of need, but the inexorable logic of the corporations' powers to buy at less than development value has led to further modifications in policy. Central Lancashire and Warrington new towns both had policies of rapid land assembly from the start: 'the corporation's policy [is] to assemble land at the earliest opportunity . . . to bring into its ownership all undeveloped land in the area' (Central Lancashire NT DC, 1973, p. 109). Public expenditure cuts in 1976 yet again resulted in the development corporations' being instructed to curtail their land acquisition (CLNT

DC, 1977, p. 93; Northampton DC, 1977, p. 210). The cycle will no doubt continue.

This policy could bring handsome profits sooner or later, notwithstanding the Community Land Act, but there are short-term risks. Housing land prices slumped in Northampton – and elsewhere:

> in 1973/74 when we were in our heyday of acquiring land at existing use value, providing infrastructure and selling off the housing land to private enterprise at £40,000 an acre. . . . Interest rates have gone up and the value of land . . . is now down to £25,000 an acre (Expenditure Committee, 1974–5a, pp. 802–3).

There is still a potential advantage to the development corporation in this capability: the problems arise from the consequent postponement of 'break-even' when that has become a major benchmark of success. As in many other areas of the new towns policy, ends and means appear to have become confused, if indeed they were ever distinct. One such objective is the 'balance and self-containment' that formed such a central part of the New Towns Committee's vision and has been the subject of more research than almost any other aspect of new town policy since then.

6 Balance and self-containment

The idea of a New Town as a self-contained and separate
entity is giving way to the newer and socially more healthy
concept of a New Town at the centre of a wider district
(Bracknell DC, 1965, p. 85).

Objectives

It has sometimes been asserted in recent writings on new towns that
balance and self-containment were ill-defined by the Reith committee. In fact, as shown in chapter 2, the committee was quite
unequivocal about at least two aspects of 'balance': it concerned
social status and the variety of employment available in a town. It is
true, however, that the desirability of the goal was not questioned
(but then the terms of reference of government committees rarely
are), nor were the means of its achievement closely examined.
While self-containment remains, as the Reith committee (New
Towns Committee, 1946c, p. 10) suggested, a (relatively) self-
evident concept, balance has been further elaborated, which has
contributed to the complexities of its definition. To confuse matters
even further, the two concepts are largely interdependent.

In the history of the new town idea, concern about the physical
and social consequences of living conditions in metropolitan areas
was supplemented, between the wars, by criticism of the contemporary response to these problems. The expansion of public and
private suburbia had improved housing conditions for many, but at
the price of expensive, tiring and time-wasting travel to work. The
visual and social homogeneity of the new housing estates were also
viewed with distaste, especially after the war, when it was expected
that the social order of wealth and status would undergo a fundamental realignment. Not merely 'homes', but a way of life, 'fit for

105

heroes' was the objective. In this climate, decentralization and renewal were quickly accepted as major goals, and the work of Barlow and Abercrombie indicated that an integrated policy of relocating homes and jobs was necessary. Commuting was rejected as a manifest (and somehow unnatural) evil. The new settlements were to have enough work for all the inhabitants, preferably within walking or bicycle distance. Lengthy journeys for regular shopping, recreation and entertainment were also to be eliminated. Self-containment, then, meant completeness in terms of work and the facilities needed for day-to-day living. (The latter consideration was of course intimately connected with the New Towns Committee's deliberations on an appropriate size for the town — and on subsequent rethinking.)

Later in the evolution of new town planning this idea of narrow spatial and functional boundaries came to be seen as quaint and outdated, and even as a rather sinister attempt to limit the choices of the residents. In the context of 1946, however, when access to cars was non-existent for most people and they were thought unlikely to become widely available, the conclusion was inevitable. The alternatives were seen as a lengthy journey to work on public transport, with all the consequences described by Young (1934) and Durant (1939), or high-density redevelopment, albeit more accessible to work, in the inner city. It was just these solutions that the post-war policy of dispersal was rejecting. Some of the positive aspects of self-containment are again becoming apparent, as will be seen later in this chapter and in the next chapter.

The employment elements of the Reith committee's interpretation of 'balance' were that there should be enough jobs available in the new town for all the population of working age, that there should be a wide variety of jobs to accommodate different skills, tastes, ages and circumstances and that the industrial base should be diverse, so that the town would not be dependent on one industry. These considerations were entailed in the idea of self-containment especially if the social-class aspect of balance were to be achieved.

The Reith committee clearly felt that the new towns should be a microcosm of contemporary British society, with all strata of income and social status represented. This has since been redefined as meaning that balance has been achieved when all social groups are represented in proportion to their incidence in the population at large. Latterly, that in turn has been extended to include 'minorities' like the single-parent family, the unemployed, the handicapped, the elderly and black and brown immigrants. To be fair to the New Towns Committee, they did not specify this degree of statistical balance, only that all groups should be represented (1946c, para. 22). They were, on the other hand, guilty of confusing prescriptive and descriptive normality, for few existing towns – especially in the 30–50,000 population range that the committee thought optimal (*ibid.*, para. 20) – are 'normal' in this way. This kind of confusion re-emphasizes, moreover, that the original conception of new towns contrived to be radical and conservative at once. Reith and his colleagues anticipated the end of social class (*ibid.*, para. 22), but did not see themselves contributing to its demise. There would be a better life for all in the new towns, but it would be a raising of standards across the board, not a redistribution of life-chances. To defend the committee, it cannot be said that such conceptual and ideological confusion lessened as the towns were built. With hindsight, the Labour government's pursuit of a 50:50 split between private and public housing in the new towns was a similar assertion that a statistical trend defined a desirable and achievable objective despite the unusual circumstances of new towns.

The New Towns Committee assumed that balance would be brought about by the attraction of industry, but equally by the provision of a variety of housing types, sizes and tenures. Earlier chapters have shown the extent to which this was frustrated in the first ten years of the new towns. Annual reports for the 1950s drew attention to this interpretation of the means to balance, for example, Harlow (Harlow DC, 1950, 1952) and Basildon in 1957 and 1964:

> the Corporation's progress in the implementation of their policy of hastening the creation of a balanced community, socially and economically, should be mentioned. The Corporation have made progress in various ways – building houses for sale to the higher income groups, attracting forms of employment in the higher salary ranges and planning amenities such as the golf course (Basildon DC, 1964, p. 35).

Later in the 1960s explicit references to the pursuit of balance of this type declined, partly to be replaced by a concern to keep jobs and housing completions 'balanced' in the sense of being in step. For the second generation of towns this was tied to the fluctuations of the economy and hence the inflow of industry. In the earlier new towns it centred on the need to attract more, and more diverse, industry (especially white-collar employment) to employ the children of the first generation of tenants.

Self-containment has rarely been discussed in the new town annual reports. To some extent this must have been because it was subsumed under the 'numbers of jobs' interpretation of balance. It was implicitly endorsed in the rejection of commuting, which let to attempts to confine sales of new town houses to existing local residents and/or employees when owner-occupation began to increase. (A parliamentary questioner complained in 1961 that Harlow, Bracknell and Crawley were all trying to do this. In Harlow the qualification was five years' residence – but not necessarily to be working there (HC Debates, vol. 639, col. 91 written).) The objective of self-containment could also be interpreted as the reason for the frequent complaints by development corporations about the lack of finance for publicly provided amenities in the first generation of new towns – and their vigorous pursuit of commercially provided facilities. This is probably better understood, however, as a wish to make the town as 'normal' and attractive as possible, rather than the calculated pursuit of self-containment.

For many towns, of course, self-containment was not a primary objective. In Scotland, meeting housing need was the overriding aim, so that the homes/jobs linkage was never as central to the new towns concept. In England and Wales, Hatfield, Aycliffe and Cwmbran all concerned themselves with providing housing for industry that existed already, outside the designated area, thus ruling out self-containment in its strictest interpretation. Given that Corby and Peterlee were also designated to meet existing industry's demand for housing and that Basildon was preoccupied with rural slum clearance, only six of the fourteen new towns in the first generation were 'typical' in conforming to the model of pursuing balance and self-containment in tandem. This group — Bracknell, Crawley, Harlow, Hemel Hempstead, Stevenage and Welwyn Garden City — came to be the subject of much of the research on the achievement of new town goals (though whether it was because they were seen as normal new towns, or happened to be pleasant and handy for London cannot now be inferred). Thus the diversity of new town circumstances was not fully acknowledged, nor were balance and self-containment recognized as what they have always been: an ideal type, against which to evaluate new town planning, not an empirical destination at which all the towns can or should arrive.

The mechanisms

When the first generation of new towns began with *carte blanche* (principally the six around London named above) it quickly became clear that a choice would have to be made between accommodating people on the basis of their housing need, or on their employment situation. By 1949 the choice had been made in favour of a close link being maintained between housing and employment in the new towns. Holding a job with a local firm would take precedence over housing need. This conformed to the Abercrombie/Reith strategy, but deeply disappointed the inner metropolitan boroughs (as was touched on in chapter 3), which had hoped for a more direct avenue to alleviating their housing problems. Thus began a dispute about the rationale and dynamic of new towns that rumbles on still.

Once there was acceptance that housing in the new towns would depend upon employment, it was inevitable that the nature of migrating industry would determine the range of skills and income in all three groups of migrants: the 'key workers' of migrant firms, those who successfully negotiated the Industrial Selection Scheme (see below) as a solution to their housing need and those who independently obtained work and were thus eligible for housing. Students of new town development disagree as to whether there was a conscious effort to limit incoming firms to clean, modern technologies with a high demand for skilled staff. Heraud (1968, p. 40) concludes that development corporations were able to be highly selective in their choice of industry. His argument is based on an undated statement from the former chief executive of Crawley, but the large number of firms who 'had discussions' with Crawley (*ibid.*) may not have borne much resemblance to the number that wished then to move, or negotiated the steeplechase of government industrial-location policies and were able to move. The statement may well have been referring to a much later time in the development of Crawley. If it did not, no chief executive would publicly declare that the new town had to grab any mobile industry it could get its hand on, though some towns did have to do so, the most notorious example being Glenrothes and Cadco (see Thomas, 1969b, p. 931 for the whole cautionary tale).

The general position typified by Thomas (1969a, p. 386) seems to be a more accurate reflection of the process. In the earliest days of the new towns, any industry was gratefully received. Later on there was the opportunity for selectivity − but within a limited range. Mobile industry was characteristically in light engineering or advanced technology, with a highly skilled work-force and/or highly automated processes. Extractive and heavy industry are not mobile, nor at the outset was there much scope to develop unskilled and semi-skilled employment in the service industries, like retailing and catering. Many low-wage industries with an unskilled work-force were likely to be found operating on a shoestring in the central city, both unwilling and unable to invest in the move to modern and relatively expensive new town accommodation. The trend towards modern, capital-intensive, high-wage, skilled employment was further amplified by the levels of new town housing rents which remained high enough to deter many lower-paid and less-skilled migrants (see chapter 3).

For the London new towns, there has been a formal system that has attempted to combine the twin objectives of meeting housing need and ensuring that all new town residents work in the town. In 1949 the Ministry of Town and Country Planning issued a Memorandum (MTCP, 1949) which proposed that London should be divided into sectors linked with a specific new town. Migrant industry would move to the new town for its sector, and as many of the workers as wanted to go with it would be housed, regardless of their origin. In conjunction with this, new town employers would notify the employment exchange in the new town, which would then contact the employment exchange acting as a clearing house in the relevant sector of London. This exchange would apply to the local authority, which held a list of people in housing need who had expressed a readiness to move to a new town, together with their skills, and arranged interviews for likely candidates. The successful candidate(s) would then be nominated for a house by the employer, and the development corporations would allocate one, but had the right not to do so. Ruddy (1969, p. 3) records that these proposals did not satisfy the London boroughs, who saw no reason to expect that industries that moved would go from the areas of greatest need, nor that their employees would be the most deserving of housing. Nevertheless the recommendations were put into effect as the Industrial Selection Scheme and operated until 1953. Within that time the sector arrangements collapsed, and the tendency of new town employers to seek skilled recruits was already established. Some candidates anyway rejected jobs because wage levels were lower and rents higher than in their current circumstances.

In 1953 the scheme was modified to be used also in town-expansion schemes built under the Town Development Act 1952 and continues to be operated – in so far as it is used – in this way to date. It has been renamed the New and Expanded Towns Scheme (NETS) and broadly similar arrangements were initiated for Birmingham, Glasgow and North Merseyside. Detailed descriptions of these schemes can be found in Ruddy (1969), Gee (1972) and Thomas (1973) while there are more succinct attempts to summarize by Thomas (1969a, p. 387); the Department of Employment (Expenditure Committee, 1974, p. 190) and Ungerson (*ibid.,* p. 374). The current situation, according to the Department of Employment's account of a somewhat labyrinthine process is as follows: people in housing need who are willing to move to a new town notify their local authority, which then classifies their need and notifies the local employment exchange, with whom the applicant has registered and given details of his experience and qualifications. At the 'other end' employers register their job requirements with the local employment exchange. If the vacancy cannot be filled 'within, generally, 48 hours' from people already living in the new town area, details are circulated to the employment exchanges of the conurbation area, or sometimes to the local authority. A short-list of possible candidates for the job is constructed, with those in greatest housing need at the top, and those on it contacted. If the person registered is interested, an interview will be arranged. If he is successful and accepts the job, the employer will nominate him for a development corporation house (Expenditure Committee, 1974, p. 190).

The procedure is manifestly cumbersome and slow and therefore needs a high level of comprehension and commitment from the (many) parties to it. Not surprisingly, for reasons discussed below, the actual numbers of migrants to new towns who arrive by means of NETS is small. This is acknowledged by the new towns themselves and in some cases towns have organized direct links with inner-city authorities to overcome this failure. In 1973 Corby, for example, albeit motivated by a labour shortage, organized a 'Come to Corby' drive with the Greater London Boroughs of Lambeth, Redbridge and Hillingdon (Corby DC, 1974, p. 119) but 'Peterborough Week' is better known. A meeting, held by Peterborough Development Corporation in conjunction with Lambeth in 1971 was attended by eight hundred people, instead of the expected maximum of four hundred:

> some 500 families registered a firm wish to come and work and live in Peterborough. And many more would have done so had not all publicity been stopped after the preliminary meeting had made it clear that the demand would otherwise have far exceeded the jobs available (Peterborough DC, 1971, p. 308).

The major weakness of the NETS attempt to weld the homes/ jobs/housing need link is, apart from its complexity, that employers are under no compulsion at all to register vacancies with the employment exchange. Most simply fill jobs by word of mouth and advertisement. If they do notify the job locally to the Department of Employment, it may of course be filled by a local resident. A large group of migrants to new towns arrive because they have heard about the possibilities there, obtained a job and therefore been nominated for a house by their employer. Key workers of migrating firms form the other major group of migrants. Which is the larger depends on the town's stage of development. Other routes are sometimes open. In 1966 a ministry circular directed that the London new towns should allocate a prescribed number of houses to unskilled workers from London and arrangements were made with London employment exchanges, but this did nothing directly to meet housing need. Changes made in 1976 explicitly to help the 'disadvantaged' are discussed in chapter 8.

Towns specifically set up to meet acute housing shortage particularly in Scotland, and Skelmersdale among others in England, have always been prepared to accept tenants by more direct means, not necessarily linked with employment. It must be said, however, that local work for all residents (and especially corporation tenants) has always been the desired objective. A more open-door policy has usually indicated a politically embarrassing and financially unhealthy stock of vacant houses. One tap of migrants that corporations have turned on and off to fill their empty houses (which has usually been associated with economic recession) is to offer them to the working-age parents of residents. Skelmersdale, which has had chronic problems with employment since its inception, offered housing direct to people on the waiting list of North Merseyside local authorities, as a response to what they considered the failure of the (then) ISS. The 'main medium of publicity' was a letter to the Skelmersdale tenants asking them to nominate eligible friends and relatives. Almost half did so, resulting in the housing of seven hundred families (Skelmersdale DC, 1970, p. 444). Again it must be emphasized that this was not, at the time, a switch in policy by the development corporation, but a short-term response to vacant housing.

To summarize: all the new towns have striven towards some degree of self-containment, and they hoped balance, by the allocation of housing to heads of household with jobs in the town. Candidates who arrived via NETS were until 1976 the first priority, where it applied, but where it did not and when it did not deliver, nomination by an employer was the next order of priority, especially if the nominee came from the exporting area. (Ex-regular-army servicemen and corporation and local-government employees have been a high, but numerically small, priority, too.) Where industrial expansion fell behind housing provision, the parents and children of residents, among others, would become eligible. Later in a town's development, the local authority frequently started to provide for these last groups, as did the Commission for the New Towns. The degree of control that the corporation exercised would have been impossible had not most of the housing been for rent, which had not of course been an explicit policy at the outset. The Reith committee seems to have assumed that provided that work was available locally, only a fool would commute, so that there was no necessary conflict between self-containment and owner-occupation. They believed, too, that private housing was a prerequisite of balance (in class terms) which may be why the development corporations appear to have been quite sanguine about moving to a much higher level of owner-occupation, which was in turn coincident with the expansion of physical mobility via car-ownership.

Apart from the homes/jobs link, the new towns strove to produce self-containment in public and commercial amenities, although these had the dual function of attracting industry by means of a direct appeal to the decision-makers, and the encouragement of their labour force to migrate. (Some towns, where housing was ahead of jobs, claimed that they could offer the industrialist a pool of labour!) A major problem for the early new towns was that many migrants, coming from London or other large cities, were quite un-prepared for the relatively low level of amenities that the new towns could offer based on their limited population. This has partly been overcome by the growth of the first generation of towns, by the tendency to designate later towns in areas of substantial existing population and infrastructure, and the interest that private and insti-tutional capital began to show in new towns in the 1960s.

The expanding field of social development is also part of the pursuit of the complete community (Horrocks, 1974). A new town's community development activities are engaged at the inter-organization, inter-group and inter-personal levels to hasten the emergence of the social relationships which are assumed to be the normal manifestations of community life. These range from the stimulation of, say, sports clubs and then the formation of a sports council, to the encouragement of a more diffuse sense of identi-fication with, and belonging to, the town. It is very much a part of the Reith heritage that new towns should be devoting at least as great a proportion of their resources to this apparently unremuner-ative exercise now as they ever have − although it has never been the recipient of lavish staffing or funds. The ambiguous position of the social development function is epitomized by its history at Milton Keynes, for which there was to have been a social plan, parallel with the physical/financial plan. There was not, but the master-plan is the most clearly articulated internal source that exists on new town social development work. It specifically refers to the importance of informal social relationships: the networks of sup-port that people use in life crises (Milton Keynes DC, 1970, vol. II, p. 119). Social development does not have the pivotal position in the corporation that was envisaged, yet it is a large and active depart-ment in that apotheosis of second-generation new towns.

The achievement

It can safely be said that the great unanticipated problem of the new towns has been age balance — or its lack. In the event nearly all migrants have been young families, as they tend to be in all other major housing schemes, both public and private. This phenomenon has produced successive potential crises of health, welfare and education provision in all the new towns, as well as the fear that the absence of the 'normal' proportion of middle-aged and elderly people would impoverish community life. It also resulted in a bulge of demand for employment at roughly the date of the first substantial housing development plus fifteen years, as a reading of the reports of the first generation of towns demonstrates. Fortunately this coincided with the expansion of office employment in the 1960s, which helped to forestall the upsurge of youngsters commuting to London that some London new towns feared. Over the course of time the age distribution of the new towns' populations had become more typical. In the event, the adjustment was brought about by growing numbers of housing applications from retired parents (who of course, present no employment/self-containment problem) as well as the ageing of the population. In Harlow, at least:

> Quite fortuitously the problem of accommodating the retired
> was found to be closely linked with demand arising from
> second generation housing needs. Both . . . were happy in the
> main to accept small dwellings generally in the form of flats.
> Given a flexible transfer policy . . . these . . . were able to
> provide for a substantial and growing demand from the two
> groups (Harlow DC, 1971, p. 185).

Champion (1978) has, however, suggested that the first generation of new towns will, by the late 1980s, have to tackle the major economic and social problems of an ageing and declining population — although this also applies *a fortiori* to the greenfield Mark Two new towns where immigration took place in the 1960s and after. With the end of induced growth, there is unlikely to be sufficient employment or housing for the adult children of the original migrants. Many will move elsewhere, leaving the new town with an ageing retired population, under-occupying the housing stock. Where there are limitless resources available, the public housing problem might be solved in the same way that Harlow approached it in its heyday, but as Champion points out, the new town housing will by that time be a local authority responsibility, and political or economic pressures might well prevent too lavish expenditure on this one item. Increasing owner-occupation can only amplify the problem because the fit of dwelling sizes to the family cycle cannot be manipulated in this way. The scenario is intriguing: a re-run of some aspects of the 'inner-city problem' with the new towns in the leading role!

The tone of much retrospective writing about new town development is that it should have been anticipated that only the young would wish to move to new towns. Possessed of more skills, needing a proper home for their new family and not held back by the low rent of an inner-city council house or private rent-controlled home, it was inevitable that there would be age imbalances in the new town population. Michael Mann has recently taken a different perspective (Mann, 1973, pp. 26ff.). If such a large proportion of early new town residents were 'key-workers', who accompanied their firm, why were there so few older families, which would surely have been represented on the firm's payroll, especially since most firms have tended to be relocations, not new branch plants (*ibid.,* p. 30)? Would not older employees, who would find it difficult to find other jobs, be more rather than less likely to accept transfer? In fact, Mann suggests, the reason is the pre-eminence of housing conditions for employees when making the choice. Older employees do not accompany the firm, because of housing and perhaps local ties. During the interval between the firm's announcing the move and its departure, the normal labour turnover, which may anyway be high, will be accentuated by what Mann calls 'selective recruitment' (*ibid.*) whereby employees join the firm precisely because it is moving, thus altering the age structure of the labour force. Presumably this process would be increased even more if new towns were to make specific efforts to attract unskilled employment, where turnover tends to be higher still.

It has been suggested that the age imbalance in new towns should be accepted and even welcomed as an inevitable consequence of the 'rather specialized' contribution of new towns to the solution of housing problems. Given the contraction of the private rented market, with controlled rents reducing the availability of inner-city accommodation still further, plus the long wait for council housing, the new towns provide one of the only means of access to decent housing of the young couple starting a family, who could not (yet) afford to buy (Hall *et al.,* 1973, vol. 2, p. 350).

The goal of self-containment in terms of commuting was the subject of two research studies in the late 1960s. In her paper 'The Self-Contained New Town', Ogilvy (1968) drew attention to the fact that the existence of enough jobs for the residents will only be a necessary condition for self-containment: it is not sufficient. Changes of employment after becoming a new town tenant, and the increasing number of secondary wage-earners, make its achievement unlikely. Using census data from 1961, Ogilvy examined the crossing journeys (i.e. journeys to work that crossed local government boundaries as opposed to local journeys that began and ended within the new town) for the eight London new towns. She found that:

The numbers of daily cross-journeys were sufficiently high to question whether any of the new towns could reasonably be labelled as 'self-dependent' at all. Even in the town with the least cross-movement, Harlow . . . 5,000 residents travelled out, while 2,500 travelled in (from a town of less than 23,000 working residents . . .) (*ibid.,* p. 45).

On further examination of the journey-to-work hinterland of the four Hertfordshire towns and Harlow, she found that most of the journeys were within a radius of between ten and twenty miles, with few people travelling to London. The most important influence on self-containment was the proximity of other substantial centres of employment. This is confirmed by Cresswell and Thomas who have drawn attention to the exceptional self-containment of Corby (Cresswell and Thomas, 1972, p. 75).

Ogilvy published a follow-up study in 1971 (Ogilvy, 1971), using data from the 1966 census, which reflected the 'take-off' of new town jobs in the 1960s. The increase in employment and the slow-down in the rate of population increase had made the towns even less self-contained, as they had become greater importers of labour. There had, however, been a slight decrease in the number of new town residents travelling out to work (*ibid.,* p. 120). Overall, there had been an increase in mobility and in the interdependence of the new towns and their hinterlands.

Cresswell and Thomas (1972) calculated the 'indices of commuting independence' (i.e. the ratio of local to crossing journeys) for all the new towns with substantial development by 1966. Of all towns, Corby headed the list with an index of 2·51. The London new towns varied between 2·05 (Harlow) and 0·96 (Basildon). (Hatfield at 0·66 is a special case.) Apart from Corby, all the other first-generation towns had ratios of less than unity, but it should be remembered that they were either not primarily intended to be self-contained, or prevented from being so by their local employment circumstances. Cresswell and Thomas (*ibid.,* p. 75) remark of Scottish new towns that many people worked, but did not live, in East Kilbride because of the disparity between new town rents and the very low levels customary elsewhere in Scotland. Cumbernauld had an overspill agreement with Glasgow and consequently had let a proportion of houses to people without employment in the town.

For the London towns, at least, the degree of long-distance commuting by residents was perhaps more a matter of concern than movements within a limited hinterland. Thomas (1969a) has also compared the commuting independence of the London new towns with other towns within a similar range of distances from London. Data for 1966 showed all the new towns to be more independent than any town at a similar distance from the capital, except Stevenage, which is surpassed by Luton. Thomas's findings, though interesting and making the best use of the limited data available, are bound to contain an element of tautology, however. Many towns in the London region have grown precisely because they are dormitories for London. That is the nature of the South East region. It is interesting that Luton, where a new townlike situation of industrial and housing expansion has happened to occur, should be so highly self-contained. That the new towns are more self-contained than elsewhere in the South East is less a measure of their success than of their not failing. To be less self-contained than a dormitory suburb would be the utter failure of the entire new towns policy.

It will, doubtless, be several more years before any equivalent work will be done for the second generation of new towns. One can speculate that the range of self-containment in terms of crossing journeys may be even larger when, for example, Peterborough, which is a large and relatively isolated development, is compared with Redditch, Skelmersdale or Livingston. The new towns for Birmingham, Liverpool and Manchester were not expected to be viable for industrial relocation or rehousing unless they were relatively close to the conurbation boundary.

Many aspects of balance are inseparable from self-containment. The most obvious is that the number of jobs available must match the number of residents of working age. This dimension was also explored by Ogilvy, and Cresswell and Thomas. The latter are able to show data for 1951, 1961 and 1966 which help to distinguish the outcome of new-town development from pre-existing circumstances. At Cwmbran and Aycliffe, for instance, the ratio fell substantially as housing was provided for the trading estates and other employment. At Basildon the ratio of jobs per hundred working population rose sharply as the area was redeveloped and employment successfully established. Other than Aycliffe at 173, the ratios in 1966 mostly varied from 126 (Bracknell) to 96 (Hatfield). The exceptions were Glenrothes, built to house miners at a pit that was then abandoned and which is located away from major communications networks, and Peterlee, which has also suffered from its isolation. Again one awaits data on the second generation of towns, some of which have had chronic employment problems. Given that most of the earliest towns have job ratios near or above unity, this element of the new towns' progress must be judged to have been a success.

Social class in the new towns

The most spirited debate about balance in the new towns has been

117

TABLE 2 *Social class in the British new towns: percentage of population in each of the Registrar-General's social classes compared with percentages for England and Wales and for Scotland as a whole*

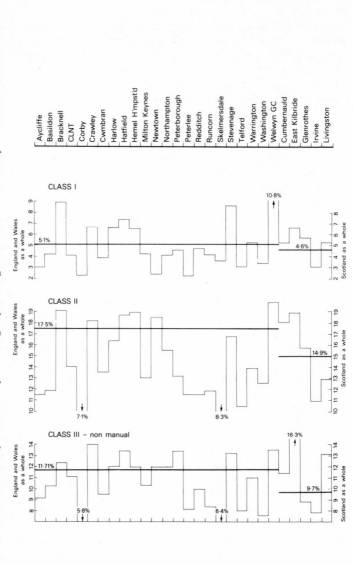

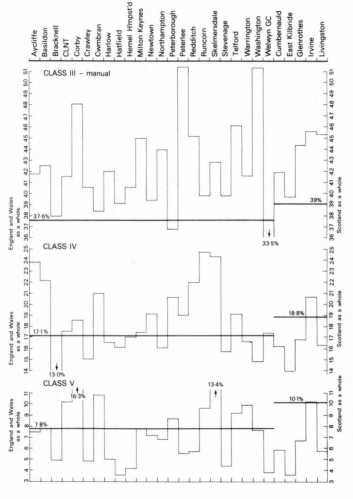

Source: Census 1971 (Office of Population, Censuses and Surveys, HMSO, 1976)

119

about the representation of the social classes. Among the wider public, new towns are pictured as exclusively working-class domains, often because no distinction is being made between developments under the New Towns Acts and large, local-authority housing estates. Material from the 1971 census bears out this assumption in one major respect: skilled manual workers are over-represented nearly everywhere and sometimes to a startling extent (see Figure 2). When defined by the Registrar-General's Class III Manual, they are over-represented in all towns except Peter-borough and Welwyn Garden City. More narrowly specified as socio-economic Group 9, skilled manual workers are still over-represented in all but Bracknell, Cwmbran, Mid-Wales (Newtown) and Welwyn, and even then the deficit is small in relation to the size of the group in all but the last two.

Apart from this striking common characteristic, however, the new towns do not all follow the same pattern of social-class distribution. They fall, rather, into two broad groupings. In the first, the upper social groups are over-represented. All the towns where Social Class I is noticeably above its national distribution are Mark One new towns in the London ring or Scotland (Bracknell, Crawley, Harlow, Hatfield, Hemel Hempstead, Stevenage, Welwyn Garden City, Cumbernauld and East Kilbride). Social Class II is over-represented in the same group with the exception of Harlow and Stevenage and addition of Mid-Wales. The distribution of Social Class III Non-manual is less systematic, but interestingly all the towns where I, II and III NM are all present in greater numbers than in the working population at large are Mark I London ring or Scottish new towns (Bracknell, Crawley, Hatfield, Hemel Hempstead, Welwyn, Cumbernauld and East Kilbride). Thomas (1969b, p. 837) has pointed out that the Scottish new towns have been considered desirable white-collar dormitories, given local housing problems and the acceptance of rented housing across all social classes in Scotland.

Where the Social Classes III Manual and above are over-represented in a new town, it tends to be at the expense of an under-representation of both Classes IV and V. The other broad grouping is of new towns in which the working population falls more than is typical countrywide into III Manual and below, with limited numbers in Classes I and II. (It should not be thought, however, that those patterns are tidily exclusive and exhaustive. Peterlee, for example is 'deficient' in Classes I, II and III NM but also in Class V, while Washington is deficient in all classes but III NM.)

All the new towns where Social Classes IV (partly skilled) and V (unskilled) are over-represented are, with the single exception of Skelmersdale, either examples of using an existing town for further development, like Runcorn, Redditch, and Irvine or where a new town was designated to provide housing for existing industry, as in Aycliffe, Cwmbran and Corby. The weighting towards less-skilled jobs therefore reflects the historical structure of heavier and less mobile industries. Some of the Mark Two new towns were deliberately sited in areas of declining traditional industries, like Telford and Peterborough, in the hope of rejuvenating the local economy. The case of Skelmersdale, which was a greenfield new town, may be explained by its history of offering houses without strict local employment qualifications. Many residents commute elsewhere in Merseyside to jobs in existing industries.

Turning from the grading of occupations by skill and prestige to types of employment and structures of opportunity — what has been called *situs* as opposed to status — it is clear that the new towns' economically active residents tend to be employed rather than self-employed. This is, perhaps, hardly surprising in the case of SEG 3, as self-employed professional practice is a static and presumably ageing and immobile sector. Many of this group working in a town may well prefer to live outside the designated area anyway. It is more interesting to speculate on the low representation of SEG 2, the non-professional self-employed. This category only appears in numbers above the national distribution in Basildon, Central Lancashire, Newtown (Mid-Wales) and Northampton, all of which had a degree of pre-existing population and infrastructure. While this pattern may not be significant, it tempts speculation as to whether it is an outcome of truly comprehensive development. Setting up in one's own business demands either obtaining premises or working from home. It is frequently observed that inner-city redevelopment can extinguish small operations dependent upon cheap premises: new towns may have cramped their potential for starting up. One solution is, of course, to work from home more or less unofficially, which would be much more difficult in a development corporation rented house where there may be — or have been — restrictions upon erecting fences, let alone running motor repairs in the back yard! Self-employment is arguably one of the avenues of social mobility for those without formal qualifications, so the question of its being restricted, albeit unintentionally, is an interesting one in the light of current preoccupations about the redistributive potential of new towns.

The lack of data about new towns is a recurring theme of this book, yet ironically where social-class material is concerned, which seems to be both detailed and plentiful, it is necessary to proceed with caution. The first set of qualifications that needs to be made is methodological. Both the Registrar-General's social classes and socio-economic groups are widely accepted to be blunt instruments:

even after the splitting of Social Class III into two, 37·7 per cent of the working population of Great Britain falls into Class III Manual. Measures of this kind fail also to capture the dynamic qualities of the changing structure of occupations and opportunities, despite periodic adjustments – resulting of course in a greater fit with contemporary conditions at the expense of longitudinal comparability. Yet it must be said that nothing more definitive has yet been generated, let alone used to gather the quantity of data that is at least available for use and criticism. (For further discussion of the Registrar-General's scale and recent attempts at greater sophistication see Goldthorpe and Hope, 1974, and Leete, 1977.)

More prosaically, the data used above is based on a 10 per cent sample of the economically active males, so some of the numbers in the cells are rather small even for the use of percentages, especially when dealing with SEGs.

Moving from the methodological part into substantive objections, it would appear that tests of significance should be applied to the differences between the distribution of classes and SEGs in new towns and nationally. The use of the national distribution is, however, a handy but ultimately misleading tool. If Maidstone or Wolverhampton or Stirling are not expected to be 'normal', why should Crawley, Telford or Cumbernauld? Indeed the concept of the normal town has bedevilled the whole idea of new towns. How can, indeed why should, experimental towns built over a very short period be expected to produce the typicality of existing towns with several centuries of physical and cultural baggage?

It is rarely clear what is at stake when the socio-economic structure of the new towns is being discussed: status, wealth, opportunities for mobility or some – usually patronizing – concept of the good life. A current criticism of the new towns is that they are not accessible to the poor, sometimes defined narrowly as the unskilled, sometimes widened to include the unemployed, unemployable, and retired. One-parent families, usually headed by women, are often singled out for mention. All these groups have two features in common: they have difficulties because of low household, rather than individual, income and they are invisible when the census data above are being used as a basis for discussion. One of the dominant themes of the inner-city studies carried out for the DOE (1977a, b, c) is that for many households it is the wife's income which makes the difference between a struggle and a reasonably comfortable life. Without material on household circumstances and women's employment opportunities in the new towns, the use of conventional employment data should be seen as only the most general indicator of broad tendencies but offering little help in formulating more interventionist policies, if that is what is needed.

The issue of 'new town housing for whom' will re-appear in later chapters, and the links between the structure of the economy, migrant industry and the skills and age of the population have already been outlined. Thomas (1969a, p. 419) provides additional arguments as to why the population of the new towns is thus biased. Not only do the new towns tend to have more of the expanding, profitable and better-paying industries than the country as a whole, but as they grow there will be even more opportunities for residents to seek a better job, and thus improve both their income and class position. Thomas also argues that the youth of the migrants will affect the class profile of the town. Younger people tend to have a higher level of education and qualifications than the total population, and when they settle in the town will probably not have reached the peak of their careers. The class origin of the migrants will quickly be concealed as the new towns tend to 'manufacture' both inter- and intra-generational upward social mobility. Even if this is true, however, it lends support to those who say that there is a need to open access to the new towns to the less skilled.

The Industrial Selection Scheme (which became the New and Expanded Towns Scheme) was intended as the medium for providing people in most housing need with a route to the new towns. These would inevitably contain a large proportion of the lower income groups. But NETS is widely acknowledged to have failed, meeting neither inner-city residents' wish to be rehoused, nor the new towns' need for tenants. In 1970 Redditch (Redditch DC, 1970, p. 365) wrote that only 3·5 per cent of families coming to the town in 1969/70 had arrived via NETS. Giving evidence to the Select Committee, Clare Ungerson reported that about 10 per cent of migration to the London new towns between 1961 and 1971 was 'planned' (Expenditure Committee, 1974, p. 375). The Department of Employment produced figures showing that a total of 625 people were placed in jobs in the first half of 1973, including 567 in the London scheme, and an incredible 1 only in the West Midlands. Part of the failure is due to employers' reluctance to use the scheme rather than direct recruitment. No details were given to the Expenditure Committee about how long it took for NETS to produce an employee, but the process described earlier in the chapter seems to indicate that it would be on the scale of weeks, not days. Viewed from the consumer's view, the scheme has also failed to communicate itself to potential registrants. Ungerson and her colleagues found that 5 people, in their sample of 500 people in two stress wards in an inner London Borough, knew of its existence (*ibid.*, p. 377).

Despite the lack of knowledge of the scheme, some people do register themselves with NETS. The total for the first half of 1973

123

was 9,893, of whom 8,700 were in London (Expenditure Committee, 1974–5a, p. 583). Why, then, were such a small proportion of registrants placed in the same period? One factor is the loss of interest of applicants. Many people still registered have in reality no intention of exploring offers of jobs. 'We do review the list to see if people wish to remain registered. Whenever we do, the list is halved' (Expenditure Committee, 1974, p. 198). On other occasions registrants get as far as the interview and then lose interest because of the costs of the move and the low wages offered. The problem may also be a shortfall of housing, so that in spite of being nominated, the candidate rejects the period of commuting involved. In the end only 15 per cent of the list are submitted to employers and only 15 per cent of these take a job (Expenditure Committee, 1974, p. 377) – and this figure includes both the new and expanded towns.

The replies of the Department of Employment to the Expenditure Committee further made it clear that NETS now confines itself neither to those in housing need, nor to the less skilled (Expenditure Committee, 1974, p. 194), although Ungerson and her colleagues showed that 20 per cent of the registrants were unskilled, compared with only 8 per cent of the population of London (*ibid.*, p. 377). It is likely, therefore, that some of the small number of people placed were anyway skilled workers in reasonable housing, thus defeating the objective of the scheme. The central and intractable problem is that such employers as do use the scheme are likely to want skilled workers, while those registered and still interested are likely not to be skilled. There is therefore no incentive for employer or would-be employee to use the scheme, as the former has no need, and the latter either does not need it if skilled, or is unlikely to benefit from it if not. The NETS has also failed to deliver jobs and housing to those in the most need because it is preoccupied with male, employed, heads of household, a bias also shared by the new towns in their nominations policy until the mid-1970s.

Changing circumstances

There was, as we have seen, a revival of interest in the possibilities of new towns in the early 1960s. It was stimulated by the soaring population projections and confirmed by the return of a Labour government for whom the new towns idea was congenial and seen as a part of the heritage of the welfare state. The second wave of designations, started in 1961, continued until 1970 (if we draw a veil over Stonehouse). Nearly all these (except Newtown) had a bigger target population than those in the first round of designations. Redditch, with a target of 70,000 and a planned increase of 38,000, was the smallest. Milton Keynes, with an existing population of 40,000 and a target of 250,000, was the largest. Nearly all the first generation of towns had their population targets raised, in some cases more than once during that period. The thinking behind this was dictated in part by the housing demands of a rising population together with continuing pressures of household fission and urban renewal. It was also apparent that the minimum population to support an acceptable standard of urban facilities was rising. Reith and his colleagues may have been concerned to provide a theatre; the planners of the 1960s were more worried by the demands of the multiple stores. Levin (1976, p. 156) reproduces a diagram drawn up by the consultants for the Central Lancashire New Town, to illustrate the catchment necessary for a hierarchy of facilities. It is, Levin argues, both arbitrary and inaccurate, but it does demonstrate the conventional wisdom of the time. A central library, town hall, swimming pool and variety stores are shown as requiring at least 60,000–80,000 potential users. Many of the smaller second generation towns fell neatly into this range, while some of the larger ones like Peterborough and Northampton, as well as CLNT itself, are developing on the basis of 'townships' of this size. As the quality of facilities improved, many new towns were anyway becoming centres for employment and shopping for a widening area. Between 1961 and 1975 the corporations of Basildon, Bracknell, Crawley, Cwmbran, Harlow and Washington all noted with satisfaction that they were becoming regional shopping centres. The Commission for the New Towns referred to all four of its towns in the same way: 'at Hemel Hempstead, for instance, analysis of returns from a car parking count just before Christmas revealed that 48 per cent of the cars parked in the town centre came from outside the town' (CNT, 1972, p. 9). The inference is clear: as long as the new towns were importing employees and shoppers, rather than exporting them, self-containment was of less interest. Size was rapidly becoming both a means and an end in itself.

Exporting workers was still, however, seen as something to be watched. The positioning of the second-generation overspill towns much nearer to their parent cities than either the first or second generation of London new towns made some commuting inevitable. The ministry's attitude seems to have been ambivalent:

> There is no specific desire to avoid commuting into and out of new towns, but in most cases there is a broad objective of keeping things in balance so one does not have too much of anything. . . . – Take a later new town . . . do you say that the objective for this particular new town is to have 30, 50 or 75 per cent of the people in employment commuting?

– It is more a matter which is left in the first instance to the development corporation itself (Expenditure Committee, 1974, p. 59).

Communications and personal mobility were key criteria in both the siting and subsequent planning of the later new towns. The new towns named in *The South East Study* (MHCG, 1964) were chosen specifically because of their access to good road transport routes, while conversely the reports of other development corporations were littered with protests that vital road links were either not yet planned or had been deferred, notably at Glenrothes, Peterlee and Telford. At the same time the capacity of the internal road networks of the newer towns was progressively raised. Milton Keynes was planned on the basis of universal car ownership. The first-generation towns, meanwhile, had problems trying to provide parking for the unforeseen car population, both in the town centre, and at the homes of residents.

Throughout the 1960s the assumption was that there would be a trend of continuous expansion of personal mobility, making self-containment increasingly irrelevant. The policy of more owner-occupation, which had at first been limited and met with mild resistance from some development corporations, was accepted as a logical consequence of the age of affluence, mobility and increased leisure. 'Flexibility' and 'choice' became the watchwords (and had their uses as the population projections fluctuated). Even the Town and Country Planning Association, which had previously rejected it, gave the new policy editorial approval in 1967 (TCPA, 1967).

While the development corporations were allowing self-containment to fade, they did not abandon the goal of employment balance, particularly because the attraction of employment was a central indicator of a town's success. For those towns with the objective of regional revitalization, like Washington, Irvine, Livingston, Telford and CLNT, it was vital. For the others it was a magnet for population, a source of pride and of income and quite probably a crucial element in the local population's and administration's acceptance of the new town package.

Social balance was not abandoned, although the mechanics of new town development continued to bias the composition of the incoming population. Ironically, the consequence of the controversial Housing Finance Act 1972 was to eliminate the differentials in cost to tenants that still existed between new town and equivalent local authority housing. Potentially, at least, one barrier to the lower-paid's benefiting from new towns was lifted, although the actual pool of new town rented housing was being contracted by sales to tenants. The industrial take-off that many towns achieved in the

1960s as well as their increased size opened up more diverse employment opportunities outside the skilled manufacturing jobs that had become characteristic of the towns. As had been seen above, in some areas an attempt was made to by-pass the fine mesh of employment qualifications and give direct access to new town housing for those in need. Such interventions were not favoured on the large scale, however. The prevailing analysis (of both political parties) was that the new towns should accept and adapt to the demands of a more affluent society. The wealth that would thus accrue would ultimately benefit more people than restrictive strategies like the pursuit of 'balance' and 'self-containment'. This principle, that the more quickly the wealthy front of the economic column moves, the sooner the back will be where the front now is, had been captured and named by Young and Willmott (1973) as 'stratified diffusion'. It fitted the logic of economic growth.

Consequences

If it is assumed that the new towns were intended to be available for all economic groups in the population, then some of these changes in new town policies and circumstances appear to favour lower income groups. The increasing heterogeneity of employment that accompanied the erosion of self-containment may paradoxically have made the achievement of some kinds of balance easier — social-class composition may become more representative of the whole population. Simultaneously the towns became importers of labour and thus less balanced in another sense. The loss of self-containment justified by increasing mobility must now, however, be seen as regressive. New town planning of the 1960s apparently had a McLuhanesque vision of the residents as totally mobile men (the noun is used advisedly) inhabiting Webber's (1964) 'non-place urban realm'. For while the number of households with access to a car continued, and continues, to increase, little real attention was given to the number of persons denied it. Thomas (Expenditure Committee, 1974—5a, p. 431) spelt it out: 'Even by the year 2000 when it is projected that there will be a car ownership of 1·4 cars per household, half the population over five years of age will be without the use of the car.' This majority, of course, includes children, those too poor to run a car, including many elderly people, those who cannot and will not drive and the legions of women at home while the family car cools in the factory or office car park. For these people the scale of recent new towns combined with the residential densities and road standards applied have merely served to increase the distance of both the central area facilities and local shops from home.

127

Such is the pressure for good central facilities that local shops have been declining (for example, Harlow DC, 1972, p. 197). The population needed to support a local general store, given new town shop rents and the keen competition from city-centre multiples, has now increased to the level where it implies a population catchment which, when multiplied by customary densities, makes the furthest houses outside acceptable walking distance! Employment for women suffers the same problems of accessibility. For men without the use of a car, too, the segregation of employment on the inevitable industrial estates creates problems of time and cost. Scattered centres of employment are unlikely to solve these problems as there is little guarantee of working at the nearest centre, and as Thomas (Expenditure Committee, 1974−5a) writes, such an arrangement will make the establishment of a financially viable public-transport network even less likely. Runcorn has attempted a radical solution to transport for the non-car owner with its famous 'figure of eight' busway, but at the price of limited expansion of population.

As has become clear from the foregoing, the door to the new towns has been closed to many groups by the pursuit of both balance and self-containment via a close linkage between employment and housing. To counter this, Heraud (1966), Thomas (Expenditure Committee, 1974−5a, p. 426) and others have recommended the adoption of large-scale policies of direct nomination from inner-city housing waiting lists, irrespective of employment status. Attractive though this is, it can only be a genuine widening of opportunities if it is still accompanied by a determined programme of providing employment. Even if full advantage is taken of rent- and rate-rebate schemes, the cost of travel on top of the cost of moving and of equipping a larger home can be crippling. It is not mere coincidence that some town expansion schemes, where commuting has always been regarded as inevitable, have had perennial problems of arrears and moonlight flits. Skelmersdale, a town with a substantial proportion of its population housed on the basis of housing need rather than employment status, and which is in a low-wage area, is one of only two new towns in England and Wales publicly to acknowledge a problem with arrears (Skelmersdale DC, 1968, p. 369; Corby DC, 1977, p. 124). The situation at Skelmersdale has not been helped by recurrent unemployment problems, shared by the Scottish new towns. For Scottish new town residents, too, as Thomas writes (1969b, p. 849), the lack of self-containment is a problem, not a sign of progress. It could be argued that while it is true that to abandon balance and self-containment may be to make the new towns more 'normal', to be normal is to be unequal. Is this a fitting fate for the new towns? 'Self-containment' may be due for rehabilitation.

Neighbourhood, community and citizenship

There is a *canard,* recently set free again by Mercer (1975, pp. 151ff.) and Bell and Newby (1976) that the concept of the neighbourhood as a social entity was a product of Ebenezer Howard's fertile imagination, and that it was then transformed into legislation by the New Towns Committee. Reading *Garden Cities of Tomorrow* (Howard, 1965) gives no justification for this view, while the Reith committee specifically rejected the idea that people should identify themselves primarily with their neighbourhood (New Towns Committee, 1946c, p. 16). Indeed, as Mercer himself details, the progenitor of the neighbourhood principle was Clarence Perry who confined himself strictly to the physical layout and facilities that would be optimal for convenience. While it is true that the Dudley Report (Central Housing Advisory Committee, 1944), the Bournville Village Trust (1941) and Reilly in his *Plan for Birkenhead* (1947) had more romantic visions of locality-based interaction and support, nothing of the kind appeared in new towns legislation. Most master-plans, new town annual reports and even the influential *The Needs of New Communities* (CHAC 1967) are both more pragmatic and prosaic. It was to be hoped that people would settle well into their new homes, but the principal means to that end were to be enough shops, clinics, phone boxes and schools, not radical social engineering at the local level.

The fundamental rationale for new town neighbourhoods has been the distance from the primary school, from which followed the shop(s), the pub and the building contract. There have, of course, been outbreaks of architectural reification (Lipman 1969; Banham 1976), but Banham's Big Metaphors are more frequently found in high-density, high-rise developments in the inner city than the medium-density, low-rise developments that residents of the new towns (and the building societies) persist in wanting.

If the town as a whole is the subject, however, the assertion that Howard and his successors had more in mind than mere housing is difficult to refute. As chapter 2 showed, Lord Reith and his colleagues could not prevent themselves from making sweeping assumptions about the nature of the civilized life, which were a good deal more specific than Howard's in may ways. While balance and self-containment deserve more defending than they have been allowed in the last twenty years, it must be admitted that they are undoubtedly prerequisites for the more questionable notion of the new town community as a 'society in miniature'. All classes were to be represented in it, and in the same distribution and relative position as in the wider society. Despite the Reith committee's visionary and partly radical orientation, the model of urban life that they were proposing implied the re-creation of a vertically integrated society, in which people would identify with the whole. Intended or not, there is a pervasive theme of control in such a model, as Bell and Newby (1976) point out when they compare it with the groupings with which people usually co-reside and identify in a horizontally integrated class society. It was suggested in chapter 1 that part of the preoccupation with some kind of organic wholeness in early new towns policy sprang from the assumed anomie of pre-war housing developments, particularly in the public sector. There may, too, have been the desire to create a local identification which would stimulate in the inhabitants a sense of their duties as citizens complementary to the dramatic extension of social citizenship rights then taking place in education, health and social insurance. The possibility that the balance between these rights (which he thoroughly endorsed) and duties might have been upset is noted by T. H. Marshall in the *locus classicus* 'Citizenship and Social Class' (in Marshall, 1963, first delivered as a public lecture in 1949). What would motivate people and fuel social change if the fear of destitution were removed, money incomes became less of a preoccupation and people came to feel of equal value to the community whatever the prestige of their occupation?

New towns (and indeed planning generally, as expressed in the 1947 Town and Country Planning Act) were undoubtedly seen as part of the new welfare state and as capable of creating more than improved health. Something of the reconstruction fervour comes through from the film *When We Build Again,* based on the Bournville Village Trust's (1941) publication of the same name. In it a soldier is seen returning home to the mean streets of a smoke-filled city, dreaming of new houses and factories, with plenty of light and fresh air. The housing would be built around greens, with communal laundries and restaurants for the continued liberation of women, set free from traditional restraints by war-time mobilization – almost a Brummie kibbutz.

Marshall's essay also suggests solutions to some of the seeming paradoxes in the philosophy of the Reith committee, the implementation of the new towns legislation and subsequent controversies. These centre on the rise of the terms class, status and equality. Both Marshall and the Reith committee were much less precise or preoccupied in their use of 'class' than is now the custom. To them it seems merely to have meant disparities of money income and institutionalized discontinuities in income between different types of occupation. Status, for Marshall, had two distinct meanings. In the more profound and important sense it meant estate, and his major assertion was that, at the time of his essay, there was (and is) only one estate in Britain. To claim the gamut of legal, political and social rights one merely had to be a sane adult citizen – unlike in medieval England or present-day caste societies. (The validation of Marshall's insights is that where this does not work in practice, for individuals or groups, it is to be solved or concealed. It is not a legitimate state of affairs.) Status in the minor sense was merely 'conventional' prestige or esteem (Lockwood, 1974). Marshall went on to say that given this baseline of citizenship rights – or equality of opportunity – it is possible for there to be continuing inequalities of wealth and prestige. The removal of really gross inequities may even serve to stabilize and perpetuate this situation, at least until some further change in the fundamental structures of legitimation in society, a possibility that Marshall foresaw. (Goldthorpe (1978) has claimed that this has now occurred.)

Seen in this light, it would not have been necessary for the new towns programme, as part of a philosophy of equality of opportunity, to have included more discriminatory policies in, for example, the allocation of housing. In the event, it was twenty years before ideas of positive discrimination began to replace the general set of assumptions since summarized as *embourgeoisement* in liberal – and even socialist – thinking. Another decade passed before the vicissitudes of new towns and their residents – expensive shops, no buses, low family incomes, isolated young mothers – were reinterpreted as the outcome of larger social and economic processes, rather than personal or local sorrows. By an irony it was these very economic processes that strangled such interventionist policies as might have been implied by Reith's vision of the rich communal life. When affluence in the 1950s and 1960s followed the stringencies of the post-war period, a more *laissez-faire* approach to the evolution of new towns, in which squash had superseded concerts, was dignified as a policy in itself.

7 Regional growth and urban decline

The building of new towns is not only an important way to relieve housing need . . . but can also play a big part in stimulating a region's economic and social development and raising the quality of its life (Cmnd 2206, 1963).

Regional policies and philosophies

The Royal Commission on the Distribution of the Industrial Population (Barlow Commission, 1940) was the first — and some would say the only — attempt comprehensively to examine the processes leading to differential economic growth and population movement in Great Britain. The strategy that it recommended included a programme of garden cities, forming a link between the new towns programme and regional policy that continues to the present day. Five of the London-ring new towns designated after the war (Basildon, Harlow, Hemel Hempstead, Stevenage, Welwyn Garden City and Hatfield) were consequences of Abercrombie's *Greater London Plan* (1945). East Kilbride and Cumbernauld were sites identified in the Abercrombie *Clyde Valley Regional Plan* (1949).

From the start there was ambiguity as to whether the towns should be understood as part of inter- or intra-regional strategies. The first generation of London new towns was unequivocally intended to operate at an intra-regional level, relieving London's housing and employment congestion by shifting part of the population to centres away from the metropolis, but still within the London region. Aycliffe, Peterlee and East Kilbride were seen in a slightly different light by the government, as became clear when public expenditure cuts were announced in 1947. These three were exempted from the slowdown on development imposed on the new towns. They were classified as 'serving immediate industrial needs' (HC Debates, vol. 443, cols 280ff.), suggesting that they were intended partly for an inter-regional objective of transfer of employment and wealth. East Kilbride was also charged with alleviating Glasgow's extreme housing problems. The twin objectives have not always been easy to pursue simultaneously, as became clear for some later new towns.

The second generation of new towns reflected the pressure of a rising birthrate and the Tory government's late conversion to a belief in economic planning. Although some of the new town sites of the second generation seem simply to have 'emerged' (or more accurately as in the case of Skelmersdale, re-emerged and been dusted off), many were part of an explicit regional strategy. Irvine and Washington were recommended in the White Papers on Scotland (Cmnd 2188, 1963) and the North East (Cmnd 2206, 1963) respectively, and had a distinct inter-regional policy focus. The three new towns that have resulted from *The South East Study* (MHLG, 1964) are, despite the location of Northampton and Peterborough just outside the technical boundary of the region, essentially intra-regional in conception, like the precursors.

When Labour was returned to power in 1964, planning was extended in scope to a level of inclusiveness which promised the orderly distribution and redistribution envisaged by Barlow. A National Plan was inaugurated in 1965, and regional economic planning councils were founded.

> The economic planning councils will be concerned with broad strategy on regional development and the best use of the region's resources. Their principal function will be to assist in the formulation of regional plans and to advise on their implementation. They will have no executive powers (HC Debates, vol. 703, cols 1829ff.).

The National Plan was destroyed by the deflation of 1966. The regional planning councils remain, but are widely acknowledged as ineffectual, even superfluous (Glasson, 1974, pp. 269ff.; Holland, 1976b, p. 50). These councils, based on the eight planning regions, are non-elective gatherings of 'the great and the good'. Lacking both executive power and adequate resources, they have been largely ignored by central government and resented by the local authorities in their areas, which in some cases have formed rival groupings to interpret the region's interests as they see them. The only immediate impact that the economic planning councils had on the new towns policy was the drastic upward revision of the designated areas and population targets of Dawley – then renamed Telford (West Midlands Economic Planning Council, 1965). The town had severe economic problems for several years thereafter, and the whole project had been criticized for a lack of adequate prior economic analysis and coherent execution (Cmnd 3998, 1969; Tolley, 1972). One of the weaknesses of Telford's situation was that it was essentially part of an intra-regional strategy to meet housing need, yet it also had more elaborate aims of clearing industrial dereliction and attracting enough population and employment to support a better level of public and private infrastructure. The former aim was frustrated by its inaccessibility and unattractiveness to Birmingham residents and employers who appear not to have seen it as a part of their region at all. The latter aim, which has more in common with the overtly inter-regional intent of Aycliffe, Washington or the Scottish new towns, was supposed to be achieved without any of the financial supports that have been considered essential to most such projects: prior commitment to better communications and the free availability of permission to relocate employment, plus cash incentives so to do. Telford was handicapped in this way precisely because, although in a very run-down area, it is technically a part of the prosperous West Midlands region and thus discriminated against by the central government's own industrial location policies.

Newtown in Mid-Wales was designated after a recommendation for a town of 70,000 in Mid-Wales (Economic Associates, 1965) and despite its modest objectives (target population at December 1977, 11,500) it is explicitly regional in concept. This was underlined by the dissolution of the development corporation and the transfer of its operations to the Development Board for Rural Wales in 1977. Central Lancashire, at the other end of the scale, is also credited with a regional objective (in this case the revival of North East Lancashire) but the history of its tortuous designation process makes clear there was a commitment to the idea before any thorough analysis of its potential was made. An 'impact' study (MHLG, 1968), commissioned to examine the economic consequences of the proposed town, followed the (planning) consultants' report and draft master-plan. Although economic consultants were working for the planning consultants and for the Department of Economic Affairs simultaneously, the study was concerned only with the size and exact boundaries of the proposed town, not with confirming that it was needed. The government's intention to act had been announced in 1965 before any research was commissioned (Levin, 1976, p. 132). *The North West Study* (DEA, 1965) published later that year was left with little option but to endorse the 'urgent decisions which . . . have already been made while this report has been in preparation' (*ibid.*, p. 3). Whether those decisions were because of the research work, or in spite of it, cannot be detected, but the sequence of events does little to suggest a well-integrated approach to new towns in a regional context.

During the latter part of the 1960s, the Town and Country Planning Association refined its position on the use of the New Towns Act. Its earlier emphasis on the need for an ever-larger programme of self-contained towns at some distance from the parent city, with its focus on the 'micro' problems of high density, high rise, etc., gave way to a 'macro' approach. The association began to lay much more stress on the regional value of new towns. In the South East, the inevitability of voluntary migration and some commuting was accepted. The use of development corporations to enable the development of areas for intensive growth, as part of an intra-regional programme of comprehensive planning to rationalize the pressures on the London area was recommended. Away from London, the TCPA endorsed the idea of 'growth points' and in its evidence to the Hunt Committee on the intermediate areas (Cmnd 3998, 1969) reaffirmed: 'the most obvious and successful growth point is a new town' (TCPA, 1968a). In its later evidence to the Expenditure Committee, the TCPA claimed that not enough use had yet been made of the inter-regional potential of new towns for 'redistribution of economic activity' (Expenditure Committee, 1974, p. 129). A major part of the Association's current platform is its advocacy of an elective regional level of government. Within this context it recommends that a body similar to a development corporation, but with more direct local representation, should have a roving commission to develop land, using the powers of purchase under the 1965 New Towns Act (ibid., pp. 143ff.). This would be combined with a revival of Ebenezer Howard's neglected concept of the 'social city' in which urban facilities would be provided in a hierarchy of mutually accessible settlements, thus reducing the need for any individual town to become as large and sprawling as is now dictated by the catchment of many urban services (ibid., p. 155). The Association has, over the last few years, increasingly drawn attention to the claimed intention of its policies, since the founding of the GCTPA, to combine the new towns programme with inner-city redevelopment, thus neatly putting some of the criticisms of the new towns' selective benefits back in central government's court!

The tone of the TCPA pronouncements has remained, as befits a pressure group, relentlessly optimistic, despite growing criticisms of the new towns' contribution to meeting housing need and latterly the assertion that there are not sufficient resources to provide new towns and reconstruct the inner city at the same time. The association collectively cannot afford to support a research programme, although individual members are themselves well known for their work on, and in, new towns. TCPA policy statements sometimes have a tone of determined hope and the certainty that comes from reiteration, rather than extensive empirical validation. If some of the early thinking about the 'self-contained' town has more than a hint of an organic analogy about it, the TCPA's recent position on regionalism seems to use what might be called the 'jug and bottle' model. From this perspective, city problems remain essentially problems of scale: too many people for the roads and the houses, too much employment for the roads, the trains, the drains, etc. The language betrays the persistent spatial (or volumetric) quality of the concepts:

> Reduction of urban *pressures* [my italics] at least makes possible an improved environment for the big city dwellers. Those in the new town are much better off than would be the *extra* [TCPA italics] population otherwise residing in the big city (Expenditure Committee, 1974, p. 127).

> a vital city will attract new functions which can best be performed in some great centre, and these functions should be given adequate *elbow-room* [my italics] (Self, 1972, p. 5).

The excess in the jug should be poured into other bottles or in the case of the South East the overflow should be channelled tidily away.

Somehow the philosophy of the TCPA has always managed to retain a wide spectrum of political support. Here the contradictions, which have enabled those who should not be able to agree to do so, become apparent. On the one hand the association has always prescribed quite Draconian powers of land assembly, rehousing and direction of industry, and from Howard and Osborn onward has has no time for sentimentality about the break-up of urban working-class 'communities'. At the same time there is only a limited recognition that the economy and polity of cities may not adjust to everyone's benefit if 'pressures' are reduced. What follows has often appeared to be endorsement of the working of market mechanisms – although it is never called that. In a 1968 executive statement on the South East, for example, the official line was to refuse to be concerned about falling populations in the central city: 'The dispersal of industrial employment from London, which will certainly continue, will free labour for central area functions . . .' (TCPA, 1968b).

Latterly the possibility that people at different wage levels might be differentially affected and that this could cause problems of access to housing and transport has come to be recognized by the Association, but a package of recommendations in a 1977 policy statement rests heavily on information, enabling and liaison, for example, to 'Give more effectively publicity to the opportunities and help that are available to move out of inner areas or into them' (TCPA, 1977).

Inter-regional policies and incentives

Despite the recommendations of the Barlow Commission, regional policies in Britain have remained fragmentary in their form and in their administration. Much intra-regional planning has been, explicitly or implicitly, under the control of what is now the Department of the Environment and local authorities, through the application of the planning acts and by financial measures such as the Rate Support Grant (although the latter has an inter-regional dimension, too). Inter-regional measures, chiefly the distribution of industrial investment and employment, have been supervised by the (now) Department of Industry. It has a variety of positive incentives and negative controls at its disposal. The positive measures have varied in detail over time, but at present they fall under three broad headings: subsidies to the capital costs of a firm, such as buildings and equipment; subsidies to variable costs, principally wages; and the provision of infrastructure and advance factories (Glasson, 1974, p. 190). The areas of the country where these incentives apply have been decided on a number of different criteria. Currently there are three tiers, called collectively the assisted areas. The largest division is the development areas, first defined by the Industrial Development Act 1966. These include most of Cornwall and North Devon, Wales, Merseyside, the Northern Region and Scotland. After 1967, a subset of these areas were designated special development areas in places of exceptionally high unemployment. Initially related specifically to pit closures, they have been extended and now 'bear a remarkable resemblance to the original Special Areas of the 1930's' (*ibid.,* p. 186). There are additional incentives for firms to migrate to the SDAs. The last category of assisted area arose out of the Hunt Committee on *The Intermediate Areas* (Cmnd 3998, 1969) which recommended that there should be less restriction upon firms wanting to locate in these 'intermediate' areas, which included the remainder of the North West, Yorkshire and Humberside, part of the East Midlands and the rest of Devon and South East Wales.

The status of the new towns at mid-1978 is as follows:

Outside the assisted areas: Basildon, Bracknell, Corby, Crawley, Harlow, Hemel Hempstead, Milton Keynes, Northampton, Peterborough, Redditch, Stevenage, Telford, Welwyn, and Hatfield.

Intermediate area: CLNT, Cwmbran, Warrington.
Development area: Mid-Wales (Newtown), Aycliffe.
Special development area: Peterlee, Runcorn, Skelmersdale,
                            Washington, Cumbernauld, East
                            Kilbride, Glenrothes, Irvine,
                            Livingston (Glenrothes and
                            Livingston have SDA status although
                            they are outside the boundary)
                            (DI, 1977).

The policies of the DI and DOE appear, however, to have co-existed rather than been integrated. While unemployment remains the main criterion for defining the boundaries of the areas, clearly there is some flexibility which allows regions to be treated in their entirety, whatever the circumstances of smaller areas within them. Despite this, the adjustment made to fit new town designations or particular new town problems have the appearance of *post hoc* tidying up, not close consultation. In 1968, for example, only part of the designated area of Washington new town was in the special development area (Washington DC, 1968, p. 434). In 1972 three of the five Scottish new towns were in the special development area, yet the other two were not. Livingston, with similar housing and industrial objectives, complained in 1971 that the special development area extended to within twelve miles (Livingston DC, 1971, p. 183). Glenrothes, too, was an odd omission, given its handicapped history. (Both were included in the SDA in 1972.) More anomalous still has been the situation at Cwmbran, which remained right at the edge of an 'island' of development area, itself bounded partly by an SDA. In 1970 Cwmbran became part of an intermediate area, but still found difficulty in attracting industry, when firms could get cash grants only a few miles away (Cwmbran DC, 1970, p. 148). It seemed peculiarly perverse that the development corporation, labouring under high unemployment and a heavy deficit arising from low rent levels and a lack of remunerative industrial property, should be thwarted by the policies of another arm of central government, yet one with overtly similar regional objectives.

The negative sanction at the disposal of the Department of Industry is the granting of Industrial Development Certificates (IDCs), which were created under the 1947 Town and Country Planning Act, since consolidated in the 1971 Town and Country Planning Act and related Scottish Act. The department can control and direct industrial movement by withholding certificates, which are needed for developments of over 12,500 square feet (1162 m²) in the South East Region and 15,000 square feet (1395m²) elsewhere outside the development areas and SDAs before local planning permission can be given. This enables the department to discriminate in favour of assisted areas, the boundaries and categorization of which are modified from time to time, as are the square footages above which a development falls within IDC control. McCrone (1969, p. 190) has described IDC control as the most rigorous of its type in Western Europe. Since 1965 there has been a parallel system of Office Development Permits (ODPs), created under the Control of Office and Industrial Development Act. The control can be extended by parliamentary order and is administered by the DOE. Although it has been used in the Midlands and Southern England (Cullingworth, 1976) it is currently (mid-1978) only applied within the South East region. New towns have tended to be the beneficiaries of the control of office development. The situation with IDCs has been more complex.

Although the DI has the power to withhold permission to develop anywhere in Britain, the present situation is that IDCs are not needed in the development or special development areas and are 'normally freely available for projects in the intermediate areas' (Expenditure Committee, 1974, p. 323). Firms wanting to move to the new towns outside the assisted areas are subject to control in the normal way, as are development corporations wishing to build advance factories. For a long period there was an informal, but explicit, policy that the new towns outside assisted areas are treated as the next best thing to a move to an assisted area by the DI. One outcome of the new policy on the inner city (see below) has been that 'certain inner areas of London and Birmingham' now take precedence over non-assisted area new towns in the DI's priorities (DI, 1977).

In the early days there were complaints from the London new towns about their being prevented from building advance factories, which have been very attractive to small employers wanting to move because of expansion. More recently development corporations in local difficulties, particularly Corby, when British Steel revised its employment forecasts downward, and Telford, when the problems of its location began to bite, have alleged a lack of support from the DI. In both cases special consultations produced a partial solution, but in response to problems, not through the anticipation of the towns' special needs (Corby DC, 1972, p. 126; Telford DC, 1970, p. 513; Expenditure Committee, 1974, p. 335).

All three of the second-generation London new towns, Milton Keynes (Milton Keynes DC, 1975, p. 188), Northampton (Northampton DC, 1971, p. 284 and HC Debates, vol. 933, col. 429) and Peterborough (Peterborough DC, 1972, p. 337), have claimed at some time to be having difficulties with IDCs. In the case of Northampton the problems were with ODPs as well, an irony, since the town was specifically supposed to develop as an office centre. Figures produced by the DI, at the request of the Expenditure Committee, revealed an anomaly, however (Expenditure Committee, 1974, p. 606). They showed that in the period 1969–71 inclusive there were five IDC refusals at Milton Keynes, one at Peterborough and none at Northampton. In 1972 (the last year for which figures were given) there were no refusals at all recorded. The inference must be that firms assumed that an application would be hopeless and/or that some firms interested in going to new towns outside the assisted areas are successfully diverted into the assisted areas by the DI, so that they never got to the stage of applying for, and failing to get, an IDC.

IDC control, despite its rigour, has limitations. The most important is that it is confined to manufacturing industry. Many new towns outside the assisted areas have been energetically promoting their locational advantages and low costs to attract warehousing, as well as the office and retail developments that are a major feature of recent new towns. 'It's an ideal centre for distribution' says an advertisement for Northampton, across the page from a *Town and Country Planning* article on the 'new towns–versus inner cities fallacy' in the February 1976 edition. It has also been claimed that firms coming from abroad have been able to dictate terms by stating baldly that if not allowed their preferred location in the South East, they will simply not invest in Britain. The DI was evasive when questioned about this issue by the Select Committee;

> 'Do you remember the case of Hoechst at Milton Keynes, the German pharmaceutical company?'
> 'I have some recollection of it. . . . The situation was: we certainly attempted to steer them to an assisted area, but eventually we allowed them something in Milton Keynes and I think there were discussions about future developments after their initial project at Milton Keynes' (Expenditure Committee, 1974, p. 331).

Given the centrality of employment to the concept of the new town, is 'fairly' close consultation adequate? The DI, in its own appearance at the hearings, conveys an impression of consistently refusing to acknowledge the pivotal role that it plays in the new towns programme. No hint was given that the new towns are taken and examined as a whole. The department even seemed to claim that its role is essentially a passive one, in that it responds to the initiatives of industry, rather than instigating movement – yet its known or imagined attitudes must have the effect of a positive policy. Questioned about attitudes to Corby and Telford (*ibid.*, pp. 336ff.), the DI gives the impression of reaction rather than action:

> 'Well, one is going through the process of discussing IDC applications with companies and suggesting to them that if they cannot move to an assisted area, perhaps they can move the thirty-odd miles to Telford? If during that process one finds that one gets a number of yeses to that proposition say [for] Redditch . . . and a series of noes [for] Telford, one begins to build up a picture of a difficult situation' (*ibid.*, p. 337).

Closer liaison with the DOE both centrally and in the regions, and contact with new town corporations themselves would be a better method of meeting such problems.

The irritation expressed by the new towns of the South East and West Midlands when government departments appear to be acting in direct opposition to one another is understandable, but the policies of the Department of Industry can be justified in terms of their overt objective of a redistribution of employment and wealth between regions. The new towns in the assisted areas, and particularly those in the development areas, should therefore be flourishing as a result of the DI's prejudices. Indeed, in the 1960s many parties to the new-towns policy assumed that a combination of development-corporation powers to assemble land and supply infrastructure and the cash incentives available in the development and special development areas could not fail to rejuvenate declining areas. This notion of concentrated public investment came to be known as 'growth-point theory'. In a more passive, 'channelling', form it appeared in the various regional plans for London and the South East. Essentially, however, it was intended as a positive policy, and was the rationale for the designations of Irvine, Washington, Warrington, Mid-Wales (Newtown) and, to an extent, Telford. It was also a key element in the thinking behind CLNT, although as Levin writes 'It is important to note that the validity of this theory in the circumstances of central and north-east Lancashire remained to be demonstrated' (1976, p. 142). Holland is rather more brutal: 'The intellectual and economic foundations of [growth pole] policy range from slim to false' (1976b, p. 48).

Broadly, the theory of a growth-point policy is to stimulate artificially a process which has occurred spontaneously as technologies have grown and differentiated. It employs the ideas of 'leading industries' and 'propulsive firms'. Leading industries will typically be new, fast-growing and using advanced technology. They will have a high income-elasticity of demand for their products and extensive linkages with other industries whose products they will either contribute to, or use themselves. Current examples in Britain are: chemicals, engineering, vehicles, metal goods and paper and printing (Glasson, 1974, p. 149). The hope is that if a 'propulsive' firm in such a sector can be attracted, then other large firms that use or contribute to its products will follow. So, too, will the multiplicity of small firms that supply or subcontract for the plants. As employment and population expand, more firms will be attracted, and gradually at least as many jobs as in the original firm will be created in the service sector. The prosperity that has arisen from such 'urbanization economies' has been observed in, for example, the development of Birmingham's light engineering (Barlow, 1940), Coventry's vehicles (Glasson, 1974) or the electronics industry in West London (Powell, 1960). It is harder, however, to identify locations where this has been deliberately created on a large scale or where the declining fortunes of one of yesteryear's growth points (often in extractive industries like coal) have been reversed. Telford, if successful, will be an instance.

The theory of growth points has been criticized not only for lack of proven examples, but also for being based on a set of out-of-date assumptions about capital and technology. Holland (1976a and b) writes that the structure of the economy has been fundamentally altered by the expansion of multinational companies. The extent of their operations now not only undermines the concept of growth points, but has caused what he calls the 'gelding' of industrial incentives and controls (Holland, 1976b, p. 42). Such firms are primarily concerned with wage costs and tax arrangements. Decisions on where to locate their new investment will be based on which country to move into, not which part of a country. This, as we have seen above, provides considerable leverage to choose a site which might not be allowed to a firm with fewer resources at its disposal. It is widely acknowledged that, ultimately, non-industrial considerations like housing, climate, schools and shopping play a large part in industrial-location decisions for firms with no specific geographical imperative. Many will, therefore, choose the South East and this process is likely to be magnified rather than diminished when the economy is in recession. At such times not even the DI can afford to be too highly principled.

For firms on a multinational scale, both transport costs and the impact of government grants in development areas are likely to be negligible, so that although they could locate away from the South East, they need not bother. Holland (1976b, p. 38) also suggests that agglomeration is not likely to follow the settlement of a branch of a multinational, if a development-area location is chosen. Most components will be manufactured by itself in another plant elsewhere. There will be very little need for the firm to interact with the local economy. The plant will therefore bring employment to the area, but the spontaneous polarization of other firms will be limited.

Another fundamental assumption of growth-point theories is that there will be a multiplier effect as the disposable income of the local population rises, stimulating other local industries and services. The extent of this depends on how much 'leakage' occurs. As the retail sector becomes dominated by multiple stores, stocking products of firms which are frequently themselves a part of a multinational conglomerate, one wonders what percentage of the income generated by the new employment will actually remain in local circulation – surely very little of that spent on food, drink, clothes or consumer durables. One is forced to conclude that to make an impact on a local economy, there would have to be a concentration of very highly paid employees indeed. Such jobs, both salaried and as employer and self-employed seem to be irredeemably concentrated in the South East.

Those who do not share Holland's gloom at the impossibility of reversing economic inequalities between regions have nevertheless suggested that inter-regional policies may be built on insecure foundations, because much of the employment that can be induced to relocate is in branch plants. Peterlee development corporation expressed concern about this in 1968, saying that 'too many of the factories are subsidiaries' (Peterlee DC, 1968, p. 272). Townroe (1975) summarized the fears about the dangers of a 'branch plant economy': that there will be few white-collar jobs and thus few higher incomes and opportunities for promotion; that there may be a high level of female employment associated with low wage-levels and the possibility of culture shock if the area is not traditionally one where women go out to work; that branches will have limited need, or permission, to buy or sub-contract locally, thus reducing spin-offs; and, above all, that branch plants will be closed when the economic climate becomes unfavourable.

Townroe then examined these fears in the light of a 1972 sample of plants that had relocated between four and six years previously, including complete transfers, subsidiary companies and branch plants. He concluded that there was little basis for the idea that branch plants would lack the power to invest autonomously and would be slow to grow. Those that grew successfully became more autonomous. Female-employing industry seemed to be more prominent than would have been expected, but Townroe pointed out that this might reflect firms with a labour shortage moving to an area of low female employment. He found no greater tendency for branches that transferred plants to employ women. 'Spin-off' effects, where a relocated company switches to local suppliers and

143

services were found to be 'disappointingly low' (*ibid.*, p. 60) for both branch plants and transfers, prompting Townroe to suggest that encouraging indigenous enterprise is more fruitful than any kind of relocation. He concluded, however, that the tendency of branches to close was not more marked than that of transferred companies and that branches in assisted areas were not more likely to close than those outside them.

Some of the nervousness about dependence on branch plants may stem from the scale of some of the best-known closures. An infamous example was the closure of Thorn's colour-television-tubes plant at Skelmersdale, with a loss of 1,400 jobs. A newspaper article described the firm as one of the two 'big league' firms, which accounted for 20 per cent of the town's employment and continued: 'It is, perhaps, not without significance that the main casualties of the present economic recession have been the 'big guns' and that by and large the smaller firms are surviving, albeit with difficulty in some cases' (*The Times*, 26 January 1976, p. 19). The other large firm was Courtaulds. After repeated rumours that it was losing money, the decision to close it was announced in October 1976. The firm employed 1,000 people. Newspaper predictions at the time were that the unemployment level in the 'ill-fated new town' could rise to 25 per cent (*The Times*, 28 October 1976).

Trends that may result in economic insecurity for new towns in the assisted areas seem to be confirmed by DI research evidence presented to the Expenditure Committee (1974–5a, pp. 976ff.). Twice as many branches were recorded as moving to new towns in the assisted areas compared with the rest of the new towns in which transfers of entire concerns predominated. More importantly, 'Average employment in branch plants was larger than in transferred plants and longer distance moves provided more jobs per move than shorter ones' (*ibid.*, p. 976). Branches of the '*Times* 500' largest UK companies and overseas firms were under-represented in new towns outside the assisted areas, suggesting that they form a larger, and maybe much larger, part of the employment in new towns within the assisted areas. This is, of course, a tribute to the efficacy of DI policies. It also suggests potential problems for towns which will inevitably have to welcome a large branch plant bringing very large employment opportunities (especially if, like Skelmersdale, they are under considerable pressure to meet housing need at the same time). Their employment base will thus be narrowed and the failure of one plant will be catastrophic. It is difficult to reject the idea that branches and subsidiaries are more vulnerable than their parent companies in contracting markets, take-overs and mergers, rationalization and asset-stripping.

An obvious solution is to encourage the movement of small

firms, which all new towns do. Such firms seem only to be able to comtemplate, or afford, a short-distance intra-regional move, however, and are now being wooed to the inner city as well. Many of these anyway fall beneath the threshold of IDC control. The pressure must therefore be on new towns in the assisted areas to accept large employers so that good results in housing and employment can be shown. Much of the problem for such towns is to show signs of dynamism in areas where it is not endemic, and thus there is a temptation to concentrate on short-term strategies.

Despite the discriminatory policies of the DI, therefore, new towns are only able to make a limited contribution to inter-regional policies of redistribution. Some of the towns in the assisted areas can claim relative success in their surrounding areas, especially East Kilbride, Washington and perhaps Aycliffe, but the inexorable logic of economic change seems to be leading more towards a polarization between new towns themselves. Changes in new town policies in the late 1960s have amplified rather than reduced the divergence. In low-wage areas, especially where accompanied by low rents, the switch to owner-occupation could only be a limited success, even when houses were offered to tenants at 20 per cent below market price. Many more new town residents in the Midlands and London new towns were able to equip themselves with that key to physical mobility and hedge against inflation: a house.

Encouraging new towns to employ private and institutional capital for office and town-centre development must also have regressive consequences between new towns, as the investors are known to favour the South and Midlands, rather than the assisted areas. Better shopping and leisure facilities do not just bring more and cheaper goods and services for new town residents, they also help in the upward spiral of better amenities, attraction of employment, more housing, commercial and industrial investment, more rate income and better local services, and so on, but not where the initial injection is lacking. Where there is less interest by investors, not only will the development corporation be less able to roll-over assets if permitted to do so but its staff are less likely to have acquired the financial and management skills which enable the maximum use of limited resources and the growing aura of success that helps the process to move along. The new towns are themselves aware of the centrality of financial success and the need to prove it – even to the Department of the Environment. In such a climate there is a widening gulf between say, Milton Keynes, Harlow and East Kilbride and the town (it shall be nameless) which, in its 1975 annual report gave building statistics in feet (the building industry officially went metric in 1968) and complained that the new system of management accounting did not yield 'benefits worth the time and effort in preparation'. The perpetuation, and even encouragement, of such a polarization of skills and resources contributes nothing whatever to any redistributive aim that the new towns programme may still be intended to have.

Intra-regional objectives and inner-city decline

Despite the period in the 1960s when new towns were harnessed to inter-regional policies, most have been primarily directed at the solution of intra-regional problems of housing need and population growth. For the London new towns it was seen as their only justification. 'They are built for one specific purpose . . . to relieve London of its housing need' (HC Debates, vol. 735, col. 1738).

As earlier discussion has shown, there has been longstanding criticism of the new towns' capacity to house those most in need, particularly from the London boroughs that had expected to be able to nominate tenants to new town houses, but found instead that the process was mediated through employment. An article by Heraud (1966) specified the alleged weaknesses of new towns in meeting London's housing problem. He drew attention to the fact that Abercrombie's intention, when formulating his decentralization policy, was that 60 per cent of the 'overspill' population should come from the old county of London (now the inner London boroughs). Using data for six of the London new towns (Basildon, Crawley, Hemel, Harlow, Welwyn and Hatfield), he showed that, although between 75 per cent (Harlow) and 82 per cent (Crawley) of their migrant population had come from London, no less than half, and in some cases many more than half, had come from the outer London area, where housing conditions were less desperate. The area sending the lowest proportion of its population to new towns (at 1·6 per thousand households, compared with the 4·6 of the outer boroughs) was the central boroughs and 'Of the nine London (Metropolitan) Boroughs shown by the Milner Holland Committee to be suffering from the greatest degree of housing stress all except one (Lambeth) have rates lower than for London as a whole . . .' (Heraud, 1966, p. 13). Many of those who did move would have been the more skilled, with better and more secure prospects, but despite this major hurdle 'approximately 46 per cent of all migrants from London to the new towns were previously on housing waiting lists. This figure varied considerably: it ranges from 37·5 per cent at Basildon to 51 per cent in Harlow' (*ibid.*, p. 15).

This would have suggested a considerable contribution to the provision of housing if the theory of 'ripple', whereby each family leaving London provided a dwelling for another household, had

146

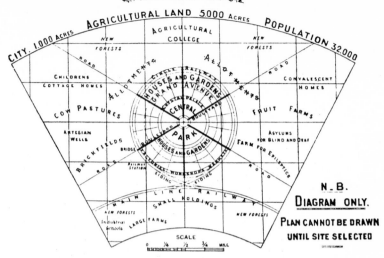

1 'Garden city and rural belt', from Ebenezer Howard's *Garden Cities of Tomorrow*, 1898

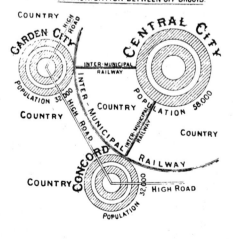

2 'Correct principle of a city's growth', from Ebenezer Howard's *Garden Cities of Tomorrow*, 1898—illustrating the idea of 'social city'

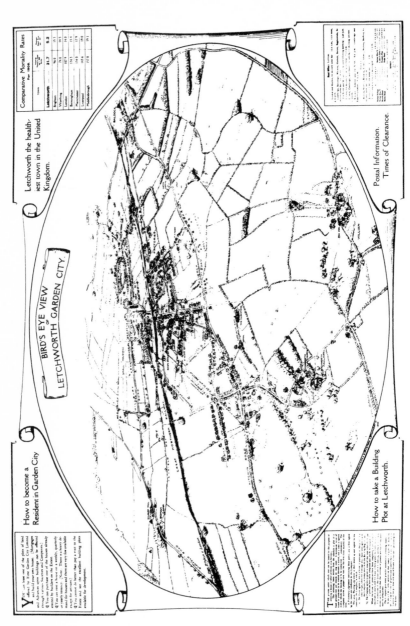

3 'Bird's eye view of Letchworth Garden City'—an early promotional poster

How to become a Resident in Garden City

YOU can lease one of the plots of land offered by First Garden City Limited and build your own house. (Mortgages and Advances upon buildings can be effected through various Societies and Companies.)

¶ You can purchase one of the houses already erected by builders on the Estate.

¶ You can rent a house on a weekly, quarterly or yearly tenancy. (Note: There is a heavy demand for houses and there are very few available except for artisans.)

¶ You cannot do better than pay a visit to the Estate and see the excellent building plots available for development.

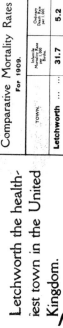

Comparative Mortality Rates
For 1909.

TOWN	Infantile Mortality Rate per 1,000 Births	Ordinary Death Rate per 1,000
Letchworth	**31.7**	**5.2**
Brighton	96.0	15.3
Worthing	74.0	14.5
London	107.9	14.0
Birmingham	134.3	15.4
Manchester	134.0	17.9
Liverpool	143.6	19.0
Middlesbrough	157.8	19.1

Letchworth the healthiest town in the United Kingdom.

How to take a Building Plot at Letchworth.

THE process under which land can be leased for the purpose of erecting a house or other premises is as follows;

The intending lessee selects from the schedule a plot at a fixed ground-rent per annum per acre, or long lease. A minimum value of house or premises to be erected thereon is stated, and a time is agreed within which the building is to be completed or (undertaken). The Company allows a pepper-corn rent for the first three months of the term.

A *Preliminary agreement* containing these particulars is first signed by the lessee and confirmed by the Company.

The usual *Building Agreement* is then drawn up and signed by the lessee and the Company, in which —

(a) *The Lessee agrees* to erect a house or premises on the plot to his own design, when the drawings shall have been agreed with the Company, in compliance with the Building Regulations.

(b) *The Company agrees* to grant a lease of the land when the house or premises have been completed and are fit for occupation.

When the house or premises have been completed, a certificate of completion is issued, and the *Lease* is then granted by the Company.

The conditions of the *Lease* are not onerous, and have only been drawn up to the end that the interests of present and future residents may be safeguarded.

The Company give every possible assistance to intending lessees. It should be clearly understood that lessees are quite at liberty to sell or dispose of their property and transfer their leases. Considerable business in the purchase and sale of houses is constantly proceeding on the Estate.

Postal Information.
Times of Clearance.

Head Office: LETTERS.

London and Hitchin, for delivery same day: 10.0 a.m., 12.0 noon, 4.35 p.m.

Cambridge, Stevenage, Welwyn, Hatfield, Barnet, Biggleswade, for delivery same day: 12.0 noon.

The North and Midlands, for delivery following morning: 5.40 p.m.

London, for delivery following morning: 7.10 p.m.

London, Cambridge, and Eastern Counties, for morning delivery: 10.0 p.m.

SUNDAYS:—London and the North: 6.0 p.m. Cambridge and Eastern Counties: 8.15 p.m.

PARCELS.

Baldock, Stotfold, Royston, Ashwell, Bedford, Shefford, for delivery same day: 2.10 p.m.

London, for delivery same day: 2.10 p.m.

London and Country, for morning delivery: 7.0 p.m.

4, 5, 6, 7   Enlargements of corners of Plate 3

8   The frontispiece of *Town and Country Planning*, vol. VI, no. 23, April/June 1938

LOOK THE SUN!   By Arthur Wragg

9   Cartoon from *London Evening News*, reproduced in *Town and Country Planning*, vol. XVI, no. 64, Winter 1948–9

"IT's not fair. I want to throw for some sites for Satellite Towns in 1949 . . .You picked them all last year."

10 Corby centre from the Corby Development Corporation's Annual Report for 1957–8

11 Town centre shops and offices in Aycliffe from the Aycliffe Development Corporation's Annual Report for 1958–9

12　The pedestrian shopping precinct at Stevenage, from the Development Corporation's Annual Report for 1958–9

13　Town centre shopping at Basildon from the Development Corporation's Annual Report for 1959–60

14   Irvine Centre, spanning the River Irvine, from the Development Corporation's
Annual Report for 1975–6

15   Milton Keynes' new city centre development at April 1978

16 Cover of 1978
publicity brochure published
by Peterlee Development
Corporation

17 Part of the first page of *A Businessman's Tour of Cumbernauld* published by
Cumbernauld Development Corporation

been demonstrated. A combination of processes acted to limit this effect. First, many people on the waiting list would have been living with relatives so that no dwelling would be released. Second, much of the accommodation was anyway substandard. Last, the local authority had no control over the reletting of the empty accommodation. It could be occupied by newcomers to London so that the 'queue' did not move at all. Heraud reports a study in East Ham by Cullingworth (1959) which:

> revealed that a third of the vacated dwellings had been occupied by families on the borough housing list and a further 23 per cent by families who considered themselves in housing need . . . [but] the fact that a large proportion of the vacated dwellings in East Ham were reoccupied by those in housing need was purely incidental (Heraud, 1966, p. 14).

More data on the contribution of the new towns to London's housing need were supplied by the GLC to the Select Committee. These showed that 45 per cent of first tenancies in seven London new towns (Basildon, Bracknell, Harlow, Milton Keynes, Northampton, Peterborough and Stevenage) went to Londoners between 1965 and 1971. The figure for the expanded towns between 1969 and 1972 varied from 88 per cent to 77 per cent. Those in housing need amongst the Londoners who did go to new towns were estimated at 81·8 per cent for 1971−2. The figure was 82·8 per cent for the expanded towns for 1970−2, but based on over 9,000 migrants, compared with the 5,258 who went to new towns (Expenditure Committee, 1974, pp. 571−2). Attention was thus focused not only on the skills of the migrants, their origin and their housing need, but on the relatively small contribution that the new towns have made to all migration from London. The South East Economic Planning Council observed that:

> It is undeniable that the new towns have been the means of moving a great many families out of London − 87,000 families or roughly 261,000 people have gone to them since the end of the Second World War . . . [in] the entire post war period the total net migration from London has been probably about 2 million people. Thus about 13 per cent of the migrants have settled in the new towns (*ibid.*, p. 561).

The problem, as the GLC and its constituent boroughs had come to see it, was that the vast bulk of migration has been unplanned and subject to only limited control. Those people that have been able to move have tended to be the younger, more skilled and wealthier, leaving behind a population containing an increasing proportion of 'dependants', and a concentration of people in housing need. The new towns should, the London local authorities felt, be one source of housing over which they could have some control, for the benefit of those less free to improve their own circumstances. The smaller the contribution of new towns' housing to the total, the more vital it was for them to recognize this responsibility.

When it gave evidence to the Expenditure Committee hearings, the GLC, despite its criticisms of various aspects of their mechanisms, reaffirmed its support for new towns:

> for a considerable time to come, London will need access to housing outside its boundaries including rented accommodation in New Towns. . . . It is to be hoped that in future the new towns will accommodate a greater proportion of Londoners in housing need and of the disadvantaged than they have been able to in the past. . . . At least one new town (Milton Keynes) has indicated its intention to take a share of the most socially dependent groups . . . [but] there would remain the tremendous problem of devising procedures whereby such families would be willing to move away from all that is familiar to them (*ibid.*, pp. 566–7).

This growing focus on the 'social composition' of the population moving to new towns, rather than its size, was put forcibly to the committee by the London Boroughs Association. Voluntary movement and the drain of manufacturing industry from the central areas was leading to a situation where the 'fairly rich' and 'very poor' were in competition for housing space. As well as the actually homeless, the Association specified unskilled and service workers, the elderly and ethnic minorities as groups for whom the new towns were one of the few hopes of decent housing. Two solutions to the barrier of the existing homes/jobs link were proposed. The first was a 'direct housing allocation' of housing available to the boroughs via the GLC. To be eligible for this a tenant would have to show the viability of commuting or be able 'reasonably' to expect to find employment in the town (*ibid.*, p. 348). Elderly nominees would be the subject of negotiations about the possibility of special financial contributions to the county social services department in the new town area. The association recognized that the priority of employers' demands for housing for workers 'can readily frustrate any chance of a special quota for unskilled workers' (*ibid.*, p. 348), and so recommended that housing for rent should be built in advance of need. Empty houses were, of course, precisely the kind of politically delicate issue that the London Boroughs Association members felt vulnerable about. So, too, was housing the groups within its second category for a housing allocation: 'urgent disadvantaged groups' (*ibid.*, p. 351). These were specified as the homeless, one-parent families and 'other special cases considered by the Social Services Department to merit special treatment'.

Giving evidence, the representatives of the LBA were very frank about the advantages, as they saw them, of the new town development corporations' less-direct political accountability:

> they are not quite as sensitive to the difficulties and vicissitudes that normally beset an elected member who, perforce, is compelled to undertake unpalatable responsibilities like putting families into homes that have been built for people who have been on a housing waiting list for 20 years . . . we sometimes fall by the wayside as a result of public pressure (*ibid.*, p. 363).

It was not, the LBA emphasized, that it wished the development corporations to continue to lack a directly democratic element, merely that 'given the existing situation, it can be more effectively used' (*ibid.*).

Part of the problem seen by the GLC and the LBA was the continuing migration of manufacturing industry. In response to this, they said that the new towns should be encouraged to recruit industry from outside London and should also attempt to take a bigger proportion of their employment from the service sector. The DI and DOE were urged to help in this process by relaxing their criteria from the granting of IDCs and ODPs (*ibid.*, p. 570). Since the time that the London local authorities made these submissions, however, the attitude of inner-city administrations to industrial migration has hardened considerably. Not only the economic problems that follow the loss of well-paid employment, but the drop in revenue for local taxation is being felt. Cities outside London seem always to have been sensitive about this. They have traditionally been reluctant to encourage industry to leave for autonomous self-contained new towns, preferring instead to build housing estates at their periphery or develop expanded-town schemes. Birmingham had not long had its two new towns at Redditch and Telford when it announced a 'policy to encourage industry to consolidate and develop within the boundaries of the city' (Redditch DC, 1972, p. 407). The city also failed to use the housing offered to it for nominated tenants (*ibid.*). Birmingham, a city of longstanding civic pride, not to say chauvinism, was followed by the GLC in January 1976 (*The Times*, 3 January 1976, p. 1), when it announced an end to its sponsorship of town-development schemes under the 1952 Town Development Act, having come to the rather belated conclusion that its longstanding policy of encouraging industrial, as well as population, emigration was mistaken.

The GLC's policy reversal attracted much public attention, but similar statements had preceded it in Wales and Scotland. Fears about the capacity of new towns to grab mobile industry had led to the demise of Llantrisant. The more dramatic casualty was Stonehouse near Glasgow, designated in 1973. In 1974 a consultants' draft report (Colin Buchanan and Partners, 1974) recommended that its postponement should be considered. Strathclyde Regional Council adopted a more uncompromising stance in June 1975:

> at the present time of economic crisis when financial resources are severely limited, the Secretary of State's continued emphasis on new town development limits the discretion of the Regional Council and could prevent the Council from making what it considers to be an equitable allocation of resources for rehabilitation in other areas. . . . If the Secretary of State is unable to provide . . . additional resources central government must accept that development in new towns can only proceed to the extent that the Regional Council is able to allocate resources for infrastructure and community facilities without damaging its ability to pay for the regeneration of other areas within the Region (Expenditure Committee 1974–5a, pp. 967—8).

The project was ended in May 1976, just as the first families moved in (*The Times,* 13 May 1976, p. 4).

The redirection of government policy

Central government's discovery of the inner-city 'crisis' was announced by the Secretary of State for the Environment, Peter Shore, in what has come to be known as the 'Manchester Speech' in September 1976 (DOE, 1976). Subsequently interpreted as marking a major shift in policy, the text was in fact equivocal. In it the minister rehearsed the issues: falling population in the inner areas with a disproportionate loss of skilled workers; the shrinkage of manufacturing industry and its well-paid jobs; the growth of the tertiary sector producing jobs which are not suitable for the population remaining – hence a growing concentration of unemployment; falling rate revenues; bad housing and a decaying environment. He then summarized the history of the post-war dispersal policy, emphasizing the link between the second-generation and thus currently active towns and the very high population projections of the early 1960s. It was, he claimed, not expected that these towns would reduce central-area populations, merely provide accommodation for future population growth. (The minister's perspective was, however, conveniently myopic. Abercrombie's *Greater London Plan* (1945), which encapsulates the strategy and tactics of post-war planning for London and elsewhere, had the explicit aim of reducing the population of the old London County Council area. The policy of dispersal and decentralization had been just that. For thirty years it had actively been pursued not only by the DI through IDCs, but by the LCC and GLC's own explicit programme of industrial emigration.)

Despite his statement on dispersal policies, however, the minister then admitted that the vast bulk of population movement had not been planned. 'For example, of the 140,000 who moved from the conurbation of Merseyside between 1966 and 1971 only 11·4 per cent moved to new towns elsewhere in the region' (DOE, 1976). Similarly, he followed his remarks on the ease with which firms had been able to move to more attractive peripheral locations by conceding that the DI study had shown that the greatest cause of inner-city job loss had been by the 'death' rather than migration of firms: 'Only 27 per cent of the loss of jobs was due to employers moving out of London' (*ibid.*). Many such deaths, however, had resulted from the 'over-zealous' exclusion of non-conforming users under development control. Faced with the cost of removal and more expensive premises, small and medium-sized firms had simply closed.

The new philosophy, announced the minister, would be to try to solve the economic problems of the city local authorities and their residents by building up manufacturing employment, especially in small and medium-sized firms. Dispersal policies should not be further 'reinforced', particularly as population loss was leading to the under-use of existing education, health, welfare, recreation, etc. infrastructure that would have to be extensively duplicated in any new peripheral development. The minister defended the new towns against the charge that they had 'stolen' industries destined for the inner city and noted the contribution that they had made to the housing stock. But, he concluded, 'objective circumstances' had changed, most importantly in regard to population, and also because of lack of funds for public investment, so 'a real question about the alternative use of resources in the inner areas or the new and expanded towns does arise. . . . If cities fail, so to a large extent does our society' (*ibid.*).

In 1977 the new policy promised by the Secretary of State was detailed in a White Paper (Cmnd 6845, 1977) and subsequently the 1978 Inner Urban Areas Act. The White Paper was clearly extensively influenced by a series of 'inner area studies' commissioned by the DOE in London, Birmingham and Liverpool (DOE, 1977a, b, c and summarized in DOE 1977d). Notwithstanding a tendency for the consultants' reports to highlight those problems and solutions most within their particular disciplinary competence to identify, a

151

number of common themes emerged. The important qualification has, however, largely been ignored in the ensuing political and academic hubbub. That is that the inner-city crisis is different as between cities. All the areas studied (Lambeth in London, Small Heath in Birmingham and a large section of the core of Liverpool) shared some characteristics: low incomes, whether from employment, unemployment or retirement; poor and overcrowded housing; inadequate publicly and privately provided infrastructure. In London, the consultants agreed with the London Borough Association's earlier diagnosis that selective dispersal policies, aimed at the disadvantaged, would still be valuable. In the other areas studied, conversely, there was a need to stabilize and then increase the population. All the studies recommended measures to raise household incomes through attraction of employment more suited to existing skills, by enabling women to work and by improving the take-up of benefits.

To a more or less explicit degree, all the reports also criticized the policies and practices of the local authorities and statutory agencies in the study areas. Cross-departmental, problem-focused teams, the devolution of middle-level decision and staff into local areas and the harmonization of boundaries between statutory agencies was urged.

The 1977 White Paper (Cmnd 6845) outlined the now familiar problems — although without the cutting edge of some of the consultants' comments — and produced a series of recommendations. They centred on three issues: industry, management and cash. Manufacturing employment was to be sustained and attracted by the relaxation of IDC control, by encouraging planning authorities to modify their 'zoning' of industrial and residential land and by new powers awarded to local authorities to assist industry. These last provisions are embodied in the 1978 Inner Urban Areas Act, a remarkably flexible document. It allows local authorities in England, Wales and Scotland, designated by the Secretary of State, to make grants and loans to industrialists for a wide variety of reclamation and rehabilitation works on sites and buildings (paras 4 to 6). Even more wide-ranging powers are available in the 'special areas' (para 8) specified by the Secretary of State as part of the 'arrangement' made between central and local government under section 7. These so-called partnership schemes (see below) allow action including 'the exercise of functions under this or any other Act (whenever passed) including, in particular, functions . . . relating to planning or the compulsory acquisition of land' (*ibid.*, para. 7(3)). Under the new régime the Location of Offices Bureau, formerly charged with moving office employment out of London, is to promote office employment in inner-urban areas — including

London. There will be a new emphasis on retraining through the Manpower Services Commission.

In certain particularly stricken local-authority areas the department proposed partnership between local authorities and central departments, schemes to identify problems and produce programmes of action, apparently aimed primarily at improving the effectiveness of existing structures and spending. Both the form of these relationships and the criteria for choosing them are fudged in the White Paper. The preliminary choice of Liverpool, Birmingham, Manchester and the Lambeth and Dockland areas of London nevertheless produced strong reaction from local authorities elsewhere, no doubt because of the link between partnership and the third and vital ingredient: money. The scheme is to be administered through an increase in spending on the England and Wales Urban Programme to £125 million per year (at 1977 prices) for ten years. This sum, immediately and unanimously condemned as ludicrously small for the scale of the problems, will be concentrated upon partnership schemes. It is implied (*ibid.*, para. 71) that partnership will entail special consideration by central-government agencies of those programmes 'in whose preparation they will have had a hand'. Funds will also be forthcoming in the Rate Support Grant (*ibid.*, para. 48). In a crucial concluding paragraph the White Paper (*ibid.*, para. 94) declares that the money is to be provided by reallocation of public funds, not by increased spending, including 'modest savings in the new towns programme'. The concurrent review of the new towns policy (described in chapter 8) produced the truly modest sum of £20 million per year by 1979/80.

Policy for the Inner Cities is certainly a significant document, but more for what it signals than what it contains. Not only is the supposed crisis to be met with no increase in public spending, but much of the money is to be at the discretion of cities themselves, through the RSG. Reliance is placed on the vapid language of community voluntary effort and corporate management. Most strikingly for a 'major review of inner city policy', emanating from a new Cabinet Committee, it does not appear to commit any other central department except the DOE to anything significant — especially the Treasury. The imperative of flexibility and a problem-oriented approach, casting aside the boundaries of little departmental empires to meet the crisis, is reserved for inner-city local authorities, not central government. There is an ironic parallel with the planning and administration of the new towns programme.

The public response of the new towns to the various government and government-sponsored pronouncements has been limited. In 1977 the general managers of Milton Keynes, Northampton and Peterborough produced a joint paper (Roche *et al.*, 1977) commenting on the Lambeth Inner Area Study (DOE, 1977b). For many Londoners in need, it asserted, only the new towns could offer the prospect of a decent home in pleasant surroundings. Only in the new towns could integrated programmes of public and private housing and the attraction of industry be effected in the short term. The general managers viewed the possibility of the consultants' proposals bearing fruit in anything less than five to seven years with scepticism:

> and even if strong executive planning and development agencies were soon established, inner area renewal would not begin to yield significant gains in much less than ten years.

> This is not an intuitive or uninformed reaction. It is firmly grounded in the experience of metropolitan and regional strategy-making in the South East over the last 20 years: planning and housing policies which have depended on inter-authority co-operation have just not been implemented. Nor is there any sound reason for believing that they would be in future (Roche *et al.*, 1977).

Accusations of 'stealing' jobs from the inner area were also rejected. The future employment in the three towns would come from expansion of existing concerns, firms migrating from the rest of the South East — which 'the recent review of the Strategy for the South East specifically recommends' — and from Europe. The last point was complementary to one made by Shostak *et al.* (1976) who had claimed that the biggest loss to London's manufacturing base had been through the death and shrinkage of firms, which had far exceeded that due to either inter- or intra-regional policies. Compared with other migrant groups, the population lost to the new towns had in fact contained more of the less-skilled (31 per cent semi-skilled, unskilled and 'other', compared with 29 per cent). Moreover, they argued, firms need to move to expand, invest and re-equip. Stunting this process would be to the long-term disadvantage of the national economy. Further evidence for this view came from a study carried out by the DI (Dennis, 1978) which concluded that, for London at least, the loss of manufacturing jobs between 1966 and 1974 was brought about primarily by a 'high rate of factory closures unconnected with industrial movement (44 per cent)', and that,

> Shrinkage of employment at plants remaining in the capital . . . comprised some 23 per cent of the total decline. Loss of manufacturing employment in London arising from movement has been due more to unplanned movement (11 per cent of the total decline) than to movement to the Assisted Areas

(9 per cent) or to the London overspill towns (7 per cent) (*ibid.*).

Dennis confirmed that small firms were more likely to close than medium-sized or large ones.

Characteristically, the TCPA is weathering the storm by renewed affirmations that the crisis is a vindication of the concerns of the Association at its founding, and that its remedies then are durable now. At the core is the issue of land values which induce high-density development. Ash (1976) claims that the irony is that this will, in itself, both maintain the advantages of new town development and deter private capital from responding to the call to re-invest in the inner city. An executive statement in 1977 (TCPA, 1977) advocated the writing down of inner-city land to current use value and more effective use of Community Land Act powers to enable land to be put to less 'profitable' uses.

The voice of the people is extensively quoted. Both Ash (1976) and Lock (1976) point out that the same centrifugal movement can be seen in cities throughout the developed world, and that it is largely due to the demand of individuals for more spacious and well-situated housing to serve their rising expectations of consumption and leisure. Subsidies to central areas (particularly London) in the form of London Weighting Allowances and the subsidy of high-rise, high-density building and of long-distance rail commuting should be abolished (TCPA, 1977). Rather than diverting funds to the inner city, the poor should be allowed to take advantage of the irreversible process occurring and be 'emancipated' from it (Hancock, 1977). Indeed Lock (1976) recalls that F. J. Osborn had a dossier of the very desirable suburban homes of the policy-makers who extolled the advantages of the inner core for the poor in the 1950s!

London is still the Great Wen for the TCPA as it was for Ebenezer Howard (although the observation must be made that its home overlooks the Mall rather than the Mersey or even Stevenage). The policy statement (TCPA, 1977) rejects the relaxation of IDC control and instead recommends the spontaneous emigration of both jobs and population from London to 'six major strategic centres' with good transport links to enable commuting – a scheme reminiscent of Social City (Howard, 1965).

On the subject of positive discrimination the TCPA is ambivalent. While it recommends use of the CLA, of regional development corporations, fiscal measures to end the poverty trap and even the spending of new town surpluses on the inner city (TCPA, 1977; Hancock, 1977), there is reluctance to advocate manipulation of new town tenancy rules or industrial mix, and firm rejection of more public housing and its 'servile' tied population (Ash, 1976). Instead,

155

the emphasis is on private and self-build housing.

Only rarely does the hint of the intractable political issues show itself through the all-party self-evidence of the language and programme, as when Hancock (1977) acknowledges that radical land policies might be difficult in the face of the new importance of land itself as an investment underpinning both public and private financial institutions. Overall, the pervading impression of the TCPA response to the inner-city issue is of *déjà vu*. The preoccupation with strong action on land but the claim that the individual should be sovereign in other respects, the execration of high densities and of flats and the preoccupation with, and generalization from, the problems of London are reminiscent of 1948, if not 1898.

8 Reappraisal 1974–8

despite changes in the legislative framework and considerable political and professional and academic interest in New Towns, there has been no comprehensive public study of New Town policy in the last quarter of a century (Expenditure Committee, 1974–5a, p. xxii).

The consultation documents

When the Labour Party was returned to government in the election of February 1974, its policy-makers had had four unlooked-for years to refine their thoughts on the future of new towns and their assets. (New policies on these had originally been scheduled for announcement in the summer of 1970.) An embargo on the sales of freehold industrial and commercial sites and on the selling of housing stock originally built for rent was introduced in the spring of 1974. In December 1974 the new government produced a 'consultation document': *New towns in England and Wales* (DOE, 1974) and a parallel statement for Scotland appeared in January 1975 (Scottish Office, 1975). The latter document, at least, was described as the outcome of a 'comprehensive review' of the new towns policy (*ibid.,* para. 17). Whatever the rigour of the evaluation the result was anodyne. Broad issues and objectives were raised, but there were few recommendations for specific action to mediate between the wishes and their fulfilment. Both documents, and in particular the version for England and Wales, were remarkable for their endorsement of the *status quo.*

After an outline history of new towns legislation and the new towns programme, the concept of 'partnership towns' was described and endorsed as a method of 'taking matters further' in respect of relationships between the development corporation and

157

the host local authority (DOE, 1974, para. 3.4). It was suggested (para. 4.2) that partnerships 'which will vary from town to town' could include a greater representation of local authority members on the new town's board, some joint planning, land assembly and management work and the establishment of a joint housing-allocation policy, paying the way for the transfer of the housing and related assets to the local authority. What can only be interpreted as a compromise solution to the issue of the political accountability of the development corporations is rather disingenuously attributed to the late Richard Crossman (para. 2.13). As we have seen in chapter 5, he more modestly gave the credit for 'cooking-up' partnership schemes to Keith Joseph and Evelyn Sharp.

The sore issue of the ownership of remunerative industrial and commercial assets was also evaded. The eventual surplus from development corporations and the additional rate revenue for local authorities were set off against one another. Any solution must take 'all such aspects fairly into account' (para. 3.5). The actual solution, which emerged in para. 3.21, was that the management (and by implication ownership) of industrial and commercial assets would pass to the Commission for the New Towns 'for the good of the whole new town programme', although no change in legislation or practice to bring this about was suggested. The 'community at large' should benefit from the betterment and surpluses arising from new town development, so in future commercial and industrial sites should be leasehold only (para. 3/19). Again, it is not clear whether the community in question is the new town itself, new towns in general through, for example, the recycling of profits into better and earlier amenity provision, potential new town residents, or the taxpayer. Present arrangements continue to favour the last.

The recommendations for Scotland differed over the transfer of assets. There being no Commission for the New Towns in Scotland, the industrial and commercial assets were destined for the Scottish Development Agency (Scottish Office, 1975, para. 9). It was also implied that, unlike in England and Wales, no transfer of housing assets would be contemplated until the development corporations were finally wound up. Sales of rented houses, conversely, were to be continued in Scotland, subject to 'the continued availability of an adequate stock of houses for rental' (*ibid.,* para. 14), and an annual governmental review of the private/rented balance in each town. In England and Wales, the further sale of housing built for rent was ended 'for the time being' (DOE, 1974, para. 4.13).

The document for England and Wales was multivalent about balance and self-containment. Balance between the population and the number of jobs available would continue to be a goal (para. 4.8). Social class, degrees of need, age distribution and stages in the family cycle appeared to be conflated in the pursuit of 'social balance' which was endorsed in para. 4.10. It was acknowledged that housing for the parents and children of the migrant generation would be desirable, but that it would in turn 'marginally reduce the priority that can be given to other categories of people'. There was ambiguity about these priorities in their turn. Earlier (para. 4.7) it had been reaffirmed that the first priority must be migrants from the city, and workers nominated by firms, but the following paragraph then declared that the requirement that the bread-winner must work in the town should be 'relaxed' and a degree of commuting accepted. But how much is self-containment to be allowed to lapse? 'This must not, however, be carried too far. The idea is to establish a happy medium between the new towns becoming mere dormitories and the new town designation area boundaries acting as an iron curtain' (para. 4.8).

The relaxation of self-containment was seen as part of a move to prevent the new towns 'beggaring the cities they serve' (para. 3/16) by the allocation of the 'proportion' of houses to those in housing stress and those who do not need a job – 'single parents or disabled' (para. 4.7). There was no guidance, however, on how these conflicting demands should be reconciled, and what actual weight should be given to employment-based housing allocation as against needs-based eligibility. Nor was there any recognition that although the modification of the employment criterion to a 'reasonable' (para. 3.16) distance from the town may do a little to solve the problem of the access to new town housing for the 'less fortunate', the cost of moving to and living in the town may be made more burdensome by placing less emphasis on the local provision of employment.

The controversy over whether the whole idea of new towns has become too expensive to maintain was dealt with by the bland assertion that:

> Constant monitoring on the part of the Government will ensure that the new towns programme does not outstrip demand or available resources . . . or adversely affect the economic, social and environmental well-being of the older urban areas (para. 4.4).

This last is typical of the tone of the whole of the document on England and Wales (less so in the Scottish version): bland, imprecise, a little self-justifying and propagandist – even patronizing. It succeeded in arousing some opposition, despite its imprecision, particularly from the Strathclyde Regional Council, which claimed, in a discussion paper, that the Scottish Consultative document 'appears to underestimate' the regional council's strategic planning role (Expenditure Committee, 1974-5a, p. 967). It was particularly concerned that the new towns should not attract all the private housing and mobile industry in the region and that tenancy 'filters' should allow for allocation of housing to the under-privileged 'without discrimination'. The transfer of commercial and industrial assets to the Scottish Development Agency was also questioned, given the scale and expertise of the local authority. As we have seen in the previous chapter, however, the prior question for Strathclyde was whether there should be new towns at all, given the current acute shortage of funds for capital projects and services in existing urban areas.

Both the Associations of County Councils and of District Councils found the document unacceptable. The counties declared: 'There should be a firm timetable for the transfer for all the assets from New Towns to local authorities . . . in the meantime, there is an urgent need to share profits with local authorities' (*ibid.,* p. 862).

The districts shared their confidence that there was no need for the Commission for the New Towns nor for the continued existence of the older development corporations. 'The Association contend that the assets could equally well be managed by the local authorities, to whom the necessary staff could also be transferred' (*ibid.,* p. 871). Outstanding debts and balances would be the only defensible basis for the transfer. Both bodies pointed out the failure of the document to get to grips with financial issues, except in its endorsement of partnership. The Association of District Councils also considered it 'essential' that the local authorities should have the right to nominate at least one representative to the Board of the Development Corporation (*ibid.,* p. 873).

The response of the development corporations either individually, or collectively through the New Towns Association, is not published. For one new town employee, writing in an internal memorandum, the 'general theme of the document is too tentative'. He contrasts the 'mere exhortation' with the more 'directive' tone that the DOE usually employs in its communications.

The Expenditure Committee

Fortunately for those interested in the new town policy — and perhaps for the towns themselves — a far-reaching examination of policy has taken place. During the 1972-3 parliament, the Environment and Home Office Sub-Committee of the Commons Expenditure Committee started hearings on the new towns. It met twelve times before it was prematurely ended by the February 1974 election. Minutes of evidence, written evidence and an interim report were then published. After the October 1974 election and the publication of the consultation documents, a new subcommittee was convened to review more specific financial issues. This met a further eleven times in 1975. The combined *Final Report* and the oral and written evidence are a rich, if unwieldy, source of material on the British new towns policy. For many issues they are the only authoritative reference.

The terms of reference of the first round of subcommittee meetings were oriented towards discovering the overall objectives of the new towns policy, the way in which specific projects were conceived and evaluated, the relations between central and local agencies in respect of new towns and the possibility of using new towns machinery in 'other planning situations' (Expenditure Committee, 1974−5a, p. xlvii).

Clearly, in an ideal world, the social, economic and financial objectives of the new towns would interact so closely with the policy about their 'number, location, size, time scale, etc.' (*ibid.*) as to be tautological. The Select Committee's hearings quickly confirmed that this was not the case. The actual process of decision about designation remained shrouded in vagueness. As we have seen, the second generation of new towns arose largely (but not exclusively) from regional plans. It is clearly central government's intention that this process should be consolidated:

> I think it will be out of this regional planning, which will also be associated with the structure planning under the new development planning techniques, that there will be exposed whether a need exists . . . for inducing growth . . . (*ibid.*, p. 63).

No specific answer emerged on the decision process about the exact location of the new town − or indeed whether there should be a new town − and the target population. There appear to be two reasons for this. First, the DOE was represented at the Expenditure Committee by administrative civil servants, and mainly by the Under-Secretary in charge of the New Town Division. Much of the crucial thinking about the 'technical' issues connected with the new towns policy − for example, which towns should be subjected to feasibility studies as was done for *The South East Study* − is carried out by the professional staff at the department which includes planners, economists, statisticians and sociologists. Many of these work to the chief planner of the department, whose perspective on the issues raised would doubtless have been different. Second, as was revealed by the committee, consultants have come increasingly to be used at all stages of the designation process. Their terms of reference vary widely in specificity: some have been limited to devising a master-plan or detailed proposals for designation, others

161

were free to determine whether a new town should be the chosen instrument. Levin (1976), however, has shown that the extent to which consultants actually reappraise the situation may be limited. The question *quis custodiet ipsos custodes?* – who decides to appoint consultants and for what? – remained unresolved.

The same lack of an overarching policy objective for the programme as a whole applied *a fortiori* to goals for individual towns, both in social, financial and economic terms.

> The only real financial objective . . . is that the town should be able to repay its loans, capital and interest, at a respectable date in the future, and I do not even think that respectable date is even set in a firm way when the new town is designated. It would be impossible to set it (*ibid.*, p. 24).

> To some extent the social goals are comprehended in the more physical and precise figures that one gives for population, employment, utilities and so on. It is generally understood that new town development corporations are expected to produce as high a quality of urban development as is consistent with the public resources available and the targets set . . . it is very difficult to quantify it more closely than that in general terms. It is rather like an elephant; one knows an elephant when one sees one (*ibid.*, p. 74).

The lack of general and specific goals has inevitably inhibited attempts both to examine policy alternatives before designation, and to evaluate new town performance once under way. It is clear that the staff of the New Towns Division accepted that the building of a new town is somehow an apolitical process. The remark about the elephant neatly encapsulates the view that a successful new town is an objectively existing and self-evident good about which there will be little dispute. It is consonant with the organic analogy implied in much of the earlier thought about the policy: that given the right preconditions and the service of men of good will, the enterprise will grow and develop in the right way. A refinement of this is the Young and Willmott (1973) principle of 'stratified diffusion', which assumes that the raising of standards and extension of opportunity will occur by providing for modal man now (with modal income and car ownership, etc.), so that the poorer will be carried along by the spontaneous growth of the system. This somewhat passive approach to policy-making is reinforced by a lack of faith in the tools currently available for its evaluation: 'I should think that it is very unlikely that one could quantify social benefits in this field with sufficient precision to calculate, so to speak, a social cost of return on the investment' (*ibid.*, p. 24).

The claimed difficulties of assessing social investment were the rationale for the department's pessimism on the possibility of comparing the costs and benefits of new towns with 'other forms of urban development' (Expenditure Committee, 1974—5a, p. 1006).

> Such a project, using current techniques, might have to be of a magnitude several times greater than anything previously contemplated . . . and even then, it might not provide a satisfactory answer in a reasonable period, if ever. The Department is therefore turning to the idea of tackling the problem piecemeal . . . .

Yet in the same Memorandum, the DOE refers to Stone's (1973) attempt to carry out just such an exercise in comparing greenfield new towns with different scales and forms of expansion of existing settlements. It must be admitted that such modelling necessarily requires a degree of abstraction from reality, through estimating and assumptions, but a number of Stone's conclusions are suggestive in the light of trends in new town thinking. He concluded, for example, that town expansion is more expensive than greenfield development (Stone, 1973, p. 248) and becomes much more so if extensive restructuring of existing settlement is contemplated. Other topics of study were the construction and recurrent costs of different densities and the effect of town size and building form on travel-to-work costs. The new conventional wisdoms about large-scale expansion of towns, as has occurred at Northampton and Peterborough, about urban form (for example, whether to have neighbourhoods or not and if so, how they should be arranged), require evaluation, particularly if there is to be more emphasis on catering for the 'dependent population' and less on purely voluntary and relatively affluent migrants. The DOE's response to Stone's work was to avoid summarizing Stone's conclusions because of a 'risk of distortion' (Expenditure Committee, 1974—5a, p. 1006) and then to damn it with faint praise because he did not have the data to be completely definite in his conclusions.

Precisely this attitude was attacked by McKinsey's (management and planning consultants) in their evidence to the Expenditure Committee. More objectives could be specified, they claimed, but further:

> There is an antipathy, we have found, to many of the available measures which do exist on two grounds: first that the knowledge and research behind them is as yet inadequate . . . and therefore we should not use them at all bcause we do not know how to use them; and secondly because of a belief, a theology, that quantifying social aims may be dangerous, because the more specific you get, the more issues both in

ideological and administrative terms that you raise (*ibid.*, p. 853).

Part of the solution adopted by central government has been to devolve responsibility on to consultants by commissioning feasibility studies, as if inexactitude and 'guestimates' are acceptable provided they are not supplied by the department itself. This does not, however, meet the problem of devising good monitoring techniques which, as DOE rightly said, will be a costly and lengthy business – and surely therefore a direct responsibility of central government. The alternative is the dignifying of current hunches into certainty by re-use and cross-referencing. A specific example is the apparent contrast between the conclusion of *The South East Study* (MHLG, 1964) that it is cheaper to raise the population of a town by 100 per cent than 50 per cent (*ibid.*, p. 68) and Stone's (1973) research. It may be that in one case the issue was development costs and the other the costs to residents – which must be a critical consideration when there is a redistributive intention, and deserves research effort devoted to it.

Until very recently, the monitoring of the new towns' performance has been through project-by-project approval of the corporation's work, and from the annual accounts, which show what has been done, but in a vacuum. The DOE has also produced cash-flow forecasts (Expenditure Committee, 1974–5a, pp. 607, 974) which indicate progress towards 'break-even'. This can only strengthen the impression that the performance of the towns is evaluated by reference to each other and not in relation to hoped-for objectives related to their individual circumstances and problems. A situation where Basildon or Telford, faced with dereliction, or the Scottish new towns, with their rents dilemma, are compared with Crawley or Harlow is unconstructive. The towns' sensitivity about such invidious comparisons manifests itself regularly in their annual reports, and prevented the publication of a study of comparative costs and returns in six English new towns appearing until seven years after it was done (Lichfield and Wendt, 1969).

The Expenditure Committee's *Report* was trenchant in its criticism of the DOE's programme of monitoring:

> We have concluded that there is nothing to suggest that the New Towns Programme is systematically evaluated in order to establish the social and economic opportunity costs of undertaking the programme, or the policies it embodies. Although extensive descriptive material has been presented to us, we have been surprised by the conspicuous lack of analysis to judge the success of New Towns . . .(Expenditure Committee, 1974–5a, p. xxxiv).

The department was 'urged to reconsider' their attitude to the possibility of major research into cost-effectiveness (*ibid.*, p. xxv). It recommended that the DOE and the Treasury should examine the 'resource implications' both nationally and for the local authorities concerned before designation, and again if a revision of target population is proposed. Targets should be set in 'both social and economic policy terms' (*ibid.*, p. xxvi).

The Select Committee also addressed itself to the co-ordination of central departments and of local authorities and statutory undertakers for the development of a new town. As we have seen in earlier chapters, ministries varied in their practice as to whether funds were earmarked for new-community projects or not. In the case of the DHSS, there has been no policy of setting aside cash for new town projects, nor of extra allocations. Road funding, now a responsibility of the DOE itself, has undergone a number of permutations, but currently is the subject of earmarked money. (The Expenditure Committee (*ibid.*, p. xxx) recommends a 'specific allocation' for all transport, not only roads, to be made to the county council within the framework of the new system of transport policies and costed programmes (TPPs).) It also became clear (1974, p. 82) that the responsibility for making representations, both to central departments and to local authorities, where facilities were either provided by or mediated through them – as in the case of education – falls on the development corporations. Whether it was done effectively or not could, therefore, profoundly influence the future of the town. We have seen that the Department of Industry and the Department of Employment have played a key part in controlling the flow of industry to the new towns, and have also been involved in the allocation of housing, through the NETS. The DI, nevertheless, seemed not to acknowledge its importance in the new town development process. As the Expenditure Committee remarked:

the Department of Industry saw the I.D.C. mechanisms as having no part to play in relation to social aspects. . . . We regret that there appears to be no movement towards (or even interest in) a more selective employment/housing policy to link New Town growth with the problems of the older cities. The lack of concern in the Departments of Industry and Employment for the relationship of their programmes to housing and planning programmes indicates to us that the widely held view that the New Towns are a good example of inter-departmental co-ordination is regrettably incorrect (1974—5a, p. xxxiii).

These observations emphasized the weakness of the DOE's

argument that positive intervention in pursuit of specified social goals is unnecessary or dangerous. The passive alternative, of allowing the new towns programme to evolve in the interstices of the departments concerned, has inevitably had real enough consequences, which are only now being considered. 'An immediate review' of the co-ordination of policies was recommended (*ibid.*, p. xxxiii), together with allocation procedures to ensure that housing for special needs 'receives due priority' and 'the Government should review the mechanisms which purport to assist the disadvantaged and unskilled to leave the cities and settle in the New Towns, with the aim of introducing more effective measures of bringing such movement about' (*ibid.*, p. xxxiii).

Relations between development corporations and the local authorities in their area have varied from good to execrable, a fact that has received remarkably little public acknowledgment by the ministry or the development corporations over the years. This hostility permeated the evidence of the Association of New Town Local Authorities (ANTLA: now part of the Association of District Councils), and it extended to relations with the DOE. ANTLA complained of the contrast in relations between the DOE and the development corporations and new town local authorities, of the secrecy of development-corporation board meetings and proceedings:

> Circulars and guidance to development corporations on matters affecting local authorities are not released to local authorities by the Department. The New Towns Handbook gives general guidance to Development Corporations on a wide variety of subjects, many of which also involve local authorities. This Handbook is treated as confidential and is not available to local authorities (1974, p. 167).

The Association, in its submission to the first set of hearings was unequivocal in its demands:

> New town local authorities have had to bear a share of the cost of build up of the town, which has created the valuable asset . . . (*ibid.*, p. 170).

> The government should then review its harsh policy of keeping new town local authorities bereft of investment income and at a considerable disadvantage to other communities (*ibid.*, p. 173).

The winding up of the Commission for the New Towns was called for and the use of development corporations for other planning situations rejected out of hand (*ibid.*, p. 169). Witnesses claimed that local authorities could be more efficient than the development corporations in housebuilding and the provision of amenities (*ibid.*, p. 181) and that some authorities had the expertise to take over the attraction of and provision for industry (*ibid.*, p. 182).

These claims did not find favour with the Select Committee, which felt that

> the interests of corporations and local authorities will not automatically co-incide and there is a need to safeguard the autonomy and independence of the Corporations if they are to fulfil satisfactorily their national role. We believe that as a town approaches maturity it may be appropriate to bring about more local involvement, but we are of the opinion that considerable caution should be exercised over raising the level of local authority representation on the Board (1974–5a, p. xxviii).

Formal joint machinery for consultation and the 'mutual exchange of information' between the development corporation, the district council and the county council was urged. A specific area of co-operation was recommended: that this new mechanism should be used to move towards a common administration of housing provision and management in new town districts (*ibid.*, p. xxix). The Select Committee also endorsed the policy, put forward in the consultation document for England and Wales (DOE, 1974), that housing and associated assets be transferred from the development corporations to the district councils. Proposals for this should be put forward at an 'early date' by the government (Expenditure Committee, 1974–5a, p. xxix).

The second set of Select Committee hearings was focused on 'selected financial issues' of which two broad areas came to the fore: the financing of local authority services in new towns, and the way in which new towns raised money and their spending was monitored. During the building of the first generation of new towns there was disquiet about the costs of the new towns on the part of ratepayers, and grumbles from the new residents about the late appearance of publicly and privately funded services and facilities. This issue remained fairly muted, however, as the towns were smaller in scale than those designated later, the population build-up was slower than had been hoped, and local-authority responsibilities were anyway more limited than they have now become. By the time the burdens were apparent, so too was the additional rate-income. From the mid-1950s to the late 1960s a continuing expansion of affluence was expected, so presumably local authorities were prepared to take a medium-term view of their 'investment'. By the 1970s the situation had altered dramatically, by the coincidence of a number of factors. The second generation of new towns were at the peak of their development, with new population arriving in large numbers. Local authority services had been extended and re-organized as in, for example, social services. A very high rate of inflation was accompanied by high interest rates and followed by central government demands to reduce local government spending by a factor which, given this inflation, meant substantial cuts. Finally, an ever-greater proportion of local finance now comes from central government's coffers via the Rate Support Grant (RSG). The figure (currently about 60 per cent) and its calculation have had a crucial effect on new town local authorities. For them, the problem formerly had been that for a short period rates might rise a bit and better facilities tend to appear a little earlier in the new town than elsewhere. By 1974, the rates rises were large and seemingly endless and the provision of facilities had become a zero-sum in some cases, that is, in the new town instead of elsewhere in the local authority's area.

A large number of local authorities, both at district and county-council level, submitted evidence to the Select Committee on their financial dilemma. One of the most detailed analyses came from six counties acting together: Buckinghamshire, Cambridgeshire, Cheshire, Lancashire, Northamptonshire and Salop, thus repre-senting all types and stages of new town development (Expenditure Committee, 1974—5a, p. 760). Their problems, necessarily over-simplified in order to be summarized, centred on the need to pro-vide facilities and services in advance of the population; Milton Keynes Borough (*ibid.*, p. 923) also illustrated the situation created by a shortfall of money allowed for locally determined schemes. Either amenities, for example in the area of leisure and recreation, would fall behind, or the council would have to sell assets to raise the cash.

The problem over revenue expenditure was even more complex because of the intricacies of the Rate Support Grant. The cal-culation of the payment to each area depends on two elements: 'needs' and 'resources'. The 'needs' element reflects the compo-sition of the population. A new town authority would attract money because of the youth of the population, but the schools have to be provided before this group would show in the population statistics employed in the annual calculation of the RSG, which always tend to be a couple of years out of date. The 'resources' element makes up rate income to a standard figure per head, which is exceeded at the moment only by 'a few local authorities outside London' (*ibid.*, p. xxiv). As the RSG accounts for more and more of local funds, therefore, the DOE's position that spending is offset by increased income becomes less defensible. For many authorities more rateable value simply results in the loss of part of their 'resources' element payment. The total is the same.

As we have seen in earlier chapters, both counties and districts claimed hardship, the former in education and other provisions and the latter in providing services like refuse disposal and street cleaning. The hardship might formerly have been seen as insignificant, but it had taken on new importance when the context was 'nil-growth' (*ibid.*, p. 963). The 'six counties' called for direct government aid for capital projects and the recasting of the RSG to allow both for provision in advance of need and equity between areas. Development corporations should make contributions to revenue expenditure and 'land needed for . . . statutory services [should be] provided free' (*ibid.*, p. 762). As we have seen, development corporations are already empowered to contribute to water and sewerage, roads and some transport services. In Peterborough, Northampton and Telford the development corporation can contribute to education and other services, once a specified threshold has been passed (*ibid.*, p. 960), although payments had only been made to Northampton up to 1975. The 1965 New Towns Act in fact allows considerable flexibility for development corporations to make contributions to local authority services, with DOE and Treasury approval, but the Select Committee came to the view that more positive help had become necessary. They recommended that such payments should be made direct to the local authority concerned, by the DOE (*ibid.*, p. xliii). Further,

> the D.O.E. should assess the capital expenditure requirements of local authorities within the New Town Area separately from their projects outside . . . and should base their allocations accordingly.

> [and] that the appropriate part of the cost of the provision of local services in New Town areas in advance of their being required should be met through D.O.E. by a specific grant to the authority, additional to R.S.G. and transport supplementary grant (*ibid.*, p. xlv).

Clearly this specific provision for new town development needed to be intimately connected with the planning of investment both locally and nationally, which the Select Committee had found wanting. The extent to which other agencies contribute to the development of a new town was emphasized by a figure produced by McKinsey's: that less than 20 per cent of public-sector current expenditure on Milton Keynes and 60 to 70 per cent of capital expenditure will come from the development corporation (1974, p. 615). With this in mind, the committee recommended that

'D.O.E. should instruct each Development Corporation to initiate discussions with all relevant agencies with a view to preparing a five year Resource Plan on a rolling basis' (1974—5a, p. xxxiv). This should be done in the context of a monitoring system established between the central departments concerned 'as a matter of urgency' (*ibid.*, p. xxxvi).

> We recommend that the D.O.E., in conjunction with other relevant Departments, including the Departments of Industry, Employment, Health and Social Security, Education and the Home Office should immediately establish a Policy Monitoring System to ensure the full contribution of the New Towns to the execution of appropriate Government social and economic policies including housing, employment and regional development policies and policies towards minority groups and the disadvantaged in inner urban areas (*ibid.*, p. xxxvii).

New town development corporations have, from the outset, only had one major source of finance, loans from the National Loans Fund, repayable over sixty years at the rate of interest in force at the time of the loan. Since 1974 they have in addition been able to use overdraft facilities up to either £500,000 or £1 million, depending on their circumstances. In 1975 the DOE communicated to the Expenditure Committee that corporations were to be allowed to borrow from each other temporarily to 'help deal with cash flow fluctuations', up to £500,000 for the 'Scottish, Welsh and English Mark I' towns and £1 million for the remainder (*ibid.*, p. 983). The Advisory Panel on Institutional Finance said that such a limited choice of finance was detrimental to the new towns, both in its written and verbal evidence to the Select Committee. 'The object of this . . . paper is to state the Panel's strongly held view that certain changes are necessary if development corporations are to continue their successful development on the most economic and efficient basis in the future' (*ibid.*, p. 994). They recommended that development corporations should be given the same freedom as local authorities to go to the money market and borrow for varying periods at different interest rates, depending on the use to which the money was to be put. They further suggested that the Commission for the New Towns' cash surplus be used in loans for corporations, and that where surpluses were generated by new towns still developing they should be able to 'Spend it internally on projects of benefit to the local community' (*ibid.*, p. 993).

Many development corporations also criticized the method by which they were financed. As Basildon gloomily observed

Whether to buy land or to buy a typewriter with its very

limited life — to have this burden for 60 years is a poor way to finance any organisation. Inevitably interest is a very heavy burden — particularly so because the Development Corporation cannot re-negotiate a loan at more advantageous terms when interest rates fall (*ibid.*, p. 985).

This reluctance to tie up cash in loan debts frequently, as Milton Keynes wrote,

> forces Development Corporations into lease and leaseback arrangements where, particularly during the early stages of development of a town, a disproportionate amount of the equity relative to the expected growth may have to be given away to the private sector, in order to attract the necessary funds (*ibid.*, p. 973).

A similar observation had been made in a memorandum from the Advisory Panel to the Secretary of State in 1972 (*ibid.*, p. 989). They acknowledge that whether or not this is a good thing 'is debatable and basically a political question', and they tellingly continue, '(New town corporations) in the North of England, in Scotland and possibly in Wales . . . tend to have to do their funding . . . on a more expensive basis in the private sector . . .' (*ibid.*, p. 990). Forward planning, too, is made difficult by the tie to the government rate of interest in force: 'For example, during 1974—75 there were no fewer than 22 changes in the year . . .' (*ibid.*, p. 985).

The Expenditure Committee supported the critics of the existing methods of funding, calling them 'unsatisfactory'. 'We do not feel that the Treasury has made out a sound case for the Development Corporations having to depend almost exclusively on 60 year fixed-interest funding' (*ibid.*, p. xli). It further observed that the newer towns may suffer from their high average rate of interest and that the housing stock may prove to be a considerable burden to the local authority when transferred.

> [They] recommend that the D.O.E. should allow Development Corporations flexibility over the period for which they borrow funds and permit higher overdraft limits, subject to Departmental and Treasury approval of the proposed arrangements [and] that borrowing from sources other than the National Loans Fund, secured by Treasury Guarantee, should be permitted to Development Corporations (*ibid.*, p. xlii).

Interestingly, the committee was much less sympathetic to the idea of surpluses being used by the Commission and the new towns themselves to provide an additional and cheaper method of finance,

171

and noted that 'a principal cause' of the surpluses was the sale of rented housing which could be expected not to yield much in the future. In the light of rising costs, the committee also expected only a very limited contribution to be made to spending by other forms of 'roll-over' of assets '. . . we are therefore unable to recommend any change in government policy towards the recovery of surpluses' (*ibid.*, p. xliii), because it would be a 'departure' from the practices applied to other public sector bodies. A consistent theme in the Expenditure Committee's *Report* is the members' apparent reluctance to allow the new towns to become any less a part of central government and a tool of national policy. Over that, at least, the Select Committee and the DOE could agree, but the committee even rejected the idea of further partnership schemes. 'It does not appear to us that there are any measurable economic benefits from partnership schemes . . .' (*ibid.*, p. xxv).

In its concluding section, the *Report* dealt with the 'role of private capital'. Over this, it was uncharacteristically circumspect, no doubt reflecting the all-party composition of the committee. The issues surrounding both the selling of the rented housing stock and limiting commercial and industrial sites to leasehold were stated, but then left in the air. 'We accept that a balance has to be struck between the gain to the private investor and a satisfactory return to the community on its considerable investment in the New Town. This must always be a matter of judgement . . .' (*ibid.*, p. xlvii). A lame, but probably inevitable, coda to what is otherwise an admirably forthright document.

Response and review

The government's response to the Expenditure Committee was embodied in a White Paper (Cmnd 6616, 1976). It noted that action was already being taken on three issues. First, the transfer of rented housing to local authorities was being legislated for under the 1976 New Towns (Amendment) Act (see below). Second, new instructions were being issued about the funding of new town roads, allowing development corporations to defray counties' expenditure on roads built earlier, or to a higher standard, than would have been the case if the new towns were not being developed (see DOE, circular 53/76). Last, the active London new towns (Basildon, Bracknell, Harlow, Milton Keynes, Northampton, Peterborough, and Stevenage) had been told to modify their tenancy allocation procedures so as to become more accessible to the 'disadvantaged'. A circular to new towns in April 1976 reiterated the general desirability of self-containment, but noted that the criterion of working in the town should no longer rigidly be applied, providing that the 'bargaining counter' of housing for migrant firms was maintained. As towns matured, this category of allocation should be 'progressively reduced'. The revised order of priorities is to be: first, Londoners in housing need with jobs in the new town or within 'reasonable daily travelling distance'. The second group is Londoners or second-generation new town households without employment, including the retired, handicapped and single-parent families. Third come the 'second generation' where the breadwinner works in or near the new town. 'Key workers' have thus been shifted from first to fourth priority. Other groups such as ex-servicemen come lower still. (A result of this directive is the appearance of figures showing the percentage of allocations to Londoners in special need in the new town annual reports, for example Bracknell DC, 1977, p. 64; Milton Keynes DC, 1977, pp. 171, 174; Northampton DC, 1977, p. 215. The latter two give specific case examples to add human interest!)

The DOE also conceded the Expenditure Committee's criticisms about the failure of co-ordination, both between central departments, and between development corporations and the local authorities and statutory bodies involved in new town developments. Consultations were planned to produce better 'performance indicators' (Cmnd 6616, para. 11) and the notion of development corporations and local authorities producing five-year rolling resource plans was enthusiastically endorsed (para. 31). The coordination of central policies is to be entrusted to Regional Economic Planning Councils (see chapter 7) and annual (*sic*) meetings of an interdepartmental working party on new towns that had been set up in 1974.

The recommendations that were rejected included the payment of sums to local authorities directly by the DOE. Instead such payments, to ameliorate the financial effects of new town capital expenditure, are to be made by the development corporations themselves under section 3(3) of the 1965 New Towns Act to county councils (para. 48). The DOE did not accept that district councils needed any such support, arguing that their services would not have to be provided in advance of population (para. 49). No alteration was allowed either in the fund-raising arrangements of new towns. It was suggested (para. 38) that the current system of funding through the National Loans Fund provides a stable basis for financial prediction and also that other forms of fund-raising might deflect cash away from 'gilt-edged' government stocks (para. 39). Yet again, scepticism about the techniques and indicators available for setting more detailed social and economic goals was expressed (para. 9), despite the statement in the opening section that more specific objectives than Reith's might now be needed. Various projects had been put in hand, however.

The uncharitable reader of the White Paper might conclude that there is a marked consistency in its responses: only one costs anything over the long run − the once-for-all payment made for some new town local authorities' locally determined schemes in 1976/7 para. 44). All the rest concern either money that is already allocated or will be recovered. Further, no change in departmental staffing or responsibilities is suggested, either centrally or in the regions. The most heartily endorsed recommendations are those involving merely liaison and co-ordination, the costs of which, if not actually nil, are at least invisible.

In April 1977 the Secretary of State announced the outcome of the regional review mentioned in the White Paper (para. 4). The programme was to maintain its momentum for seven or eight years with the twin objectives of an increased emphasis on owner-occupation and taking more of the 'disadvantaged' (HC Debates, vol. 929. cols 1110ff.). Thereafter, however, the new towns' activities were to be curtailed by cutbacks in their target populations. A number of longstanding queries were resolved. There would be no enlargement of the designated areas of Bracknell, Harlow, Skelmersdale or Stevenage, nor expansion of Basildon, Corby, Redditch or Runcorn. The vexed issue of CLNT was also settled — for the time being: it is to continue on a 'much reduced scale' (col. 1114). (Its target population is currently 285,000 by the mid-1980s instead of the original 480,000 by 2001. For details of the revised figures, subsequently announced in July 1977 and particularly affecting the larger active London new towns, see Table 2.)

More details of the review and its rationale emerged in the routine debate on a new towns money bill in July 1977 (HC Debates, vol. 933, cols 392ff.), where the Secretary of State conceded that 90 per cent of inner-city emigrants had not gone to new towns (col. 397) and that the decline in the birthrate would not show up as a decline in household formation for another ten years. Nevertheless, the winding up of eight development corporations was announced. (These were subsequently named as Corby, Stevenage, Harlow, Runcorn, Bracknell, Redditch, Washington and Basildon. See chapter 5 for details of the history of this issue.)

In an unusually lively debate, both government and opposition MPs criticized the incoherence of the new towns policy and the lack of specificity in the proposals to add £500 million to the Public Sector Borrowing Requirement, with an option on another £500 million. The policies of the DI and DHSS in planning and providing new town facilities and services were singled out for comment. Conservative members again expressed the opinion that new town assets should be 'rolled-over', that is that property should be sold or leased and the profits ploughed back into the programme (col. 439). At current rates of interest, many of the development corporations' assets were more like liabilities! As a protest against the lack of detailed proposals for spending the extra cash, the opposition pressed a division. It was won by the government, which had defended the proceedings on the ground that things had always been done this way . . . (col. 460).

The New Towns (Amendment) Act 1976

Thirty years after the first New Towns Act, a major modification to the legislation was introduced by the Minister for Planning and Local Government, John Silkin, the son of Lewis Silkin, who was responsible for the original 1946 measure. The symmetry was not lost on the Commons, and the bill was claimed both to be 'redeeming a pledge of long standing' (HC Debates, vol. 908, col. 244) and a return to the path intended in the visionary days of new towns.

The bill put before parliament was essentially straightforward, covering two issues. A single clause (para. 15) raised the number of board members of a development corporation to a maximum of eleven, plus chairman and deputy chairman. Even the major item, the transfer of rented housing, was dealt with simply. The bill (which applies only to England and Wales) provided that schemes can be prepared to transfer the housing and related assets (i.e. neighbourhood shops, play areas and other open spaces) from the development corporations, or the Commission for the New Towns, to the district council in those towns that are either already transferred to the Commission for the New Towns or where fifteen years have passed since designation or are 'substantially complete' (para. 2(2)). The simplicity of the measure lay in the acceptance of a transfer of outstanding debts and balances rather than any form of sale, so that the council could 'stand in the shoes' of the corporation or commission, in the way that the CNT had recommended to Cullingworth and Karn (1968, p. 50). Such a transfer scheme can be initiated either by the Secretary of State, or, where a town had been designated for at least fifteen years, the corporation and the district council can approach each other and the Secretary of State to initiate a scheme for the transfer of all or part of the housing. Any scheme will be subject to central approval, but where this is withheld, either of the authorities concerned may request renewed consultations after a three-year interval (para. 8). A transfer scheme must also contain details of the arrangements proposed to protect and compensate the new town staff affected (paras 13ff.) and of the period for which the corporation will continue to have some

175

TABLE 2 *Facts and figures on British new towns*

	Date of designation **	Source of designation	City housing need	Housing needs of industry	Regional regeneration	Putting in infrastructure	Land reclamation	Arresting rural depopulation	Original population **	Target population at designation	Subsequent targets	Target population at 31.12.77 †***	Present population **
Aycliffe	19.4.47		✓	✓					60	10,000	1957 20,000 / 1966 45,000	Undecided 45,000	27,500
Basildon	4.1.49	Advisory Committee for London Regional Planning 1946	✓			✓ ?	✓		25,000		1951 80,000 by 1975 / 1960 86,000 / 1967 103,000 by 1976	103,600 / 130,000	91,420
Bracknell	17.6.49		London ✓						5,000	25,000	1961 54,000	55–60,000 / 55–60,000	47,500
Central Lancs New Town	26.3.70		London ✓		✓				234,500	430,000 by 1991	1973 420,000 in 2001	285,000 in mid 80s	248,200
Corby	1.4.50	Local initiative	Manchester	Steel		✓ ?	✓		15,700	40,000	1963 55,000	not estimated / Not estimated 70,000	53,500
Crawley	9.1.47		✓ London						9,100	60,000 by 1965		CNT††	75,500
Cwmbran	4.11.49		London	✓		✓ ?			12,000	55,000		55,000	45,000
Harlow	25.3.47	Greater London Plan 1944	✓						4,500	?	1961 71,000 by 1966	Undecided / Undecided	79,500
Hemel Hempstead	4.2.47	Greater London Plan 1944 (as Redbourn)	London ✓						21,000	60,000	1961 63,500 by 1963	65,000 / 85,000 now CNT	78,500
Milton Keynes	23.1.67	The South-East Study 1964	London ✓						40,000	250,000 by 1990/s		150,000 / 200,000	80,000
Mid Wales (Newtown)	18.12.67	1965 A New Town for mid-Wales 1964	London			✓		✓	5,000	11,500	13,000	11,500 / 13,000	7,900
Northampton	14.2.68	The South-...	✓						133,000	?	1969 230,000 by 1987 / 180,000	173,000 / 180,000	147,000

Town	Date	Local initiative / Study	City					Initial pop.	Target	Target	Target (by 1985)	1985 target
Peterlee	10.3.48	Local initiative / ✓ Mining	London				✓	200	by 1985 25,000		160,000 28,000	
Redditch	10.4.64	✓ ?	✓ Birmingham			✓		32,000	70,000 by 1979		30,000 70,000	27,500 56,000
Runcorn	10.4.64	✓	✓ Liverpool					28,500	70–75,000 by 1979		90,000 71,000 by 1980 90–95,000	57,900
Skelmersdale	9.10.61	Lancashire Development Plan 1956	✓					10,000			52,000 60,000	40,000
Stevenage	11.11.46	Liverpool	✓						70,000 by early 1980s			
Telford	12.12.68	Greater London Plan 1944 Started as Dawley—expanded after 1965 W. Midlands Economic Planning Council report	London ✓		✓			7,000 70,000	? 21,000 70,000	1967 80,000 by 1965 90,000 by 1978 220,000 by late 80s	Both under review 130,000 150,000	74,500 98,500
Warrington	28.4.68		Birmingham ✓		✓	✓		122,300	?		160,000 170,000	135,400
Washington	26.7.64	The North-East Cmnd 2204	Manchester			✓		20,000	65,000 by 1983		65,000 80,000	48,000
Welwyn Garden City and Hatfield	20.5.48	Advisory Committee for London Region Housing 1946	✓ London (Welwyn)	de Havillands (Hatfield)				18,500	36,500	42,000	42,000 50,000 (CNT)	41,000
Cumbernauld	9.12.55	Clyde Valley Plan 1949	✓					8,500	25,000	100,000	25,000 29,000 (CNT) 70,000	26,000
East Kilbride	6.5.47	Clyde Valley Plan 1949	Glasgow ✓		✓ ?			3,000	70,000		70,000	45,600
Glenrothes	30.6.48		Glasgow ✓ Glasgow (mining)					2,400 1,100	82,500 55,000	90,000 70,000	82,000 90,000 55,000 70,000	73,000 35,000

177

TABLE 2 *(continued)*

	Date of designation **	Source of designation	City housing need	Housing needs of industry	Regional regeneration	Putting in infrastructure	Land reclamation	Arresting rural depopulation	Original population **	Target population at designation	Subsequent targets	Target population at 31.12.77 †**	Present population **
Irvine	9.11.66	*Central Scotland: a Programme for Development* 1964	✓		✓ ?				34,600	116,000	120,000	116,000 120,000	57,300
Livingston	16.4.62		Glasgow ✓ Glasgow		✓		✓		2,000	70,000	100,000	70,000 100,000	33,340

† Two figures are given: the first is the population size when planned migration is to stop, the second the projected ultimate population, allowing for natural increase.
†† Handed over to Commission for New Towns.
* Expenditure Committee, 1974, p. 545, and *Town and Country Planning*, February 1976.
** *Town and Country Planning*, February 1978.

nomination rights over the houses (para. 7). This could be either a mutually agreed period, or alternatively five years, or until the cor-poration is wound up. A very broad clause allowed the DOE to make grants to meet any 'undue financial burden' on the district council as a result of the transfer.

Both the policy changes embodied in the bill were broadly accept-able to the two main political parties. Indeed, it was members from the government side who raised objections that the changes in the size of the board did not do enough to meet demands for democracy in development corporations. The Labour member for Hemel Hempstead also called for the abolition of the Commission for New Towns, which he had described in an earlier debate as 'a latter-day feudal baronetcy, invented by the Conservatives to act as a shock absorber between tenants and local democracy' (HC Debates, vol. 892, col. 82). Apart from the rehearsal of familiar local grievances, there was sufficient agreement on the substantive issues in the measure for it to be passed without division.

The passage of the bill, did, however, provide the opportunity for a full-scale party-political dispute over the sale of the new town rented-housing stock (see chapter 5).

New towns in 'other planning situations'?

Part of the remit of the Expenditure Committee was to consider the value of using the New Towns Act in, for example, inner-city redevelopment. This possibility had been raised in another set of hearings on the future of London's docklands (Expenditure Com-mittee, 1974−5b) but the response of the committee was equivocal. They concluded that support and opposition for such a body was equal, but that 'the establishment of a special agency would involve the comparatively lengthy process of a hybrid bill in parliament . . .' (ibid., p. xiii). Their report on new towns made no recommendation on the issue, neither did witnesses devote much attention to it. Those that did adopted predictable stances: the TCPA and New Towns Association in favour, and the Associations of the District and County Councils against. Their arguments were subsumed under the position they had taken on the virtues or vices of develop-ment corporations in existing new towns. The local authority representative did, however, incidentally draw attention to a cluster of legislative changes which will profoundly affect the context in which new town development corporations operate and the justi-fication for their existence. These new developments are the out-come of the Town and Country Planning Act 1971, local govern-ment reorganization in 1974 and the Community Land Act (CLA) 1975.

The 1971 Town and Country Planning Act (consolidating the 1968 Act) introduced a new departure in planning procedures. It attempted to move away from what has been described as 'blue-print' and 'end-state' land-use planning, in which the emphasis was on producing an agreed map of land use for an area, and then ensuring that subsequent development conformed to the plan. Under the new regime, such detailed prescriptions would be left to district councils (in the main) who would prepare local plans for areas in which projects were planned. These local plans would be part of a higher-level, but less-detailed, strategic plan, executed by county authorities, who would not limit themselves to land use, but attempt to set out economic and social objectives with the methods and time-scale of their achievement, too, preferably in conjunction with the Regional Economic Planning Council and other county authorities if relevant. To date (mid-1978) it is difficult to judge the achievement of the new system, as very few of the new-style structure plans have come to the stage of implementation. This process has not been speeded up by the intervening reorganization of the bodies responsible for preparing the plans, nor by the cuts in public spending which have affected staffing. For the new system to be of value, a large volume of social and economic research is implied, together with constructive analysis of the findings. Expenditure cuts will not have helped here either.

When the new planning framework has established itself, there will undoubtedly be pressure for the new town development cor-porations to relate themselves to the local planning mechanisms. Indeed, the idea of an autonomous master-plan as a separate strategy (although, unlike the strategic plan once approved, it has never been a statutory document), and the planning powers of the development corporation forming a 'hole' in the county, may seem anomalous. The DOE issued a circular (7/74) drawing attention to the need for compatibility between the plans, but how this may be brought about remains to be seen.

Local-government reorganization is closely linked with the operation of the new planning system. It will have a more funda-mental impact on the new towns through its unification of local government units in new town areas. Most designated areas are now coterminous with a district, or are part of one. Liaison between the development corporation and the local authorities will become more coherent, but where relations are poor, the opposition will be capable of unified action. It is unlikely that the transfer of the housing stock could have been contemplated in the pre-existing situation, but it is also clear that the district councils are now more able to flex their muscles as they have in the case of commercial industrial assets, although in vain. It is less easy to defend the idea of development corporations than it was when the designated area was divided between a motley collection of small and impoverished rural and urban district councils.

The reorganization has already produced some difficulties of a different kind where, for instance, counties have lost a more affluent part of their area, as has occurred for Buckinghamshire, and thus find themselves with a smaller revenue base. Changes in the powers of local authorities have complicated some relationships. In Northampton the town has become a county district and thus lost some of the functions it had as a county borough. These included education and some planning powers, so that the dyadic partnership with the development corporation has become a triad, to the regret of the general manager, at least (Expenditure Committee, 1974−5a, p. 799).

By far the most significant piece of legislation for new towns would appear to be the Community Land Act 1975. The intention behind this measure is that betterment value (i.e. the difference between the value of land in its existing use and with permission to develop) should accrue to the community. This is to be achieved by the application of a Development Land Tax at increasingly penal rates and by awarding to local authorities the power to acquire land net of tax, either for their own use or to sell to developers. In principle, this gives to local authorities even greater advantages in land acquisition than that which the new town development corporations have enjoyed since 1946, and which has been a pivotal element in their national and international reputation. District councils will be able to acquire more land more cheaply, turn their share of the profit (the Treasury has the other part) to community good, and build up a lucrative land-bank. Apparently a development corporation would become redundant.

Likely practice is expected to be different from the theory, at least for a few years to come. The structure of local authorities will not be altered, nor will the direct political pressures upon them, which are absent in a development corporation. New towns also have a fund of experience in acquiring, managing and developing land, while it was found in 1975 that over half of the district councils in England and Wales did not have any valuation staff of their own, and had to use the district valuer. Eddison (1976) suggested that the enforced contact between the finance, planning, legal, estates and housing departments should bring about greater competence and flexibility, but it will not occur instantaneously. In the meantime, local authorities will continue to be vertically, rather than horizontally, integrated and responsible to a number of semi-autonomous committees. Eddison was optimistic that the CLA will give an impetus to the integration of local and structure plans, but that too

181

will take time.

Despite the sweeping powers that the CLA confers on the local authorities, they will be more hamstrung than development corporations by the existence of 'excepted sites'. These, which include owner-occupied houses and gardens up to an acre and certain other uses, are the subject of a slower process of objection and inquiry than under the new town development corporation's powers in its designated area. Any town-centre area that is either among the most valuable for development, or most in need of renewal, will be 'pepper-potted' with such sites. For the time being the DOE is encouraging the district councils to concentrate on sites which are easier to acquire and develop (and show the efficacy of the CLA), which will tend to be at the edge of urban areas. A major DOE circular (26/76) on the 'acquisition, management and disposal' of land for private development under the CLA laid considerable stress on the need to cultivate good relations between local authorities and builders, and the desirability of 'keeping to a minimum' the period for which land is held, hopefully showing a profit within two-to-three years. Building up land-banks and the over-zealous use of compulsory purchase orders was specifically discouraged, although it might be thought that both are crucial to the overall goal of community benefit, both financial and otherwise. It has also been said that many land-owners may refuse to sell, in the hope that any future Conservative government would repeal the CLA.

Finally, as ever, there is a cash problem. The money for the local authorities to buy land is to come from central government funds. The total set aside for 1976—7 was a mere £31·3 million, and the 'Land Fund' to which the Treasury's share of profit will go was not officially (in 1976) expected to be in profit until 1983. The December 1976 public expenditure cuts further restricted the funds available for purchasing in 1977—8 to £35 million instead of the expected £76 million, although the figure for 1978/9 was £100 million. Limitations upon the cash available, upon the use of any profit for further purchases, and the instructions not to use the more radical powers that the Act bestows upon them, suggest that local authorities will be at a disadvantage to new town development corporations for some time to come. It is, however, significant that the city of Sheffield has embarked upon a large-scale comprehensive development at Mossborough using the CLA and its existing housing powers. In the event, no doubt, the future use of development corporations as agencies will depend less on principles of accountability and democracy than on demographic and economic change. The recent review of the new towns policy was understood by many members of the public to be the ending of the programme. This is hardly the case. Savings have been made in money not yet spent on population which has not been born. (Real savings for 1979/80 are only expected to be around £20 million – an insignificant sum, HC Debates, vol. 929, col. 1114.) Further dramatic changes in the birthrate may yet result in the rediscovery of the new towns.

9 What is the 'new towns policy'?

> They have caught the eye and imagination of architects and planners, and many others, all over the world. They are visited and photographed, admired and disparaged, praised and criticized by thousands of people every year. The architecture has been described as dull, drab and visually-uninspired. But illustrations of development in London's new towns adorn every substantial book on planning (Thomas, 1969a, p. 373).

The British new towns are the subject of both public curiosity and self-congratulation. The DOE, the TCPA and members of parliament refer frequently to their international reputation. New town annual reports routinely give a roll-call of their visitors with their diverse and colourful origins. Students of architecture, planning, sociology, geography, social policy and social work are keen to visit them, read about them and write about them. Even members of the lay public, as the writer well knows, are almost equally ready to discuss the new towns, although their eyes tend to glaze over if a detailed distinction is made between towns built under the New Towns Acts, inner-city redevelopment and peripheral local authority housing estates – crucial though the distinction is for the topic under discussion, which is usually employment (or its lack), travel facilities and costs or the reputation of high-density/high-rise public housing. Despite this widespread interest in the new towns, few people realize how many new towns there are and are surprised to hear Northampton or Runcorn called a 'new town'. Thomas (1969b, p. 811) remarks that the non-London new towns have an 'indistinct and cloudy image', and goes on to say that many people do not know even how to pronounce Cwmbran or Glenrothes.

Publicly, both government and others interested in the new towns tend to refer to the British new towns as the outcome of a unified policy. One of the many valuable insights that the Expenditure Committee hearings of 1973–5 produced was, however, that not even the DOE sees the new towns in this way:

> It will be evident that the new towns were not conceived as, and do not constitute a single programme so much as a series of programmes resulting from decisions taken at a number of points since 1964 (Expenditure Committee, 1974, p. 3).

The unapologetic tone of this, the DOE's main submission to the first sitting of the Select Committee, suggests that the *ad hoc* developments are seen retrospectively as a form of flexibility and adaptation to change. It is one of the main contentions of this book that, on the contrary, it has resulted in a regrettable lack of clarity about what objective or objectives were being pursued, a set of policies with centrifugal tendencies and the dilution of a truly visionary social programme.

Attitudes and mechanisms

It is not currently fashionable to explain social structure or social policy in terms of individual personality or actions, but no account of the new towns policy is possible without recognizing certain key figures. Ebenezer Howard produced an idea that was both inspiring and apparently within reach. F. J. Osborn had devoted nearly all his very long life to keep the idea of garden cities, and then new towns, on the political agenda. Frank Schaffer administered first the New Towns Division of the (then) Ministry of Housing and, later, the Commission for the New Towns. His book *The New Town Story* (1972) is a widely used source as, of course, are several of Osborn's publications. A crucial figure in the evolution of new towns as a part of the social policy of successive governments was Evelyn (now Lady) Sharp, Permanent Secretary in charge of the Ministry of Housing for an unprecedented period from the early 1950s until her retirement in 1966. Richard Crossman (1975) wrote vividly of her commitment to the new towns, although his account should be interpreted with a little caution, since the two clearly had a volatile relationship. He suggests that Evelyn Sharp did not credit local government with the foresight or skill to execute a similar policy. 'I am sure that at the back of the Dame's mind is the idea that unless the Ministry runs and controls the new building, the local authorities will fall down on the job . . .' (*ibid.*, p. 307). An essay by Lady Sharp herself reinforces this impression:

> The one question was whether the local authorities might not
> take the job on; but it was plainly beyond their financial
> competence. Further, their rate-payers seldom want to see a
> new town built around them — at any price . . . only deter-
> mined government action and under-writing by government
> money could secure them (Sharp, 1972, p. 41).

This belief in central direction is fitting for a senior civil servant
whose dedication to state service Crossman also writes about (1975,
p. 616). Holding the post of Permanent Secretary presumably made
it possible to take a 'macro' view of the nation's problems and their
solution. No doubt from that perspective the local authorities'
complaints must have seemed parochial and petty-minded.
Schaffer's writing is also permeated by a slight impatience with the
grumbles of local politicians. He is, for example, quite unconvinced
that democracy in development corporations need be any more
direct than by means of the accountability of the board to the
minister and of the government to the electorate at large.

For whatever reason, the DOE has resisted the claims of new
town local authorities to be treated as a discrete interest group in the
formulation of new towns policy. The parties concerned seemed
rather to have been defined as the government, the development
corporations, employers and residents, even if the last have been
treated as an abstraction. Although there has been not one policy,
but several, decisions have been based on the new towns in relation
to the ministry and each other, not to their local political context.
The representatives of the local authorities expressed their
grievance about this to the Select Committee very bluntly:

> 'We have tried communicating by writing letters and lobbying
> M.P.'s; we have tried all the normal democratic ways . . .
> They are resting entirely on their laurels, "we do not
> recognize this Association" ' (Expenditure Committee, 1974,
> p. 177).

During the 1958 debates on the proposed Commission for the
New Towns, the Conservative government had expressed the view
that the role of local government was essentially a limited one: to
provide services. It would not be appropriate for it to venture
further into the ownership or management of property (HC
Debates, vol. 596, col. 848). Despite Labour's heated rejection of
this view at that time, and Crossman's liking for local democracy,
expressed through his preference for expanded towns rather than
new town corporations (1975, p. 307), successive governments have
held back from any devolution of new town development. The programme remains administered by people with commitment to the

overall view and central control, and this conception was endorsed by the Expenditure Committee.

Belief in a programme is not by itself enough. Resources are needed for effective monitoring and direction. As we have seen, the lack of interdepartmental co-ordination at central government level, complained of from time to time in new town annual reports, was roundly condemned by the Expenditure Committee. Anyone who takes an interest in new town policy soon becomes aware that, notwithstanding the orgy of self-congratulation that the new towns produce in public debates, the new towns have never been of much interest to central government. Whether this is because they have not delivered housing on a sufficiently large scale, are thought to be too expensive or are simply not sufficiently 'political' is difficult to interpret. It is sometimes asserted that the Conservative government was ready to let the first round of designations run their course and then allow the policy quietly to disappear. The cynical might feel that the new towns were saved then by the international interest they had aroused. Latterly their potential profitability may have had more to do with their survival.

A major consequence of the peripheral importance attached to the new towns had been the shortage of resources in the New Towns Division of the DOE, which is said to be both isolated and over-burdened. McKinsey remarked on this in their written evidence to the Expenditure Committee:

> we have been struck by the consistency with which people in widely differing positions in the new towns have commented on the extreme pressure on the Directorate − pressure that makes it extremely difficult for it to 'stand back' and perform a critical evaluation role (Expenditure Committee, 1974, p. 644).

Until very recently the division's control of new town policy was through detailed project-by-project approvals, so that the lack of a flow of statistical and other research data on the new towns in any centralized and compendious way is hardly surprising. (There was a research and intelligence unit at the inception of the policy, but it was rationalized out of existence in the late 1940s when public-spending cuts and a clash of personalities coincided.) An MP complained in a 1975 debate on the new towns that information on them was 'even slower and more painful' to obtain than on other topics (HC Debates, vol. 892, col. 78). Anyone who has carried out research or teaching on the new towns will be compelled to agree with him.

Staffing and resources in the New Towns Division are not yet much increased. In 1973 a system of management accounts was introduced for the new towns, with the aim first of allowing the development corporations more flexibility and autonomy to work within a set of performance criteria. Second, they were intended to provide the DOE with a tool to evaluate the new towns' performance and profitability, rather than merely to tot up what had been done. The *Report* of the Expenditure Committee comments that the accounts are 'of use, but only within a limited concept of New Town development – a concept suggesting that the whole exercise is one of optimising . . . the physical objectives of providing a town of a certain size at a certain speed' (1974–5a, p. xxxv). But even with this crucial reservation, 'witnesses questioned whether D.O.E. made the best possible use of the Accounts' (*ibid.*).

> The staff responsible for the control of expenditure are architects by professional training although they are assisted by an accountant in the Finance Directorate. . . . The Welsh Office . . . informed us that the analysis of the Accounts was in the hands of planners 'who of necessity apply a layman's approach to the subject . . .' (*ibid.*, p. xxxix).

This was because the necessary expertise was 'not available'. As we have seen, (chapter 8) the need for more appropriately skilled staff was conceded in the DOE's response to the Expenditure Committee. They will be needed. In 1977 the spending limit was raised by £500 million to £2,750 million – with an option on another £500 million within the two-year period currently customary between New Town Money Bills. To keep the Directorate fully occupied, new towns are now required to make quarterly financial returns.

Research and intelligence on and in new towns has, because of the lack of a central capacity, been carried out in the towns individually, and a parallel lack of spare resources has prevented any correlation of the mass of data potentially available from them. In 1970 the new town chairmen's conference set up a permanent secretariat called the New Towns Association to service their standing committee: 'for the purpose of pooling information and considering joint action on matters of common interest' (Schaffer, 1972, p. 64). It is a shoestring operation not, apparently, equipped for or geared to research, nor to sharing information with outsiders. The financing of the Town and Country Planning Association is hardly lavish either, but it has had to fill the vacuum left by official bodies. Its digest of new town statistics, published yearly in the February edition of *Town and Country Planning,* is an invaluable source of descriptive data on the new towns. The editorial content of the journal consists of brief articles geared to the interested layman. Their range has widened in recent years, particularly into issues of the countryside, the regions, natural resources and similar issues abroad. On the new towns, *Town and Country Planning* remains resolutely propagandist and even missionary – and why not? The Association is, after all, one of the most effective pressure groups operating openly in this country. Given its vested interest, though, it has been to the detriment of constructive criticism of the new towns that the systematic production of statistical data, articles and even books has been left almost entirely to the Association. Such is the commitment of many prominent members of the TCPA to the new towns movement, that detached comment or attempts to clarify concepts have been interpreted at best as irrelevant, or even as destructive criticism. Not untypically, the reviewer of Ray Pahl's influential *Whose City?* (1970) lambasted him for 'aloof professionalism', under the heading 'Where are the social reformers?' More recently, the eminent reviewer of the TCPA's own collection *New Towns: The British Experience* (Evans, 1972) felt compelled to recant in a subsequent letter. The TCPA's unique position has even led to its journal being described as 'official' by a new town development corporation (East Kilbride DC, 1969, p. 53)! They cannot be alone in their misunderstanding.

In this climate it is hardly surprising that fundamental questions about the concept, direction and future of new towns have seldom been raised, let alone discussed. Both the TCPA and the DOE have, as the Expenditure Committee vividly illustrated, seen the new towns as essentially the physical outcomes of a physical conception, embodied in the master-plan. Maps and photographs are a tellingly indispensable (and of course fascinating) element of *Town and Country Planning*, new town plans and the annual reports. In both employment and industrial development, progress is often dealt with quite apart from the 'social aspects', which are themselves often interpreted in purely demographic terms or as a catalogue of facilities and organizations.

The genius of the TCPA for gathering support from all shades of the political spectrum has been commented on earlier in this book, and also by Foley (1962) in his paper on the history of the Association. We have also seen that, apart from some rather stylized confrontations about the ownership of new town assets, the definition of the new towns policy as outside the party political arena has somehow survived, perhaps aided by the covert lack of interest in them by most central government departments. Neither the administrative nor the professional staff of the DOE are likely to wish to politicize the issues involved, and the TCPA is apparently unable to see them as the subject of possible controversies over social or political philosophies and goals. Part of the explanation for the lack of debate must lie in British town planning's definition of its operations as drawing their justification from a world of apolitical and universal verities. Another Foley paper (1960) describes the profession as having at least three definitions of its objective and describes this 'ideological ambivalence' as an 'adaptive mechanism'. New towns fall within the third and broadest of these ideologies:

> as part of a broader social programme . . . responsible for providing the physical basis for better urban community life; the main ideals toward which town planning is to strive are *a*. the provision of low density residential areas *b*. the fostering of local community life and *c*. the control of conurbation growth (*ibid.*, p. 218).

The continuing ability of town planners to see their function as one of tidying up the environment, using techniques that do not involve value judgment, is explained by Ruth Glass (1959) as stemming from the disciplines from which planning draws recruits. These, including surveying, engineering, architecture and geography, draw on essentially linear models of cause and effect, which lead to an over-simplified interpretation of social life and the city as a system. Since that paper was written, disciplines with more emphasis on the complexity of the social world and the pervasiveness of political choice (not necessarily in any party sense) have been more closely associated with the planning profession and its education programmes, but it is too soon for their influence to be extensively felt in the evaluation of policy from within. In 1969 the 'official' line was still that planning is not a political affair. This was expressed memorably by the Skeffington Report (MHLG, 1969) on public participation in planning, which declared that although they had been 'urged to recommend that the public should be involved from the start in the broad aims or goals that the community wish to see achieved. We doubt the necessity for that in this country' (para. 136). Any notion of 'pluralist' or even advocacy planning in Britain was thus rejected.

Whatever the taken-for-granted quality of the perspective of the new towns' proponents, it cannot be denied that their insulation from local and central government horsetrading must have had advantages both for the towns themselves, and for the New Towns Division. The mechanisms for building new towns was recommended by the Reith committee (New Towns Committee, 1946a, b, c) at a time when national unity seemed real and central control both natural and desirable. When the community of adversity disintegrated as peace was established, there was, as we have seen, no inclination to alter the structure of new town administration. For a long time, new town designations were not accessible to parliamentary debate. In 1964 a Private Member's Bill made it possible for parliament to annul a designation order within forty sitting days – but only if the local planning authority was among the objectors (Schaffer, 1972, p. 45). Even this limited power is diluted by the fact that no future proposed new town is likely to get to that late stage without extensive agreement with the local authorities concerned. The DOE's reluctance to become involved in setting and monitoring social objectives for the new towns was clearly not only based on scepticism about the possibilities of doing so, and the fear of not having the resources available even to attempt it, but also on a half-explicit acknowledgment that such issues have more apparent political dimensions than the pseudo-objectivity of the physical master-plan approach. Thus the tendency not to acknowledge the political content of the new towns policy becomes complementary to the lack of resources within the responsible section of the DOE. Too many parliamentary debates or questions, let alone a full-blown party political spectacular, would overstretch those resources intolerably – and the same is true of the TCPA if it felt impelled to step up its lobbying. For all the Select Committee's recommendations about the DOE's need for more resources, more skill and a change of attitude, it too made no recommendation that would subject new town administration to more public scrutiny – only that the policy-making should be more *technically* capable.

New town development corporations are not electorally accountable bodies. This aspect of their structure was not popular with either major party when the New Towns Act 1946 was being debated, but it was accepted, on the assumption that the corporations would be short-lived. It was also assumed that local government boundary changes would be made so that the new town would operate within a unified area, providing both ease of administration and coherent representation for the residents. As earlier chapters have shown, this rationalization of boundaries has only recently and coincidentally occurred. It is hard to think that such an untidy structure can have aided the provision of amenities or services, yet there appears to have been no pressure from the corporations for any large-scale revisions. Presumably the diffusion of political control and pressure with the possibility of 'divide and rule' must have entered into the new towns' calculations. The ministry clearly felt little need to make development corporations more a part of the local political structure, and continues to resist direct nominations from local authorities or election to the board. As we have seen, the necessity of development corporations has been turned into a virtue, even by such unlikely allies as the London Boroughs Association (Expenditure Committee, 1974, pp. 343ff.). The Select Committee showed no inclination to modify this aspect

191

of new towns practice either, thus endorsing the bias towards pursuing effectiveness rather than accountability.

So it has come about that a web of persons and circumstances has kept the new towns apart from party-political debate, or even from discussion about the social philosophy of their objectives. This lack of evaluation from without and within has allowed the perpetuation of contradictions within the policy and even their compounding as other elements of the political and economic situation have affected the new towns. The decisions were indeed 'taken at a number of points' (1974, p. 3) and some of the most critical ones were not aimed directly at the new towns. Those that were seem to have been based on commonsensical notions about society and the economy and/or to have been dominated by short-run expedients.

New town designation itself, even after thirty years, follows no standard procedure of evaluation and costing, as the Expenditure Committee made painfully clear. Proposals have arisen primarily from housing demands, spurred on by demographic projections. The second generation of new towns was designated to meet a rising population and thus a shortfall of housing, which it was assumed to be beyond the capacity of the local authorities to remedy. An additional rationale came from the unverified theory of 'growth points'. But why were the sites themselves chosen? Some choices were subjected to careful analysis, like those recommended in *The South East Study* (MHLG, 1964). In addition to looking for the basic requirements of having water supply, drainage, good communications, and not being on (too much) prime agricultural land, the searchers based their efforts on locating towns capable of doubling their size, and the mapping of hinterlands. Even in such an 'objective' framework, however, Milton Keynes bears a close resemblance to the pre-existing North Bucks new town proposal – 'Pooleyville' after the influential county planner, Fred Pooley. Since it is doubtful that any development in the South East over the last thirty years could have been a total failure, the effectiveness of the elusive decision-making on some designations has not been put to the test.

Outside the South East, the lack of prior evaluation has been more visible. Even Cumbernauld, sanctified by the Clyde Valley Plan (Abercrombie, 1949), famous for its lack of neighbourhoods and for its use of a high-density, high-rise plan for the town centre, has been roundly condemned for its siting, by no less than a leading member of the TCPA (Whittick, 1970). Latterly, economic problems have been more pressing, as in Telford, where the thinking seemed to be based on a 'growth-point' strategy, but with no parallel commitment from the departments concerned with public infrastructure and the direction of industry. Telford also shared with Warrington a massive burden of industrial dereliction. Astonishingly, the cost of its clearance seems not to have been assessed. Crossman says of Dawley (later Telford): 'Money could have been no object in [Evelyn Sharp's] mind since it will cost a fortune to turn this into a modern urban area' (1975, p. 307) − an observation which has particular piquancy in view of Lady Sharp's own insistence that new towns should be chosen in the light of their potential for economic success (1972, p. 42)! When the DOE were examined by the Expenditure Committee, Warrington was discussed:

> there must have been a very considerable investigation as to whether it was really worthwhile financially?

> There was an investigation of the broad financial picture, but at that stage it is extremely difficult to get it right. . . . What I am trying to say is that there were other considerations than financial ones which probably determined the choice of Warrington (Expenditure Committee, 1974, p. 24).

In time, the perspicacity behind choosing difficult rather than cheap sites may well be revealed, but it is extraordinary that powerful arguments to back such a leap of faith were not marshalled for use if needed.

These two examples are far from unusual, because, as we have seen, a detailed rationale has often followed rather than preceded designation. Where consultants have been drafted in, one suspects that on some occasions their role was of legitimation through their independent status, rather than to undertake a radical evaluation of the whole proposal. Levin (1976) writes in detail about the new town designation mechanism. He lays particular emphasis on the non-rational elements in the process, and his view is the more interesting given his earlier work, which rested on the assumption that such events could be described as a logical sequence of positive decisions − if only the researcher would put in the effort. In *Government and the Planning Process,* Levin compares the decisions to embark on Central Lancashire new town (CLNT) and to extend the expansion scheme at Swindon. Much of their respective histories are explained in terms of individuals' and groups' 'commitment' to policies, producing a definition of the situation which will then determine both their view of relevant information and the use to which it is put. It thus becomes very difficult to contemplate redirection and reappraisal, because both self-esteem and resources are at stake. Levin goes on to detail the 'strategies' (*ibid.,* pp. 40ff.) that generate commitment. These include personal or group acts or attitudes, which he classifies under espousal, the undertaking, and the public or semi-public declaration. All these are particularly important in local and central party politics, much of which centres on charges and counter-charges about declarations.

Commitment is also established by the application of sequential administrative processes, goodwill, effort, time and staff. When, as now, economic stringencies have made many projects a zero-sum, there will be considerable resistance to the cost of modifying a strategy. The alternatives will be seen as abandoning it, or carrying through the original conception, however dubiously arrived at. Abandonment will cause personal loss of face and the embarrassment of resources devoted to the production of nothing. CLNT is a particularly choice example of these processes, but other new towns could doubtless be interpreted in the same way. Stonehouse, on the other hand, is an example of the political costs of continuing outweighing those of calling a halt — especially since the agency was the still-active East Kilbride Development Corporation, which would simply continue as before. Levin makes the valuable observation that new town designation is especially unfitted to the simultaneous evaluation of alternative strategies because it is a 'single proposal statutory procedure' (*ibid.*, p. 49) which

> may lead to alternatives being penalized not only by virtue of the delay that becomes attached to them, but also by virtue of the investment of effort and the multiple clearance involved in formulating the original proposal and putting it through the procedural hoops.

Similar procedures have to be gone through for major extensions to the designated area of a town, hence the débâcle over the future of Stevenage and Harlow. First proposed for expansion, together with Basildon, in *The South East Study*, Stevenage provoked, through the rise in population, the 'Hertfordshire rebellion'. The residents, the local authorities and members of parliament were ranged on one side and the development corporation and ministry on the other. Crossman (1975, p. 66) declared in his diary, just before the public inquiry in 1965, 'and of course Stevenage is right', but no decision was taken. Local opposition in Stevenage and a new downward trend in population forecasts helped to keep both Stevenage and Harlow in limbo. Stevenage was without a masterplan between 1958 and 1966, when limited expansion to 80,000 was agreed. Major extension to 150,000 was again proposed in the early 1970s (it was this which had provoked the rebellion) and accepted by the ministry in January 1974. This was quickly followed by another instruction to limit development to 1,000 acres (Stevenage DC, 1974, p. 400) and then to prepare proposals for a target 100,000 people by the 1990s (*ibid.*, 1975, p. 374). Harlow corporation remarked in 1974: 'The need for expansion is beyond question. That it should have been under consideration in various forms for twelve years has led to criticism and uncertainty' (Harlow DC, 1974, p. 154). The definitive decision – to do nothing – was finally announced in 1977 (HC Debates, vol. 929, col. 1110). Both will be wound up in 1980. Clearly the designation of new towns is a cumbersome and rather rigid process. The absence of coherent higher order goals for the policy and of routine procedures of evaluating alternative strategies has not helped towards the production of an integrated programme. What has emerged has the appearance of a collection of more or less successful pet projects – and a Boot Hill of failed hunches which could not be quickly rethought or replaced because of the slowness of the legitimation process: Llantrisant, Ipswich, the GLC's project at Hook in Hampshire, Manchester's at Lymm and Moberly. CLNT is not, after all, to join them, but is consigned to the living death of having its expansion target cut to 27 per cent of the original.

Incremental and haphazard decision-taking – or non-decision – has figured in other parts of the new towns programme. As we have seen, the constraints on house-building and the composition of the new town housing stock produced rent levels that were high, compared with similar local authority housing. Gradually the new towns were able to cross-subsidize their newer from their older housing, and many introduced rebate schemes. No move was apparently made by central government either to monitor or to intervene in this situation, although the (intended) NETS hurdles to new town housing were heightened by the high rents, and effectively debarred many of the most needy. NETS itself in its various forms was criticized extensively by the new towns and the exporting authorities, yet in that crucial area of the new towns philosophy of homes and jobs together, no major central initiative was taken, either to streamline NETS, or to make it more widely known.

The Expenditure Committee hearings brought out very clearly that not only are other statutory agencies involved in the planning and building of a new town, but that they contribute a large proportion of the public spending. At present this can be over 80 per cent of current expenditure and 30 to 40 per cent of capital expenditure. Nevertheless the DOE consistently refused until 1976 to produce guidelines to help development corporations in their frequent 'who should pay for what' disputes, leading to delays, acrimony and an expensive waste of staff time and other resources. Even then, the help consisted only in advocating the formulation of rolling resource programmes (Cmnd 6616, 1976). There seems, in addition, to have been no attempt to encourage other central departments to take account of new town developments in their own planning, or to produce a formula for compromise where, as for example with the DI and its policies over the assisted areas, objectives might diverge. The New Towns Division's lack of resources and status may account for this.

The decisions that show the most striking lack of careful thinking-through must surely be those taken by the Labour government between 1966 and 1970. (Their perpetuation and amplification by the Conservatives thereafter can at least be rationalized, if not necessarily defended, by their consistency with a belief in market mechanisms.) A policy of owner-occupation was announced, with a target of 50 per cent ownership in England and Wales and 25 per cent in Scotland. Little account appears to have been taken of the composition, the price and the mortgageability of the new town housing stock. The figure of 50 per cent seems to have been crude extrapolation from the national trend in house ownership, ignoring the much more varied price and type of housing available overall, and the routes by which people enter and move through the housing market. When Cullingworth and Karn (1968) produced their conclusions, the latent unfulfilled desire for house ownership that they had uncovered in the new towns was taken as a *post facto* justi-fication of the initial policy decision. Their equally important analysis of how few new town residents would actually be able to afford to buy their houses, or would recast themselves as potential home-owners was overlooked, and the policy of selling the rented stock got off to a very slow start. The Conservative government paid heed to the advice and offered the houses at a substantial dis-count, which helped to fuel an explosion of house prices. By 1974 there were growing waiting lists, to the discomfiture of both parties. The incoming Labour administration stopped the sales, remarking rather smugly in the 1974 Consultation document (DOE, 1974) that the Conservative government had 'tipped the balance for the time being too strongly in favour of owner occupation' (para. 3.14). Yet in no case had more than 30 per cent of the rented stock been sold (*ibid.*) and in most towns it was far less. In the older towns it was only possible to raise the level of owner-occupation by selling rented houses, as the Labour government itself had acknowledged. What they criticized in 1974 was probably the consequence of what they had themselves tried, and failed to bring about before 1970. Ironically, when sales were curtailed, the development corpora-tions found themselves without a significant source of revenue, upon which they had based some of their plans and forecasts. No additional cash or advice seems to have been forthcoming from the DOE however, so yet again a decision had been taken without its wider implications and consequences being assessed.

The Labour government also announced a greater emphasis on the use of private capital in the new towns, which undoubtedly has a logic in times of economic expansion. In a static economy, however, the lack of public investment will affect towns differentially, yet the same policy was apparently applied to all. The differences in amenities and employment prospects which already existed between the Midlands and South East new towns and those elsewhere were exacerbated on the principle, amply demonstrated in the new towns programme, that nothing suceeds like success.

Other aspects of new town finance were even more contradictory. The evidence to the Select Committee contains quite explicit statements that the pushing of development corporations towards private and institutional finance, before their reliability as an investment was proven, led to the use of devices such as lease and lease-back. In some cases this produced a situation where a greater proportion of the profit went to the private sector than had been hoped, largely because the development corporations had little choice between the terms offered by the investor or the traditionally rigid framework of government lending – if central funds were available at all. And this at a time when the financial potential of the new towns programme was becoming both the major justification of its existence and a central preoccupation of the towns themselves.

Both the Consultation documents (DOE, 1974; Scottish Office, 1975) and the Report of the Expenditure Committee (1974/5a) laid considerable stress on the advantages of living in a new town being available to a wide cross-section of the population. We have seen that the Expenditure Committee urged that steps be taken to facilitate this, and that the active London new towns have been instructed so to do. To be effective, however, implies an increased programme of rented housing with vacant stock available to respond to urgent nominations of those in need, and particularly the commitment of all the local statutory agencies to a greater provision of social and other services. In chapter 8 it was shown that the DOE's help in doing this consisted more of encouraging words than cash on the table. Such payments as development corporations may make are to be to the capital spending of counties, and that funded from their existing budgets.

Overall, therefore, it is not difficult to illustrate the DOE's own declaration that there has not been a unified new towns policy. The key question is whether there were a number of policies developed to meet special problems and situations or whether the 'policies' were the coming together of reactive, unrelated and incremental decision-making. The evidence points to the second interpretation.

197

The changing ideology of the new towns

It is often assumed that the new towns policy has been explicitly concerned with reconstructing the social order, and in particular with the redistribution of wealth. A brief review of the new towns movement and later national policy throws some doubt on whether this was ever true or could be true in future without radical changes in administration and attitudes.

The original garden city projects, at Letchworth and Welwyn, were of course privately financed. Cheaper housing was provided by subsidiary companies and private investors, but the whole venture depended entirely upon voluntary initiative and voluntary migration. Both Ebenezer Howard and F. J. Osborn had been Fabian socialists in their youth, but the legacy of this was an egalitarian concern for the welfare of all people, whatever their social position. It did not extend to changing relativities of wealth and status. The garden cities would merely be a medium for a more healthy life for all. Howard's original scheme envisaged a minimum of central government control, once the reticulation of new towns was established and the great cities were in their inexorable decline. The garden cities movement between the wars was, as we have seen, decentralized and individualist with respect to discussions of the social planning that should go into their organization. Osborn continually scoffed at those who wanted to impose 'community' life on migrants to new towns and new estates. At the same time, however, the TCPA and other groups committed to the idea of new towns were willing to see state intervention on a massive scale, in order to bring the programme about. Rigorous control of land, industrial development, housing and population movement – and by implication the autonomy of individuals and local government – were espoused as the means to the individualist destination.

For a brief period after the Second World War, social policy was formulated as if the nation was one monolithic interest group. Coalition government and a degree of common purpose made radical and comprehensive social programmes seem feasible. The traditional order of status and deference was upset. Centralized socialism was the order of the day. Charges of both naïvety and of architectural determinism are sometimes levelled at the new towns movement and at the Reith committee for their belief that a garden and some sunshine would bring about a social revolution. This is both more and less than the truth. The protagonists of the new towns movement between the wars, and particularly the TCPA, were, it is true, obsessed with the quality of the environment, but for them garden cities were very much a solution to health problems. (We simply forget that rickets and tuberculosis were still major urban scourges, and that today, too, many people's health would be drastically improved by a better house in a better climate.) Social revolution was not on their agenda. After the war massive social change was expected, and was being legislated for in other welfare state programmes. The Reith committee can probably be better interpreted as seeing in new towns a receptacle for the new world of equality of opportunity rather than radical redistribution of wealth. Their naïvety, which is all too easy to identify thirty years on, was to expect the changes in the social structure and social processes quickly to come about.

The mood was of collectivism, but the only aspect of new towns legislation that specifically embodied it was the concentration on new towns' being centrally chosen, centrally funded and centrally controlled. The powers of development corporations themselves, especially over land assembly, would have been considered intolerably radical before the war. Indeed, even the controversial Community Land Act 1975 is equivocal in comparison (and becoming more so). As we have seen, however, the problems of economic instability soon overtook the new social programmes. By the end of the 1940s the crucial choice had to be made as to whether housing need or employment status should have primacy in the allocation of new town houses, since the economy simply could not produce a flow of jobs to match the flat-out production of new town houses. A determination not to repeat the inter-war errors of public housing triumphed, so that the economic inequalities of the nation were reproduced in the new towns. Again, it is easy to mock now when the less attractive consequences of these decisions are working themselves through, but what value would there have been in building dormitory settlements in the middle of nowhere?

After the early 1950s, new town policy became essentially passive. For a time there was a confidence that poverty and gross inequality were being abolished by a combination of the welfare state and economic expansion. Positive redistribution seemed an irrelevance. As the two main political parties have moved towards one another, Labour embracing the mixed economy and the Tories willing to accept extensive central direction of both capital and labour, the new towns have become an excellent example of what Pahl and Winkler (1974) have described as the 'corporate state'. The characteristics of this include order, unity and 'success', interpreted through ends (primarily economic) rather than means. Issues would increasingly be defined as apolitical, and the only party divergence would be over the 'extent of their commitment to a goal of egalitarian redistribution of incomes' (*ibid.,* p. 75).

The Expenditure Committee instructed the DOE to find ways of making the new towns more accessible to the 'disadvantaged', implying a renewal or perhaps creation of a redistributive goal for the new towns policy. Similar claims have been made for the 1976 New Towns (Amendment) Act, which moves towards a slightly less centralized conception of new towns, although cash and initiatives are still flowing from the centre. More than mere direct nomination is needed, however. Most of the policy changes and trends in the last fifteen years have been towards perpetuating regional and individual economic disparities.

New town rents, the changing structure of employment and consequent composition of mobile industry constricted entry to new towns. Current recommendations to overcome these tendencies include attracting a wider variety of employment, especially unskilled service jobs and industrial retraining. The latter can only be described as an old chestnut of a solution, given the scarcity of places on these courses and the risks that individuals must accept in order to make the leap. Moving to and living in a new town remains an expensive business which suggests that more comprehensive solutions are needed than importing a few more low-wage jobs. One strategy would involve providing plenty of part-time employment for women and day-care facilities for pre-school children to enable women's wages to raise household incomes. Day-care is not, however, a paying proposition and current DOE instructions are that all corporation projects must pay their way . . .

The ambitious private enterprise new town of Columbia in Maryland at least attempted a novel exercise in producing alternative social strategies. Instead of extrapolating from existing structures and services (so many schools, parks, libraries and telephone boxes) as *The Needs of New Communities* (CHAC, 1967) suggested, they tried to construct the lives of typical potential residents and infer from that what traditional and innovatory social facilities would be needed. Among the variables used were age, sex, marital status, income and ethnicity, which are often used as indicators in their aggregated form in new town planning. Stripped of the undoubted element of public relations razzmatazz, such an approach to British new town policy would at least have had the virtue of re-emphasizing, before the recent discovery of the inner city, that there is a need to extend the conception of the new town resident beyond that of a toolmaker of twenty-nine with a Ford Cortina, a child of two and a wife expecting another child before the hospital is built.

Lower-wage households are also at a disadvantage in entering owner-occupation in new towns, while in most inner urban areas there are still relatively cheap houses for first-time buyers, with council mortgages (sometimes) available. A counter-solution is, of course, drastically reduced house prices to new town tenants, which merely serves to make the situation more iniquitous for those who still cannot move to the new towns.

In addition to inequalities of access for individuals to new towns, there are inequalities between new towns. Industrial and commercial investment is more diverse and more concentrated in the new towns of the Midlands and South East. While so much reliance is placed upon private capital for retail and leisure amenities, both opportunities for and the prospects of profitability are likely to be limited in the new towns in the assisted areas. There is little evidence that central government is willing to make up the shortfall by allowing more loan finance for 'frills' in the assisted areas than elsewhere. The same criteria of 50 per cent private capital and a 10 per cent rate of return on investment were imposed across the board. Nor are the better-placed new towns permitted to give or lend their cash surpluses to the weaker projects. Apparently the statement that somewhere will be a growth point is considered sufficient. Lower wage levels have also restricted the range of new town residents able to take up the opportunity to buy their houses, so that fewer have been able to acquire what is for most people their most valuable capital asset. To that extent the policy of owner-occupation in new towns has been regressive.

Theories of growth points for inter-regional redistribution have foundered in the face of industrial contraction and public spending cuts, which have eroded the provision of publicly provided infrastructure to attract industry. Industrial location controls themselves have weakened while there is an absolute shortage of investment. The sadly limited extent of the economic miracle in new towns was revealed in the answer to the parliamentary written question about unemployment in January 1976 (HC Debates, vol. 904, col. 110 written). The towns with the lowest rate of male unemployment were, in ascending order: Crawley, Hatfield with Welwyn, Hemel Hempstead, Peterborough and Harlow (where the rate was 5·4 per cent of the working population). At the other end of the scale were Peterlee (10·8 per cent), Cumbernauld, Irvine, Skelmersdale and Washington (13·2 per cent).

Meeting housing need and inter-regional redistribution have always been in latent conflict in the new towns. The former goal implies building as many rented houses in as short a time as possible and if necessary, reducing the subtlety of layout and landscape. Their occupants may have to commute, but local employment, where available, should have a high proportion of unskilled and part-time work. Many of those in the most acute housing need will not be working at all. None of this is appropriate to a policy

201

which hopes to raise the level of prosperity in the new town and its hinterland. To do that a selective policy geared towards high-paying industries with a skilled labour force is indicated, together with rented housing for key workers plus a high level of owner-occupation as an incentive to migration. On this basis, the hope will be to attract good-quality shops and other services (somewhere to take clients for lunch, etc.) to impress yet more potential new town employers and retailers. Cash and staff resources will have to be spent on liaison, on attractive landscaping and civic design. It may even be necessary to accept a lower rate of growth in order to select industry and to integrate the development.

The end of the new towns policy?

A wistful statement from a leading member of the TCPA in February 1976 held that:

Now is the time to make a statement of faith. As we all pull in our belts, as the nation's aspirations contract, it is easy to assume that there can be no developments . . . let the convinced, therefore, now stand up and be counted. Planning, as the TCPA understands it, was never the creature of growth . . . (Ash, 1976).

Despite this, it is clear, from a more detached examination, that the new towns' fortunes have advanced and receded with the state of the economy. Ironically, given the new towns' centralized adminis-tration, this has been true *a fortiori* of those with the goal of inter-regional distribution. In 1977 as in 1949 national economic prob-lems reduced spending on the infrastructure vital to new towns, reduced the provision of amenities and services by local authorities, especially in advance of population, reduced public and private house-building, reduced building standards and limited the staff and cash available for any hope of innovatory social research and planning. It is hard to resist the conclusion that the new towns, which are such a striking example of long-term planning and the triumph of hope over certainty, have been among the first to suffer when the economic screws tighten. They have always been a risky venture, needing a high level of central and local government cash and commitment. It appears that as the going gets tough, little has been forthcoming. When, therefore, economic problems were accompanied by dramatic downward trends in both the birthrate and population projections, it was inevitable that the new towns programme would be modified. If genuine commitment is lacking at the centre it is probably preferable that the targets should be explicitly curtailed, rather than perpetuate the chronic uncertainty that many new towns (and the CNT) have lived with for a number of years. No doubt the piquancy of the first public and systematic review of the new towns' target taking place in order to prune and save money has not been lost on those who work in them.

The government's declared intention of shifting spending out of the new towns to the inner cities is, however, more apparent than real, for not only is the £20 million involved in 1979/80 puny compared with the potential £1,000 million agreed for the period 1977–9, but most of the 'savings' are rather a decision not to spend over the middle term. One might conclude that the new towns are a convenient focus for action that would particularly appease the inner-city politicians who have come to use them as an easy explanation for processes that are rather to be understood in the society and economy at large. Besides, even after the wind-up of eight development corporations by 1983, at least thirteen are likely to be active (the Secretary of State was, at mid-1978, considering the future of Aycliffe, Peterlee and Skelmersdale (HC Debates, vol. 946, col. 569 written)). They will be concentrated around London and Glasgow, a situation that Abercrombie would have endorsed.

It is not impossible that they will once more be rediscovered. The policy for the inner cities is at best untried and at worst may be a futile attempt to reverse major economic and social trends without significant resources. While industry is being urged to divest itself of excess labour and outworn capital equipment and is, without being urged, forming itself into ever vaster multinational conglomerates, it is a curious logic that also expects sufficient labour-intensive small firms suddenly to emerge from the economic woodwork to make a dent in urban employment and fiscal problems. It is also hard to imagine, say, a pharmaceutical giant from the EEC eagerly looking for a disused mill in Salford for conversion. Again, why should the political, administrative and territorial framework within which the urban crisis occurred, suddenly be able or willing to mobilize itself to reverse the trends merely in response to a rather woolly White Paper and some permissive legislation, but very little cash?

Apart from the brouhaha about employment, there is also the issue of housing. Rehabilitation, as prescribed for inner Birmingham, for example, is not cheap and, as critics have pointed out, only delays and amplifies the problem of obsolescence (Inner City Working Group, 1977, as part of a valuable commentary on the inner area studies). The TCPA may be evangelist and even naïve in their view of the inexorable trend to paradise at twelve houses to the acre but it is hard to deny that suburban life is the people's choice. One of Deakin and Ungerson's (1977) most interesting findings

203

was the widespread and unsentimental desire to leave the inner city, even on the part of those born and bred there. (Admittedly their reasons were sometimes the 'wrong' ones from the policy-maker's point of view!) The apparent goal of freezing the physical expression of urban process, as if rapid change is pathological, is lacking in historical perspective. Arguably the shape of our cities is less fluid now than at any time since the industrial revolution, as a reading of Anderson (1971) or Hall *et al.* (1973) soon reveals. Pain and inequity is likely to be caused less by active intervention in the processes at work than by ineffective attempts to forestall them. 'Small area' philosophies were surely shown to be inadequate by the history of the Community Development Project (CDP, 1977b). The theoretical basis of the current effort is more middle-range but is still essentially concerned with tinkering with symptoms.

The team from the University of Birmingham (Inner City Working Group, 1977) concluded that there is no solution to urban problems without large-scale public investment and the same is true of the new towns, where so much has already been spent. To help the disadvantaged, it is not sufficient for a government − especially a Labour government − to tell new town corporations, in effect, to make sure they find some and ship them in. There must be a positive commitment to providing jobs (where is the National Enterprise Board as far as new towns are concerned?) and public facilities and services as well as housing. Now that the admirable decision has been made to retain new town commercial and industrial investments under public control, via the CNT, there is a real opportunity to reinvest the surplus, not simply by handing it to inner-city authorities but by devising a coherent strategy of using new towns to give opportunities to inner-city residents − for the inner-city crisis is theirs, not an attribute of some reified urban system. Simply clawing back surpluses into general revenue is half-baked gradualism, and less defensible than a full-scale policy of roll-over of assets. New towns may have an entrepreneurial dimension, but they are not directly analogues to the Coal Board or the Post Office, nor should they be directed to operate as such. Given more appropriate performance criteria that laid less emphasis on financial break-even as a goal, but more importantly more political will and cash, they might even become in actuality what they have always been reputed to be: a bold social experiment.

Outline chronology

1898	Ebenezer Howard publishes *Tomorrow: a Peaceful Path to Real Reform* (Howard, 1965)
1899	Howard *et al.* found Garden Cities Association
1902	Garden City Pioneer Company founded
1903	Pioneer Company starts Letchworth
1912	F. J. Osborn goes to work at Letchworth
1918	*New Towns after the War* by F. J. Osborn *et al.* published (Osborn, 1942)
1919	Howard buys land for Welwyn Garden City
1920	Welwyn started
1921	Chamberlain's Unhealthy Areas Committee reports
1933	*A Hundred New Towns for Britain* published by A. Trystan Edwards under the pseudonym Ex-serviceman J47485
1935	Marley's inter-departmental committee on garden cities and satellite towns reports
1936	F. J. Osborn becomes virtually full-time worker for Garden City and Town Planning Association
1937	Barlow Royal Commission on Distribution of Industrial Population set up
1940	Barlow's report published
1942	*New Towns after the War* republished. Uthwatt Committee on Compensation and Betterment reports. Scott Committee on Land Utilization in Rural Areas reports
1945	Lewis Silkin appoints New Towns Committee under John Reith
1946	January: Reith committee publishes *Interim Report* (New Towns Committee, 1946a)
	March: Stevenage announced
	April: New Towns Bill introduced into Commons

	April:	Reith committee publishes *Second Interim Report* (New Towns Committee, 1946b)
	July:	*Final Report* of Reith committee published (New Towns Committee, 1946c). New Towns Bill completes parliamentary passage
	November:	Stevenage designated under New Towns Act
1947–50	Thirteen other towns designated in England, Wales and Scotland	
1952	Town Development Act passed	
1955	Cumbernauld designated	
1959	New Towns Act passed, setting up Commission for the New Towns	
1961	Skelmersdale designated. Fourteen more towns designated between 1962 and 1973, ending with Stonehouse	
1965	New Towns Act passed, amending and consolidating first two major acts	
1966	Government announces shift to 50 per cent owner-occupation	
1968	Parallel Act to 1965 Act for Scotland	
1974	Expenditure Committee starts hearings. Consultative Document for England and Wales (DOE, 1974) published	
1975	Consultation Document for Scotland (Scottish Office, 1975) published. Expenditure Committee publishes *Final Report* (Expenditure Committee, 1974/5a)	
1976	May:	Stonehouse new town ended
	September:	Government response to Expenditure Committee published as White Paper (Cmnd 6616). Peter Shore's 'Manchester Speech'. New Towns (Amendment) Act passed, allowing for transfer of rented housing to local authorities
1977	New Towns (Scotland) Act passed allowing for winding up of development corporations (the 1959 Act did not apply to Scotland)	
	April:	Result of review of new towns' targets announced
	September:	White Paper on the inner city (Cmnd 6845) published
1978	Inner Urban Areas Act passed	

Bibliography

General

House of Commons Debates (Hansard or the Official Parliamentary
  Record)
Annual Reports of the New Town Development Corporations
Annual Reports of the Commission for the New Towns
Acts of Parliament
DOE Circulars
All these have complete references in the text and are not listed in the
bibliography, e.g.: HC Debates, vol. 929, col. 1110; Stevenage DC, 1974,
p. 400; CNT, 1974, p. 13; New Towns Act 1965, section 6(1); DOE
Circular 26/76. The Annual Reports are published as parliamentary
papers on 31 March.

Books and articles

ABERCROMBIE, P. (1945), *Greater London Plan 1944*, HMSO, London.
ABERCROMBIE, P. (1949), *The Clyde Valley Regional Plan*, HMSO,
  Edinburgh.
ANDERSON, M. (1971), *Family Structure in Nineteenth Century Lancashire*,
  Cambridge University Press
ASH, M. (1976), 'Planning, Growth — and Change: the New Towns versus
  Inner City Fallacy', *Town and Country Planning*, vol. 44, no. 2,
  February 1976.
ASHWORTH, G. (1954), *The Genesis of Modern British Town Planning*,
  Routledge & Kegan Paul, London.
BAER, M. (1978), 'Political Participation in New Towns: the Case of
  Britain', *British Journal of Political Science*, vol. 8, no. 2, pp. 237–45.
BANHAM, R. (1976), 'Groundscraping', *New Society*, 12 August, pp. 352–3.
BARLOW COMMISSION (1940), See: Royal Commission on the Distribution of
  the Industrial Population (1940).
BELL, C. R., and NEWBY, H. (1976), 'Community, Communion, Class and
  Community Action: the Social Sources of the New Urban Politics',
  in Herbert, D. T., and Johnston, R. J. (1976).

BELLAMY, E. (1951), *Looking Backward: 2000–1887,* Random House, New York, (first published 1887).

BOURNVILLE VILLAGE TRUST (1941), *When We Build Again,* Allen & Unwin, London.

BRETT, L. (1953), 'Failure of the New Towns?', *Architectural Review,* August, pp. 119–20.

BUCKINGHAM, J. S. (1849), *National Evils and Practical Remedies with a Plan of a Model Town,* Peter Jackson, London.

CHAC (1944), *The Design of Dwellings* ('The Dudley Report'), HMSO, London.

CHAC (1967), *The Needs of New Communities,* HMSO, London.

CHAMPION, A. G. (1978), 'Are the New Towns likely to face Population Decline in the next Decade?', *Town and Country Planning,* vol. 46, no. 2, February, pp. 64–8.

CHAMPION, A. G., CLEGG, K., and DAVIES, R. L. (1977), *Facts and Figures about the New Towns. A Socio-economic Digest,* Retailing and Planning Associates, Corbridge, Northumberland.

CHERRY, G. E. (1972), *Urban Change and Planning. A History of Urban Development in Britain since 1750,* Foulis, Henley-on-Thames.

CMND 1952 (1963), *London: Employment, Housing, Land,* HMSO, London.

CMND 2188 (1963), *Central Scotland: a Plan for Development and Growth,* HMSO, London.

CMND 2206 (1963), *The North East: a Plan for Development and Growth,* HMSO, London.

CMND 3998 (1969), *The Intermediate Areas* ('The Hunt Report'), HMSO, London.

CMND 6616 (1976), *New Towns. Government Observations on the Thirteenth Report from the Select Committee on Expenditure,* HMSO, London.

CMND 6845 (1977), *Policy for the Inner Cities,* HMSO, London.

COLIN BUCHANAN and PARTNERS (1974), *West Central Scotland, a Programme of Action: Consultants' Draft Report,* W. Central Scotland Planning Team, Glasgow.

COMMITTEE ON LAND UTILIZATION IN RURAL AREAS (1942), *Report,* Cmnd 6378, ('The Scott Report') HMSO, London.

COMMUNITY DEVELOPMENT PROJECT (1977a), *The Costs of Industrial Change,* CDP, London.

COMMUNITY DEVELOPMENT PROJECT (1977b), *Gilding the Ghetto,* CDP, London.

CRESSWELL, P., and THOMAS, R. (1972), 'Employment and Population Balance', in Evans, H. (ed.) (1972).

CROSSMAN, R. (1975), *The Diaries of a Cabinet Minister,* Vol. I, *Minister of Housing and Local Government,* Hamish Hamilton and Jonathan Cape, London.

CULLINGWORTH, J. B. (1959), 'Some Administrative Problems of Planned Overspill', *Public Administration,* vol. 37, Winter.

CULLINGWORTH, J. B. (1976), *Town and Country Planning in Britain,* (6th edition), Allen & Unwin, London.

208

CULLINGWORTH, J. B., and KARN, V. A. (1968), *The Ownership and Management of Housing in the New Towns*, HMSO, London.

DEA (1965), *The North West: a Regional Study*, HMSO, London.

DEAKIN, N., and UNGERSON, C. (1977), *Leaving London. Planned Mobility and the Inner City*, Heinemann, London.

DENNIS, R. (1978), 'The Decline of Manufacturing Employment in Greater London: 1966–74', *Urban Studies*, vol. 15, no. 1, 1978.

DEPARTMENTAL COMMITTEE ON GARDEN CITIES AND SATELLITE TOWNS (1935), *Report* ('The Marley Report'), HMSO, London.

DI (1977), *Incentives to Industry in the Areas for Expansion*, HMSO, London.

DOE and THE WELSH OFFICE (1974), *New Towns in England and Wales. A Consultation Document* (see also Expenditure Committee, 1974–5a, pp. 1007–18), DOE, London.

DOE (1976), 'Inner Urban Policy', *Press Notice 835*, DOE, London.

DOE (1977a), *Unequal City* (Inner-area study of Small Heath, Birmingham by Llewellyn-Davies, Weeks, Forestier, Walker and Bor), HMSO, London.

DOE (1977b), *Inner London: Policies for Dispersal and Balance* (Inner-area study of Lambeth by Shankland, Cox and Associates), HMSO, London.

DOE (1977c), *Change and Decay* (Inner-area study of Liverpool by Hugh Wilson & Lewis Womersley, *et al.*), HMSO, London.

DOE (1977d), *Inner Area Studies: Liverpool, Birmingham and Lambeth. Summaries of Consultants' Final Reports*, HMSO, London.

DURANT, R. (1939), *Watling*, P. S. King & Sons, London.

ECONOMIC ASSOCIATES (1965), *A New Town in Mid-Wales*, HMSO, London.

EDDISON, T. (1976), 'The Challenge of the Community Land Act – 13. A Final Check List', *Municipal Journal*, vol. 84, no. 17, 23 April 1976.

EDWARDS, A. TRYSTAN (1933), *'A Hundred New Towns for Britain'*, Simpkin Marshall, London (published under the pseudonym 'J47485').

Estates Gazette (1973), 'Compensation Claims: Land Tribunal Decisions', (the case of Myers *et al.* v Milton Keynes DC), *Estates Gazette*, vol. 225, 20 January and 27 January, 3 February and 10 February 1973, pp. 443–52, 623–32, 804–12, 999–1008.

EVANS, H. (ed.) (1972), *New Towns: the British Experience*, London, Charles Knight.

EXPENDITURE COMMITTEE (1974), *Second Report*, New Towns, vols II and III, HC 305 II and III (pp. 1–715) (see also Expenditure Committee 1974–5a), HMSO, London.

EXPENDITURE COMMITTEE (1974–5a), *Thirteenth Report*, New Towns, vols I, IV and V, HC 616 I, IV and V (see also Expenditure Committee 1974), HMSO, London.

EXPENDITURE COMMITTEE (1974–5b), *Fifth Report*, Docklands, HC 348, HMSO, London.

EXPERT COMMITTEE ON COMPENSATION AND BETTERMENT (1942), *Report*, Cmnd 6386 ('The Uthwatt Report'), HMSO, London.

FOLEY, D. (1960), 'British Town Planning: One Ideology or Three?', *British Journal of Sociology*, vol. 11, no. 3.

FOLEY, D. (1962), 'Idea and Influence. The Town and Country Planning Association', *Journal of Sociology of the American Institute of Planners*, vol. 28, no. 1, February.

FORSHAW, J. H., and ABERCROMBIE, P. (1943), *The County of London Plan*, Macmillan, London.

FRAZER, W. M. (1950), *A History of English Public Health 1834–1939*, Ballière, Tindall & Cox, London.

GEE, F. (1972), *Homes and Jobs for Londoners in New and Expanded Towns*, HMSO, London.

GLASS, R. (1959), 'The Evaluation of Planning: Some Sociological Considerations', *International Social Science Journal*, vol. 11, no. 3.

GLASSON, J. (1974), *An Introduction to Regional Planning*, Hutchinson, London.

GOLDTHORPE, J. H., and HOPE, K. (1974), *The Social Grading of Occupations: A New Approach and Scale*, Clarendon, Oxford.

GOLDTHORPE, J. H. (1978), 'The Current Inflation: Towards a Sociological Account', in Hirsch, F., and Goldthorpe, J. H. (1978).

HALL, P. (1976), 'The South East: Britain's Tarnished Golden Corner', *New Society*, 7 July, pp. 228–31.

HALL, P. *et al.* (1973), *The Containment of Urban England* (2 vols), Allen & Unwin, London.

HANCOCK, T. (1977), 'An Inner City Programme', *Town and Country Planning*, vol. 45, no. 2, February, pp. 82–7.

HARLOE, M. (1975), *Swindon: a Town in Transition*, Heinemann, London.

HERAUD, B. J. (1966), 'The New Towns and London's Housing Problem', *Urban Studies*, vol. 3, no. 1, February, pp. 8–21.

HERAUD, B. J. (1968), 'Social Class and the New Towns', *Urban Studies*, vol. 6, no. 1, February, pp. 33–58.

HERBERT, D. T., and JOHNSTON, R. J. (1976), *Social Areas in Cities*, Vol. I, *Spatial Perspectives on Problems and Policies*, Wiley, Chichester.

HIRSCH, F., and GOLDTHORPE, J. H. (1978), *The Political Economy of Inflation*, Martin Robertson, London.

HOLLAND, S. (1976a), *Capital Versus the Regions*, Macmillan, London.

HOLLAND, S. (1976b), *The Regional Problem*, Macmillan, London.

HORROCKS, M. (1974), *Social Development Work in the New Communities*, Occasional Paper no. 27, University of Birmingham Centre for Urban and Regional Studies, Birmingham.

HOWARD, E. (1965), *Garden Cities of Tomorrow* (first published in 1898 as *Tomorrow: a Peaceful Path to Real Reform*), Faber, London.

INNER CITY WORKING GROUP (1977), *Inner Area Studies: a Contribution to the Debate*, University of Birmingham Joint Centre for Regional, Urban and Local Government Studies, Birmingham.

LANCASHIRE COUNTY COUNCIL (1956), *Development Plan*, Lancashire County Council, Preston.

LEETE, R. (1977), 'Registrar General's Social Classes: Origins and Uses', *Population Trends*, no. 8, HMSO, London.

LEVIN, P. (1976), *Government and the Planning Process,* Allen & Unwin, London.

LEYBOURNE-WHITE, G., and WHITE, K. (1945), *Children for Britain,* Pilot Press, London.

LICHFIELD, N., and WENDT, P. (1969), 'Six English New Towns', *Town Planning Review,* vol. 40, pp. 283–314.

LIPMAN, A. (1969), 'The Architectural Belief System and Social Behaviour', *British Journal of Sociology,* vol. 20, no. 2, June.

LOCAL GOVERNMENT BOARD (1918), *Committee on Building Construction in Connection with the Provision of Dwellings for the Working Class – Report,* ('The Tudor Walters Report'), HMSO, London.

LOCK, D. (1976), 'Planned Dispersal and the Decline of London', *Planner,* vol. 62, no. 7, November.

LOCKWOOD, D. (1974), 'For T. H. Marshall', *Sociology,* vol. 8, no. 3, September.

MCCRONE, G. (1969), *Regional Policy in Britain,* Allen & Unwin, London.

MACFADYEN, D. (1933), *Sir Ebenezer Howard and the Town Planning Movement,* Manchester University Press.

MANN, M. (1973), *Workers on the Move,* Cambridge University Press.

MARCHANT, J. (ed.) (no date), *Rebuilding Family Life,* Odhams, London.

MARSHALL, T. H. (1963), *Sociology at the Crossroads,* Heinemann, London.

MERCER, C. (1975), *Living in Cities,* Penguin, Harmondsworth.

MHLG (1964), *The South East Study 1961–81,* HMSO, London.

MHLG (1967), *Central Lancashire – Study for a City,* HMSO, London.

MHLG (1968), *Central Lancashire New Town Proposal – Impact on North East Lancashire,* HMSO, London.

MHLG (1969), *People and Planning,* ('The Skeffington Report'), HMSO, London.

MILTON KEYNES DEVELOPMENT CORPORATION (1970), *The Plan for Milton Keynes* (2 vols), Milton Keynes DC, Bletchley.

MINISTRY OF TOWN AND COUNTRY PLANNING (1949), 'Memorandum on Movement of Population to New and Expanded Towns', unpublished circular.

MORRIS, W. (1891), *News from Nowhere, or an Epoch of Rest . . . ,* limited edition, London.

MUMFORD, L., and OSBORN, F. J. (1971),*The Letters of Lewis Mumford and Frederic J. Osborn* (ed. Hughes, M.), Adams & Dart, Bath.

NEW TOWNS COMMITTEE (1946a), *Interim Report* (Cmnd 6759), HMSO, London.

NEW TOWNS COMMITTEE (1946b), *Second Interim Report* (Cmnd 6794), HMSO, London.

NEW TOWNS COMMITTEE (1946c), *Final Report* (Cmnd 6876), ('The Reith Report'), HMSO, London.

NORTH WEST JOINT PLANNING TEAM (1974), *Strategic Plan for the North West,* HMSO, London.

OGILVY, A. A. (1968), 'The Self-Contained New Town', *Town Planning Review,* vol. 39, pp. 38–54.

211

OGILVY, A. A. (1971), 'Employment Expansion and the Development of New Town Hinterlands', *Town Planning Review,* vol. 42, pp. 113–29.

ORLANS, H. (1952), *Stevenage: A Sociological Study,* Routledge & Kegan Paul, London.

OSBORN, F. J. (1942), *New Towns after the War,* Dent, London.

OSBORN, F. J. (1954), 'Success of the New Towns', *Town and Country Planning,* vol. 22, no. 117, January, pp. 10–12.

OSBORN, F. J. (1955a), 'High Land Prices and High Buildings', *Town and Country Planning,* vol. 23, no. 131, March, pp. 117–18.

OSBORN, F. J. (1955b), 'Housing Subsidies and Density in City Development', *Town and Country Planning,* vol. 23, no. 137, September, pp. 407–14.

OSBORN, F. J. (1955c), 'Housing Subsidies and Interest', *Town and Country Planning,* vol. 23, no. 139, November, pp. 503–4.

OSBORN, F. J. (1955d), 'Housing Subsidies and City Congestion', *Town and Country Planning,* vol. 23, no. 140, December, pp. 549–50.

OSBORN, F. J., and WHITTICK, A. (1969), *The New Towns: the Answer to Megalopolis,* Leonard Hill, London.

PAHL, R. (1970), *Whose City?* Longman, London (1975 edn, Penguin, Harmondsworth).

PAHL, R., and WINKLER, J. (1974), 'The Coming Corporatism', *New Society,* 10 October, pp. 72–6.

PERKS, R. (1974), 'Trends in Architecture: from Sculptural Form to Human Functioning', an unpublished dissertation of the University of Nottingham.

PETERSEN, W. (1968), 'The Ideological Origins of Britain's New Towns', *Journal American Institute of Planners,* vol. 34, no. 3, May, pp. 160–70.

Planning (1944), 'Location of Employment', no. 224, August.

POWELL, G. (1960), 'The Recent Development of Greater London', *Advancement of Science,* May, pp. 76–86.

PRICE, F. (1972), 'Shops and Shopping', in Evans, H. (ed.) (1972).

PURDOM, C. B. (1949), *The Building of Satellite Towns,* Dent, London.

'REGIONALITER' (1942), *Regional Government,* Fabian Research Series no. 63, The Fabian Society, London.

REILLY, C. (1947), *Outline Plan for Birkenhead,* County Borough, Birkenhead.

RICHARDS, J. M. (1953), 'Failure of the New Towns', *Architectural Review,* July.

ROCHE, F. L., THOMAS, W., and WESTON, J. (1977), 'Lambeth Inner Area Study: comments of Milton Keynes, Peterborough and Northampton New Town Development Corporations on the summary of the consultants' report published in January 1977', Milton Keynes Development Corporation, Milton Keynes.

RODWIN, L. (1956), *The British New Towns Policy,* Harvard University Press, Cambridge, Mass.

ROWNTREE, B. S. (1941), *Poverty and Progress,* Longman, London.

ROYAL COMMISSION ON THE DISTRIBUTION OF THE INDUSTRIAL POPULATION (1940), *Report,* Cmnd 6153 ('The Barlow Commission'), HMSO, London.

RUDDY, S. (1969), *Industrial Selection Schemes,* Occasional Paper no. 5, University of Birmingham Centre for Urban and Regional Studies, Birmingham.

SCHAFFER, F. (1972), *The New Town Story,* Paladin, London.

SCOTT REPORT (1942), see Commission on Land Utilization in Rural Areas (1942).

SCOTTISH OFFICE (1975), *The Scottish New Towns: a Consultative Document* (see also Expenditure Committee, 1974–5a, pp. 931–5), Scottish Office, Edinburgh.

SELF, P. (1972), 'A New Vision for New Towns', *Town and Country Planning,* vol. 40, no. 1, January, pp. 4–9.

SHARP, E. (1972), 'The Government's Role', in Evans, H. (ed.) (1972).

SHOSTAK, L. *et al.* (1976), 'New Towns, Inner Urban Areas and Community Development Corporations', unpublished paper delivered at National Voluntary Housing Conference, 1976.

SIMON, E. D. (1945), *Rebuilding Britain – A Twenty Year Plan,* Gollancz, London.

SKEFFINGTON REPORT (1969), see MHLG (1969).

STONE, P. A. (1973), *The Structure, Size and Costs of Urban Settlement,* Cambridge University Press.

TCPA EXECUTIVE (1960), 'Planning Problems of the Large Towns', *Town and Country Planning,* vol. 38, June, pp. 200–5.

TCPA (1967), 'Editorial', *Town and Country Planning,* vol. 35, no. 1, January, pp. 1–2.

TCPA (1968a), 'TCPA Evidence to Hunt Committee', *Town and Country Planning,* vol. 36, no. 5, May, pp. 237–55.

TCPA (1968b), 'Executive Statement', *Town and Country Planning,* vol. 36, no. 9, September, pp. 395–401.

TCPA (1977), 'TCPA Policy Statement. Inner Cities of Tomorrow', *Town and Country Planning,* vol. 45, no. 5, May, pp. 265–77.

THOMAS, R. (1969a), 'London's New Towns', *PEP Broadsheet 510,* Political and Economic Planning, London.

THOMAS, R. (1969b), 'Aycliffe to Cumbernauld', *PEP Broadsheet 516,* Political and Economic Planning, London.

THOMAS, W. (1967), 'Housing Choice in the New Towns', *Town and Country Planning,* vol. 35, no. 1, January, pp. 1–2.

THOMAS, W. (1972), 'The Management Task', in Evans, H. (ed.) 1972.

THOMSON, C. (1973), *The Industrial Selection Scheme – a Study of Conflicting Objectives in Urban and Regional Planning,* CES Working Paper 81, Centre for Environmental Studies, London.

TITMUSS, R. M. (1949), *Problems of Social Policy,* HMSO and Longmans, Green, London.

TOLLEY, R. S. (1972), 'Telford New Town', *Town Planning Review,* vol. 43, pp. 343–60.

TOWNDROW, F. E. (ed.) (1941), *Replanning Britain,* Faber, London.

TOWNROE, P. (1975), 'Branch Plants and Regional Development', *Town Planning Review,* vol. 46, no. 1, January, pp. 47–62.

UNHEALTHY AREAS COMMITTEE (1921), *Second and Final Report,* HMSO, London.

UTHWATT REPORT (1942) see: Expert Committee on Compensation and Betterment (1942).

WEBBER, M. (1964), 'The Urban Place and the Non-Place Urban Realm', in Webber, M. *et al.*, *Explorations in Urban Structure*, Pennsylvania University Press, Philadelphia.

WEST MIDLANDS ECONOMIC PLANNING COUNCIL (1965), *The West Midlands: A Regional Study*, HMSO, London.

WHITTICK, A. (1970), 'Cumbernauld – Outstanding Success or a Failure?' *Town and Country Planning*, vol. 38, no. 5, May, pp. 236–40.

WIRZ, H. (1975), *Social Aspects of Planning in New Towns*, Saxon House, Farnborough.

YOUNG, M., and WILLMOTT, P. (1957), *Family and Kinship in East London*, Routledge & Kegan Paul, London.

YOUNG, M., and WILLMOTT, P. (1973), *The Symmetrical Family*, Routledge & Kegan Paul, London.

YOUNG, T. R. (1934), *Becontree and Dagenham*, The Pilgrim Trust, London.

Index

Routledge Social Science Series

Routledge & Kegan Paul   London, Henley and Boston

39 Store Street, London WC1E 7DD
Broadway House, Newtown Road,
Henley-on-Thames, Oxon RG9 1EN
9 Park Street, Boston, Mass. 02108

Contents

*Authors wishing to submit manuscripts for any series in
this catalogue should send them to the Social Science Editor,
Routledge & Kegan Paul Ltd, 39 Store Street,
London WC1E 7DD*

●*Books so marked are available in paperback*
All books are in Metric Demy 8vo format (216 × 138mm approx.)

International Library of Sociology

General Editor   John Rex

GENERAL SOCIOLOGY

Barnsley, J. H. The Social Reality of Ethics. *464 pp.*
Brown, Robert. Explanation in Social Science. *208 pp.*
● Rules and Laws in Sociology. *192 pp.*
Bruford, W. H. Chekhov and His Russia. *A Sociological Study. 244 pp.*
Burton, F. and **Carlen, P.** Official Discourse. *On Discourse Analysis, Government Publications, Ideology. About 140 pp.*
Cain, Maureen E. Society and the Policeman's Role. *326 pp.*
●**Fletcher, Colin.** Beneath the Surface. *An Account of Three Styles of Sociological Research. 221 pp.*
Gibson, Quentin. The Logic of Social Enquiry. *240 pp.*
Glucksmann, M. Structuralist Analysis in Contemporary Social Thought. *212 pp.*
Gurvitch, Georges. Sociology of Law. *Foreword by Roscoe Pound. 264 pp.*
Hinkle, R. Founding Theory of American Sociology 1883-1915. *About 350 pp.*
Homans, George C. Sentiments and Activities. *336 pp.*
Johnson, Harry M. Sociology: *a Systematic Introduction. Foreword by Robert K. Merton. 710 pp.*
●**Keat, Russell** and **Urry, John.** Social Theory as Science. *278 pp.*
Mannheim, Karl. Essays on Sociology and Social Psychology. *Edited by Paul Keckskemeti. With Editorial Note by Adolph Lowe. 344 pp.*
Martindale, Don. The Nature and Types of Sociological Theory. *292 pp.*
●**Maus, Heinz.** A Short History of Sociology. *234 pp.*
Myrdal, Gunnar. Value in Social Theory: *A Collection of Essays on Methodology. Edited by Paul Streeten. 332 pp.*
Ogburn, William F. and **Nimkoff, Meyer F.** A Handbook of Sociology. *Preface by Karl Mannheim. 656 pp. 46 figures. 35 tables.*
Parsons, Talcott, and **Smelser, Neil J.** Economy and Society: *A Study in the Integration of Economic and Social Theory. 362 pp.*
Podgórecki, Adam. Practical Social Sciences. *About 200 pp.*
Raffel, S. Matters of Fact. *A Sociological Inquiry. 152 pp.*
●**Rex, John.** (Ed.) Approaches to Sociology. *Contributions by Peter Abell,* Sociology and the Demystification of the Modern World. *282 pp.*
●**Rex, John** (Ed.) Approaches to Sociology. *Contributions by Peter Abell, Frank Bechhofer, Basil Bernstein, Ronald Fletcher, David Frisby, Miriam Glucksmann, Peter Lassman, Herminio Martins, John Rex, Roland Robertson, John Westergaard and Jock Young. 302 pp.*
Rigby, A. Alternative Realities. *352 pp.*
Roche, M. Phenomenology, Language and the Social Sciences. *374 pp.*
Sahay, A. Sociological Analysis. *220 pp.*

Strasser, Hermann. The Normative Structure of Sociology. *Conservative and Emancipatory Themes in Social Thought. About 340 pp.*
Strong, P. Ceremonial Order of the Clinic. *About 250 pp.*
Urry, John. Reference Groups and the Theory of Revolution. *244 pp.*
Weinberg, E. Development of Sociology in the Soviet Union. *173 pp.*

FOREIGN CLASSICS OF SOCIOLOGY

● **Gerth, H. H.** and **Mills, C. Wright.** From Max Weber: *Essays in Sociology. 502 pp.*
● **Tönnies, Ferdinand.** Community and Association. *(Gemeinschaft and Gesellschaft.) Translated and Supplemented by Charles P. Loomis. Foreword by Pitirim A. Sorokin. 334 pp.*

SOCIAL STRUCTURE

Andreski, Stanislav. Military Organization and Society. *Foreword by Professor A. R. Radcliffe-Brown. 226 pp. 1 folder.*
Carlton, Eric. Ideology and Social Order. *Foreword by Professor Philip Abrahams. About 320 pp.*
Coontz, Sydney H. Population Theories and the Economic Interpretation. *202 pp.*
Coser, Lewis. The Functions of Social Conflict. *204 pp.*
Dickie-Clark, H. F. Marginal Situation: *A Sociological Study of a Coloured Group. 240 pp. 11 tables.*
Giner, S. and **Archer, M. S.** (Eds.). Contemporary Europe. *Social Structures and Cultural Patterns. 336 pp.*
● **Glaser, Barney** and **Strauss, Anselm L.** Status Passage. *A Formal Theory. 212 pp.*
Glass, D. V. (Ed.) Social Mobility in Britain. *Contributions by J. Berent, T. Bottomore, R. C. Chambers, J. Floud, D. V. Glass, J. R. Hall, H. T. Himmelweit, R. K. Kelsall, F. M. Martin, C. A. Moser, R. Mukherjee, and W. Ziegel. 420 pp.*
Kelsall, R. K. Higher Civil Servants in Britain: *From 1870 to the Present Day. 268 pp. 31 tables.*
● **Lawton, Denis.** Social Class, Language and Education. *192 pp.*
McLeish, John. The Theory of Social Change: *Four Views Considered. 128 pp.*
● **Marsh, David C.** The Changing Social Structure of England and Wales, 1871-1961. *Revised edition. 288 pp.*
Menzies, Ken. Talcott Parsons and the Social Image of Man. *About 208 pp.*
● **Mouzelis, Nicos.** Organization and Bureaucracy. *An Analysis of Modern Theories. 240 pp.*
Ossowski, Stanislaw. Class Structure in the Social Consciousness. *210 pp.*
● **Podgórecki, Adam.** Law and Society. *302 pp.*
Renner, Karl. Institutions of Private Law and Their Social Functions. *Edited, with an Introduction and Notes, by O. Kahn-Freud. Translated by Agnes Schwarzschild. 316 pp.*

Rex, J. and **Tomlinson, S.** Colonial Immigrants in a British City. *A Class Analysis. 368 pp.*

Smooha, S. Israel: Pluralism and Conflict. *472 pp.*

Wesolowski, W. Class, Strata and Power. *Trans. and with Introduction by G. Kolankiewicz. 160 pp.*

Zureik, E. Palestinians in Israel. *A Study in Internal Colonialism. 264 pp.*

SOCIOLOGY AND POLITICS

Acton, T. A. Gypsy Politics and Social Change. *316 pp.*

Burton, F. Politics of Legitimacy. *Struggles in a Belfast Community. 250 pp.*

Etzioni-Halevy, E. Political Manipulation and Administrative Power. *A Comparative Study. About 200 pp.*

●**Hechter, Michael.** Internal Colonialism. *The Celtic Fringe in British National Development, 1536–1966. 380 pp.*

Kornhauser, William. The Politics of Mass Society. *272 pp. 20 tables.*

Korpi, W. The Working Class in Welfare Capitalism. *Work, Unions and Politics in Sweden. 472 pp.*

Kroes, R. Soldiers and Students. *A Study of Right- and Left-wing Students. 174 pp.*

Martin, Roderick. Sociology of Power. *About 272 pp.*

Myrdal, Gunnar. The Political Element in the Development of Economic Theory. *Translated from the German by Paul Streeten. 282 pp.*

Wong, S.-L. Sociology and Socialism in Contemporary China. *160 pp.*

Wootton, Graham. Workers, Unions and the State. *188 pp.*

CRIMINOLOGY

Ancel, Marc. Social Defence: *A Modern Approach to Criminal Problems. Foreword by Leon Radzinowicz. 240 pp.*

Athens, L. Violent Criminal Acts and Actors. *About 150 pp.*

Cain, Maureen E. Society and the Policeman's Role. *326 pp.*

Cloward, Richard A. and **Ohlin, Lloyd E.** Delinquency and Opportunity: *A Theory of Delinquent Gangs. 248 pp.*

Downes, David M. The Delinquent Solution. *A Study in Subcultural Theory. 296 pp.*

Friedlander, Kate. The Psycho-Analytical Approach to Juvenile Delinquency: *Theory, Case Studies, Treatment. 320 pp.*

Gleuck, Sheldon and **Eleanor.** Family Environment and Delinquency. *With the statistical assistance of Rose W. Kneznek. 340 pp.*

Lopez-Rey, Manuel. Crime. *An Analytical Appraisal. 288 pp.*

Mannheim, Hermann. Comparative Criminology: *a Text Book. Two volumes. 442 pp. and 380 pp.*

Morris, Terence. The Criminal Area: *A Study in Social Ecology. Foreword by Hermann Mannheim. 232 pp. 25 tables. 4 maps.*

Podgorecki, A. and **Łos, M.** *Multidimensional Sociology. About 380 pp.*

Rock, Paul. Making People Pay. *338 pp.*

● **Taylor, Ian, Walton, Paul,** and **Young, Jock.** The New Criminology. *For a Social Theory of Deviance. 325 pp.*

● **Taylor, Ian, Walton, Paul** and **Young, Jock.** (Eds) Critical Criminology. *268 pp.*

SOCIAL PSYCHOLOGY

Bagley, Christopher. The Social Psychology of the Epileptic Child. *320 pp.*

Brittan, Arthur. Meanings and Situations. *224 pp.*

Carroll, J. Break-Out from the Crystal Palace. *200 pp.*

● **Fleming, C. M.** Adolescence: Its Social Psychology. *With an Introduction to recent findings from the fields of Anthropology, Physiology, Medicine, Psychometrics and Sociometry. 288 pp.*

● The Social Psychology of Education: *An Introduction and Guide to Its Study. 136 pp.*

Linton, Ralph. The Cultural Background of Personality. *132 pp.*

● **Mayo, Elton.** The Social Problems of an Industrial Civilization. *With an Appendix on the Political Problem. 180 pp.*

Ottaway, A. K. C. Learning Through Group Experience. *176 pp.*

Plummer, Ken. Sexual Stigma. *An Interactionist Account. 254 pp.*

● **Rose, Arnold M.** (Ed.) Human Behaviour and Social Processes: *an Interactionist Approach. Contributions by Arnold M. Rose, Ralph H. Turner, Anselm Strauss, Everett C. Hughes, E. Franklin Frazier, Howard S. Becker et al. 696 pp.*

Smelser, Neil J. Theory of Collective Behaviour. *448 pp.*

Stephenson, Geoffrey M. The Development of Conscience. *128 pp.*

Young, Kimball. Handbook of Social Psychology. *658 pp. 16 figures. 10 tables.*

SOCIOLOGY OF THE FAMILY

Bell, Colin R. Middle Class Families: *Social and Geographical Mobility. 224 pp.*

Burton, Lindy. Vulnerable Children. *272 pp.*

Gavron, Hannah. The Captive Wife: *Conflicts of Household Mothers. 190 pp.*

George, Victor and **Wilding, Paul.** Motherless Families. *248 pp.*

Klein, Josephine. Samples from English Cultures.
  1. Three Preliminary Studies and Aspects of Adult Life in England. *447 pp.*
  2. Child-Rearing Practices and Index. *247 pp.*

Klein, Viola. The Feminine Character. *History of an Ideology. 244 pp.*

McWhinnie, Alexina M. Adopted Children. *How They Grow Up. 304 pp.*

● **Morgan, D. H. J.** Social Theory and the Family. *About 320 pp.*

● **Myrdal, Alva** and **Klein, Viola.** Women's Two Roles: *Home and Work. 238 pp. 27 tables.*

Parsons, Talcott and **Bales, Robert F.** Family: Socialization and Inter-action Process. *In collaboration with James Olds, Morris Zelditch and Philip E. Slater. 456 pp. 50 figures and tables.*

SOCIAL SERVICES

Bastide, Roger. The Sociology of Mental Disorder. *Translated from the French by Jean McNeil. 260 pp.*

Carlebach, Julius. Caring For Children in Trouble. *266 pp.*

George, Victor. Foster Care. *Theory and Practice. 234 pp.*
Social Security: *Beveridge and After. 258 pp.*

George, V. and **Wilding, P.** Motherless Families. *248 pp.*

● **Goetschius, George W.** Working with Community Groups. *256 pp.*

Goetschius, George W. and **Tash, Joan.** Working with Unattached Youth. *416 pp.*

Heywood, Jean S. Children in Care. *The Development of the Service for the Deprived Child. Third revised edition. 284 pp.*

King, Roy D., Ranes, Norma V. and **Tizard, Jack.** Patterns of Residential Care. *356 pp.*

Leigh, John. Young People and Leisure. *256 pp.*

● **Mays, John.** (Ed.) Penelope Hall's Social Services of England and Wales. *About 324 pp.*

Morris, Mary. Voluntary Work and the Welfare State. *300 pp.*

Nokes, P. L. The Professional Task in Welfare Practice. *152 pp.*

Timms, Noel. Psychiatric Social Work in Great Britain (1939-1962). *280 pp.*

● Social Casework: *Principles and Practice. 256 pp.*

SOCIOLOGY OF EDUCATION

Banks, Olive. Parity and Prestige in English Secondary Education: a Study in Educational Sociology. *272 pp.*

● **Blyth, W. A. L.** English Primary Education. *A Sociological Description.* 2. Background. *168 pp.*

Collier, K. G. The Social Purposes of Education: *Personal and Social Values in Education. 268 pp.*

Evans, K. M. Sociometry and Education. *158 pp.*

● **Ford, Julienne.** Social Class and the Comprehensive School. *192 pp.*

Foster, P. J. Education and Social Change in Ghana. *336 pp. 3 maps.*

Fraser, W. R. Education and Society in Modern France. *150 pp.*

Grace, Gerald R. Role Conflict and the Teacher. *150 pp.*

Hans, Nicholas. New Trends in Education in the Eighteenth Century. *278 pp. 19 tables.*

● Comparative Education: *A Study of Educational Factors and Traditions. 360 pp.*

● **Hargreaves, David.** Interpersonal Relations and Education. *432 pp.*

● Social Relations in a Secondary School. *240 pp.*

School Organization and Pupil Involvement. *A Study of Secondary Schools.*

● **Mannheim, Karl** and **Stewart, W.A.C.** An Introduction to the Sociology of Education. *206 pp.*

● **Musgrove, F.** Youth and the Social Order. *176 pp.*

● **Ottaway, A. K. C.** Education and Society: An Introduction to the Sociology of Education. *With an Introduction by W. O. Lester Smith. 212 pp.*

Peers, Robert. Adult Education: *A Comparative Study. Revised edition. 398 pp.*

Stratta, Erica. The Education of Borstal Boys. *A Study of their Educational Experiences prior to, and during, Borstal Training. 256 pp.*

● **Taylor, P. H., Reid, W. A.** and **Holley, B. J.** The English Sixth Form. *A Case Study in Curriculum Research. 198 pp.*

SOCIOLOGY OF CULTURE

Eppel, E. M. and **M.** Adolescents and Morality: *A Study of some Moral Values and Dilemmas of Working Adolescents in the Context of a changing Climate of Opinion. Foreword by W. J. H. Sprott. 268 pp. 39 tables.*

● **Fromm, Erich.** The Fear of Freedom. *286 pp.*

● The Sane Society. *400 pp.*

Johnson, L. The Cultural Critics. *From Matthew Arnold to Raymond Williams. 233 pp.*

Mannheim, Karl. Essays on the Sociology of Culture. *Edited by Ernst Mannheim in co-operation with Paul Kecskemeti. Editorial Note by Adolph Lowe. 280 pp.*

Zijderfeld, A. C. On Clichés. *The Supersedure of Meaning by Function in Modernity. About 132 pp.*

SOCIOLOGY OF RELIGION

Argyle, Michael and **Beit-Hallahmi, Benjamin.** The Social Psychology of Religion. *About 256 pp.*

Glasner, Peter E. The Sociology of Secularisation. *A Critique of a Concept. About 180 pp.*

Hall, J. R. The Ways Out. *Utopian Communal Groups in an Age of Babylon. 280 pp.*

Ranson, S., Hinings, B. and **Bryman, A.** Clergy, Ministers and Priests. *216 pp.*

Stark, Werner. The Sociology of Religion. *A Study of Christendom.*
Volume II. *Sectarian Religion. 368 pp.*
Volume III. *The Universal Church. 464 pp.*
Volume IV. *Types of Religious Man. 352 pp.*
Volume V. *Types of Religious Culture. 464 pp.*

Turner, B. S. Weber and Islam. *216 pp.*

Watt, W. Montgomery. Islam and the Integration of Society. *320 pp.*

SOCIOLOGY OF ART AND LITERATURE

Jarvie, Ian C. Towards a Sociology of the Cinema. *A Comparative Essay on the Structure and Functioning of a Major Entertainment Industry. 405 pp.*

Rust, Frances S. Dance in Society. *An Analysis of the Relationships between the Social Dance and Society in England from the Middle Ages to the Present Day. 256 pp. 8 pp. of plates.*

Schücking, L. L. The Sociology of Literary Taste. *112 pp.*

Wolff, Janet. Hermeneutic Philosophy and the Sociology of Art. *150 pp.*

SOCIOLOGY OF KNOWLEDGE

Diesing, P. Patterns of Discovery in the Social Sciences. *262 pp.*

● **Douglas, J. D.** (Ed.) Understanding Everyday Life. *370 pp.*

Glasner, B. Essential Interactionism. *About 220 pp.*

● **Hamilton, P.** Knowledge and Social Structure. *174 pp.*

Jarvie, I. C. Concepts and Society. *232 pp.*

Mannheim, Karl. Essays on the Sociology of Knowledge. *Edited by Paul Kecskemeti. Editorial Note by Adolph Lowe. 353 pp.*

Remmling, Gunter W. The Sociology of Karl Mannheim. *With a Bibliographical Guide to the Sociology of Knowledge, Ideological Analysis, and Social Planning. 255 pp.*

Remmling, Gunter W. (Ed.) Towards the Sociology of Knowledge. *Origin and Development of a Sociological Thought Style. 463 pp.*

URBAN SOCIOLOGY

Aldridge, M. The British New Towns. *A Programme Without a Policy. About 250 pp.*

Ashworth, William. The Genesis of Modern British Town Planning: *A Study in Economic and Social History of the Nineteenth and Twentieth Centuries. 288 pp.*

Brittan, A. The Privatised World. *196 pp.*

Cullingworth, J. B. Housing Needs and Planning Policy: *A Restatement of the Problems of Housing Need and 'Overspill' in England and Wales. 232 pp. 44 tables. 8 maps.*

Dickinson, Robert E. City and Region: *A Geographical Interpretation. 608 pp. 125 figures.*

The West European City: *A Geographical Interpretation. 600 pp. 129 maps. 29 plates.*

Humphreys, Alexander J. New Dubliners: *Urbanization and the Irish Family. Foreword by George C. Homans. 304 pp.*

Jackson, Brian. Working Class Community: *Some General Notions raised by a Series of Studies in Northern England. 192 pp.*

● **Mann, P. H.** An Approach to Urban Sociology. *240 pp.*

Mellor, J. R. Urban Sociology in an Urbanized Society. *326 pp.*

Morris, R. N. and **Mogey, J.** The Sociology of Housing. *Studies at Berinsfield. 232 pp. 4 pp. plates.*

Rosser, C. and **Harris, C.** The Family and Social Change. *A Study of Family and Kinship in a South Wales Town. 352 pp. 8 maps.*

● **Stacey, Margaret, Batsone, Eric, Bell, Colin** and **Thurcott, Anne.** Power, Persistence and Change. *A Second Study of Banbury. 196 pp.*

RURAL SOCIOLOGY

Mayer, Adrian C. Peasants in the Pacific. *A Study of Fiji Indian Rural Society. 248 pp. 20 plates.*

Williams, W. M. The Sociology of an English Village: *Gosforth. 272 pp. 12 figures. 13 tables.*

SOCIOLOGY OF INDUSTRY AND DISTRIBUTION

Dunkerley, David. The Foreman. *Aspects of Task and Structure. 192 pp.*

Eldridge, J. E. T. Industrial Disputes. *Essays in the Sociology of Industrial Relations. 288 pp.*

Hollowell, Peter G. The Lorry Driver. *272 pp.*

● **Oxaal, I., Barnett, T.** and **Booth, D.** (Eds) Beyond the Sociology of Development. *Economy and Society in Latin America and Africa. 295 pp.*

Smelser, Neil J. Social Change in the Industrial Revolution: *An Application of Theory to the Lancashire Cotton Industry, 1770–1840. 468 pp. 12 figures. 14 tables.*

Watson, T. J. The Personnel Managers. *A Study in the Sociology of Work and Employment. 262 pp.*

ANTHROPOLOGY

Brandel-Syrier, Mia. Reeftown Elite. *A Study of Social Mobility in a Modern African Community on the Reef. 376 pp.*

Dickie-Clark, H. F. The Marginal Situation. *A Sociological Study of a Coloured Group. 236 pp.*

Dube, S. C. Indian Village. *Foreword by Morris Edward Opler. 276 pp. 4 plates.*

India's Changing Villages: *Human Factors in Community Development. 260 pp. 8 plates. 1 map.*

Firth, Raymond. Malay Fishermen. *Their Peasant Economy. 420 pp. 17 pp. plates.*

Gulliver, P. H. Social Control in an African Society: a Study of the Arusha, Agricultural Masai of Northern Tanganyika. *320 pp. 8 plates. 10 figures.*

Family Herds. *288 pp.*

Jarvie, Ian C. The Revolution in Anthropology. *268 pp.*

Little, Kenneth L. Mende of Sierra Leone. *308 pp. and folder.*

Negroes in Britain. *With a New Introduction and Contemporary Study by Leonard Bloom. 320 pp.*

Madan, G. R. Western Sociologists on Indian Society. *Marx, Spencer, Weber, Durkheim, Pareto. 384 pp.*

Mayer, A. C. Peasants in the Pacific. *A Study of Fiji Indian Rural Society. 248 pp.*

Meer, Fatima. Race and Suicide in South Africa. *325 pp.*

Smith, Raymond T. The Negro Family in British Guiana: *Family Structure and Social Status in the Villages. With a Foreword by Meyer Fortes. 314 pp. 8 plates. 1 figure. 4 maps.*

SOCIOLOGY AND PHILOSOPHY

Barnsley, John H. The Social Reality of Ethics. *A Comparative Analysis of Moral Codes. 448 pp.*

Diesing, Paul. Patterns of Discovery in the Social Sciences. *362 pp.*

● **Douglas, Jack D.** (Ed.) Understanding Everyday Life. *Toward the Reconstruction of Sociological Knowledge. Contributions by Alan F. Blum, Aaron W. Cicourel, Norman K. Denzin, Jack D. Douglas, John Heeren, Peter McHugh, Peter K. Manning, Melvin Power, Matthew Speier, Roy Turner, D. Lawrence Wieder, Thomas P. Wilson and Don H. Zimmerman. 370 pp.*

Gorman, Robert A. The Dual Vision. *Alfred Schutz and the Myth of Phenomenological Social Science. About 300 pp.*

Jarvie, Ian C. Concepts and Society. *216 pp.*

Kilminster, R. Praxis and Method. *A Sociological Dialogue with Lukács, Gramsci and the early Frankfurt School. About 304 pp.*

● **Pelz, Werner.** The Scope of Understanding in Sociology. *Towards a More Radical Reorientation in the Social Humanistic Sciences. 283 pp.*

Roche, Maurice. Phenomenology, Language and the Social Sciences. *371 pp.*

Sahay, Arun. Sociological Analysis. *212 pp.*

Slater, P. Origin and Significance of the Frankfurt School. *A Marxist Perspective. About 192 pp.*

Spurling, L. Phenomenology and the Social World. *The Philosophy of Merleau-Ponty and its Relation to the Social Sciences. 222 pp.*

Wilson, H. T. The American Ideology. *Science, Technology and Organization as Modes of Rationality. 368 pp.*

International Library of Anthropology

General Editor Adam Kuper

Ahmed, A. S. Millenium and Charisma Among Pathans. *A Critical Essay in Social Anthropology. 192 pp.*
  Pukhtun Economy and Society. *About 360 pp.*

Brown, Paula. The Chimbu. *A Study of Change in the New Guinea Highlands. 151 pp.*

Foner, N. Jamaica Farewell. *200 pp.*

Gudeman, Stephen. Relationships, Residence and the Individual. *A Rural Panamanian Community. 288 pp. 11 plates, 5 figures, 2 maps, 10 tables.*

The Demise of a Rural Economy. *From Subsistence to Capitalism in a Latin American Village. 160 pp.*

Hamnett, Ian. Chieftainship and Legitimacy. *An Anthropological Study of Executive Law in Lesotho. 163 pp.*

Hanson, F. Allan. Meaning in Culture. *127 pp.*

Humphreys, S. C. Anthropology and the Greeks. *288 pp.*

Karp, I. Fields of Change Among the Iteso of Kenya. *140 pp.*

Lloyd, P. C. Power and Independence. *Urban Africans' Perception of Social Inequality. 264 pp.*

Parry, J. P. Caste and Kinship in Kangra. *352 pp. Illustrated.*

Pettigrew, Joyce. Robber Noblemen. *A Study of the Political System of the Sikh Jats. 284 pp.*

Street, Brian V. The Savage in Literature. *Representations of 'Primitive' Society in English Fiction, 1858–1920. 207 pp.*

Van Den Berghe, Pierre L. Power and Privilege at an African University. *278 pp.*

International Library of Social Policy

General Editor   Kathleen Jones

Bayley, M. Mental Handicap and Community Care. *426 pp.*

Bottoms, A. E. and **McClean, J. D.** Defendants in the Criminal Process. *284 pp.*

Butler, J. R. Family Doctors and Public Policy. *208 pp.*

Davies, Martin. Prisoners of Society. *Attitudes and Aftercare. 204 pp.*

Gittus, Elizabeth. Flats, Families and the Under-Fives. *285 pp.*

Holman, Robert. Trading in Children. *A Study of Private Fostering. 355 pp.*

Jeffs, A. Young People and the Youth Service. *About 180 pp.*

Jones, Howard, and **Cornes, Paul.** Open Prisons. *288 pp.*

Jones, Kathleen. History of the Mental Health Service. *428 pp.*

Jones, Kathleen, with **Brown, John, Cunningham, W. J., Roberts, Julian** and **Williams, Peter.** Opening the Door. *A Study of New Policies for the Mentally Handicapped. 278 pp.*

Karn, Valerie. Retiring to the Seaside. *About 280 pp. 2 maps. Numerous tables.*

King, R. D. and **Elliot, K. W.** Albany: Birth of a Prison—End of an Era. *394 pp.*

Thomas, J. E. The English Prison Officer since 1850: *A Study in Conflict.* *258 pp.*

Walton, R. G. Women in Social Work. *303 pp.*

● **Woodward, J.** To Do the Sick No Harm. *A Study of the British Voluntary Hospital System to 1875. 234 pp.*

International Library of Welfare and Philosophy

General Editors   Noel Timms and David Watson

● **McDermott, F. E.** (Ed.) Self-Determination in Social Work. *A Collection of Essays on Self-determination and Related Concepts by Philosophers and Social Work Theorists. Contributors: F. B. Biestek, S. Bernstein, A. Keith-Lucas, D. Sayer, H. H. Perelman, C. Whittington, R. F. Stalley, F. E. McDermott, I. Berlin, H. J. McCloskey, H. L. A. Hart, J. Wilson, A. I. Melden, S. I. Benn. 254 pp.*

● **Plant, Raymond.** Community and Ideology. *104 pp.*

Ragg, Nicholas M. People Not Cases. *A Philosophical Approach to Social Work. About 250 pp.*

● **Timms, Noel** and **Watson, David.** (Eds) Talking About Welfare. *Readings in Philosophy and Social Policy. Contributors: T. H. Marshall, R. B. Brandt, G. H. von Wright, K. Nielsen, M. Cranston, R. M. Titmuss, R. S. Downie, E. Telfer, D. Donnison, J. Benson, P. Leonard, A. Keith-Lucas, D. Walsh, I. T. Ramsey. 320 pp.*

●   (Eds). Philosophy in Social Work. *250 pp.*

● **Weale, A.** Equality and Social Policy. *164 pp.*

Primary Socialization, Language and Education

General Editor   Basil Bernstein

Adlam, Diana S., *with the assistance of Geoffrey Turner and Lesley Lineker.* Code in Context. *About 272 pp.*

Bernstein, Basil. Class, Codes and Control. *3 volumes.*

●   1. *Theoretical Studies Towards a Sociology of Language. 254 pp.*

     2. *Applied Studies Towards a Sociology of Language. 377 pp.*

●   3. *Towards a Theory of Educational Transmission. 167 pp.*

Brandis, W. and **Bernstein, B.** Selection and Control. *176 pp.*

Brandis, Walter and **Henderson, Dorothy.** Social Class, Language and Communication. *288 pp.*

Cook-Gumperz, Jenny. Social Control and Socialization. *A Study of Class Differences in the Language of Maternal Control. 290 pp.*

● **Gahagan, D. M** and **G. A.** Talk Reform. *Exploration in Language for Infant School Children. 160 pp.*

Hawkins, P. R. Social Class, the Nominal Group and Verbal Strategies. *About 220 pp.*

Robinson, W. P. and **Rackstraw, Susan D. A.** A Question of Answers. *2 volumes. 192 pp. and 180 pp.*

Turner, Geoffrey J. and **Mohan, Bernard A.** A Linguistic Description and Computer Programme for Children's Speech. *208 pp.*

Reports of the Institute of Community Studies

Baker, J. The Neighbourhood Advice Centre. A Community Project in Camden. *320 pp.*

● **Cartwright, Ann.** Patients and their Doctors. *A Study of General Practice. 304 pp.*

Dench, Geoff. Maltese in London.*A Case-study in the Erosion of Ethnic Consciousness. 302 pp.*

Jackson, Brian and **Marsden, Dennis.** Education and the Working Class: *Some General Themes raised by a Study of 88 Working-class Children in a Northern Industrial City. 268 pp. 2 folders.*

Marris, Peter. The Experience of Higher Education. *232 pp. 27 tables.*

● Loss and Change. *192 pp.*

Marris, Peter and **Rein, Martin.** Dilemmas of Social Reform. *Poverty and Community Action in the United States. 256 pp.*

Marris, Peter and **Somerset, Anthony.** African Businessmen. *A Study of Entrepreneurship and Development in Keyna. 256 pp.*

Mills, Richard. Young Outsiders: *a Study in Alternative Communities. 216 pp.*

Runciman, W. G. Relative Deprivation and Social Justice. *A Study of Attitudes to Social Inequality in Twentieth-Century England. 352 pp.*

Willmott, Peter. Adolescent Boys in East London. *230 pp.*

Willmott, Peter and **Young, Michael.** Family and Class in a London Suburb. *202 pp. 47 tables.*

Young, Michael and **McGeeney, Patrick.** Learning Begins at Home. *A Study of a Junior School and its Parents. 128 pp.*

Young, Michael and **Willmott, Peter.** Family and Kinship in East London. *Foreword by Richard M. Titmuss. 252 pp. 39 tables.*

The Symmetrical Family. *410 pp.*

Reports of the Institute for Social Studies in Medical Care

Cartwright, Ann, Hockey, Lisbeth and **Anderson, John J.** Life Before Death. *310 pp.*

Dunnell, Karen and **Cartwright, Ann.** Medicine Takers, Prescribers and Hoarders. *190 pp.*

Farrell, C. My Mother Said. . . . *A Study of the Way Young People Learned About Sex and Birth Control. 200 pp.*

Medicine, Illness and Society

General Editor W. M. Williams

Hall, David J. Social Relations & Innovation. *Changing the State of Play in Hospitals. 232 pp.*

Hall, David J., and **Stacey, M.** (Eds) Beyond Separation. *234 pp.*

Robinson, David. The Process of Becoming Ill. *142 pp.*

Stacey, Margaret *et al.* Hospitals, Children and Their Families. *The Report of a Pilot Study. 202 pp.*

Stimson G. V. and **Webb, B.** Going to See the Doctor. *The Consultation Process in General Practice. 155 pp.*

Monographs in Social Theory

General Editor Arthur Brittan

● **Barnes, B.** Scientific Knowledge and Sociological Theory. *192 pp.*

Bauman, Zygmunt. Culture as Praxis. *204 pp.*

● **Dixon, Keith.** Sociological Theory. *Pretence and Possibility. 142 pp.*

Meltzer, B. N., Petras, J. W. and **Reynolds, L. T.** Symbolic Interactionism. *Genesis, Varieties and Criticisms. 144 pp.*

● **Smith, Anthony D.** The Concept of Social Change. *A Critique of the Functionalist Theory of Social Change. 208 pp.*

Routledge Social Science Journals

The British Journal of Sociology. *Editor – Angus Stewart; Associate Editor – Leslie Sklair. Vol. 1, No. 1 – March 1950 and Quarterly. Roy. 8vo. All back issues available. An international journal publishing original papers in the field of sociology and related areas.*

Community Work. *Edited by David Jones and Marjorie Mayo. 1973. Published annually.*

Economy and Society. *Vol. 1, No. 1. February 1972 and Quarterly. Metric Roy. 8vo. A journal for all social scientists covering sociology, philosophy, anthropology, economics and history. All back numbers available.*

Ethnic and Racial Studies. *Editor – John Stone. Vol. 1 – 1978. Published quarterly.*

Religion. Journal of Religion and Religions. *Chairman of Editorial Board, Ninian Smart. Vol. 1, No. 1, Spring 1971. A journal with an inter-disciplinary approach to the study of the phenomena of religion. All back numbers available.*

Sociology of Health and Illness. *A Journal of Medical Sociology. Editor – Alan Davies; Associate Editor – Ray Jobling. Vol. 1, Spring 1979. Published 3 times per annum.*

Year Book of Social Policy in Britain, The. *Edited by Kathleen Jones. 1971. Published annually.*

Social and Psychological Aspects of Medical Practice

Editor Trevor Silverstone

Lader, Malcolm. Psychophysiology of Mental Illness. *280 pp.*
● **Silverstone, Trevor** and **Turner, Paul.** Drug Treatment in Psychiatry. *Revised edition. 256 pp.*
Whiteley, J. S. and **Gordon, J.** Group Approaches in Psychiatry. *256 pp.*

Printed in Great Britain by
Lowe & Brydone Printers Limited, Thetford, Norfolk